Daoist Ritual, State Religion, and Popular Practice

Zhenwu, or the Perfected Warrior, is one of the few Chinese Deities that can rightfully claim a countrywide devotion. Religious specialists, lay devotees, the state machine, and the cultural industry all participated, both collaboratively and competitively, in the evolution of this devotional movement. This book centers on the development and transformation of the godhead of Zhenwu, as well as the devotional movement focused on him. Organized chronologically following the development of Zhenwu worship in Daoist ritual, state religion, and popular practice, it looks at the changes in the way Zhenwu was perceived and the historical context in which those changes took place.

The author investigates the complicated means by which various social and political groups contested with each other in appropriating cultural-religious symbols. The question at the core of the book is how, in a given historical context, human agency and social structures shape the religious world to which they profess devotion. The work offers a holistic approach to religion in a period of Chinese history when central, local, official, clerical, and popular power are constantly negotiating and reshaping established values.

Shin-yi Chao is Assistant Professor in the Department of Philosophy and Religion at Rutgers University, Camden campus, US. Her research focuses on Daoism and Chinese popular religion in pre-modern and modern times.

Routledge Studies in Taoism

Series Editors: T.H. Barrett, School of Oriental and African Studies, University of London; Russell Kirkland, University of Georgia; Benjamin Penny, Australian National University and Monica Esposito, Kyoto University

The *Routledge Studies in Taoism* series publishes books of high scholarly standards. The series includes monographic studies, surveys and annotated translations of primary sources and technical reference works with a wide scope. Occasionally, translations of books first published in other languages might also be considered for inclusion in the series.

Daoism in History
Essays in Honour of Liu Ts'un-yan
Edited by Benjamin Penny

Daoist Ritual, State Religion, and Popular Practice
Zhenwu Worship from Song to Ming (960–1644)
Shin-yi Chao

Daoist Ritual, State Religion, and Popular Practice

Zhenwu Worship from Song to Ming (960–1644)

Shin-yi Chao

Routledge
Taylor & Francis Group

LONDON AND NEW YORK

First published 2011
by Routledge
2 Park Square, Milton Park, Abingdon, Oxon, OX14 4RN

Simultaneously published in the USA and Canada
by Routledge
270 Madison Avenue, New York, NY 10016

Routledge is an imprint of the Taylor & Francis Group, an informa business

© 2011 Shin-yi Chao

The right of Shin-yi Chao to be identified as author of this work has been asserted by her in accordance with sections 77 and 78 of the Copyright, Designs and Patents Act 1988.

All rights reserved. No part of this book may be reprinted or reproduced or utilised in any form or by any electronic, mechanical, or other means, now known or hereafter invented, including photocopying and recording, or in any information storage or retrieval system, without permission in writing from the publishers.

Trademark notice: Product or corporate names may be trademarks or registered trademarks, and are used only for identification and explanation without intent to infringe.

British Library Cataloguing in Publication Data
A catalogue record for this book is available from the British Library

Library of Congress Cataloging-in-Publication Data
Chao, Shin-yi.
Daoist ritual, state religion, and popular practice : Zhenwu worship from Song to Ming (960–1644) / Shin-yi Chao.
p. cm. -- (Routledge Studies in Taoism)
Includes bibliographical references and index.
ISBN 978-0-415-78066-7 (hardback) -- ISBN 978-0-203-81783-4 (ebook) 1. Taoism--China--History. 2. God (Chinese religion) 3. China--Religious life and customs. I. Title. II. Title: Zhenwu worship from Song to Ming (960–1644).
BL1910.C45 2011
299.5'14211--dc22
2010047721

ISBN13: 978-0-415-78066-7 (hbk)
ISBN13: 978-0-203-81783-4 (ebk)

Typeset in Times
by Integra Software Services Pvt. Ltd, Pondicherry, India

Printed and bound in Great Britain by
CPI Antony Rowe, Chippenham, Wiltshire

To my parents,
Chao Chi-lin and Tseng Su-chen

Contents

List of figures and tables		viii
Abbreviations		ix
Chronology		x
Acknowledgments		xi
	Introduction	1
1	A god in formation	13
2	A god in full	29
3	A god in transition	47
4	A god and his mountain	78
5	The whole and the parts	104
	Appendix 1	116
	Appendix 2	120
	Notes	123
	Bibliography	137
	Index	151

Figures and tables

Figures

I.1	A stone inscription of the *Scripture of Zhenwu* carved in 1099.	5
1.1	A tile with the design of a turtle encircled by a snake, Eastern Han dynasty.	15
1.2	The Four Animals in a tomb in Yi'nan, Shandong province. Eastern Han dynasty.	18
1.3	The Four Saints, attributed to Wu Daozi (CE 680–740), but more likely from the thirteenth century.	25
1.4	The Four Saints, detail.	26
3.1	Thunder God by the Japanese artist Tawaraya Sōtatsu, fl. early seventeenth century.	49
3.2	Thunder God, detail.	49
3.3	The 12 "earthly branches" and eight trigrams on a hand.	54
3.4	Zhenwu talisman from the *Secret Essential* j. 2.	56
3.5	Xuanwu-Heisha talisman from the *Shangqing tianxin zhengfa* j. 3.	57
3.6	Chart for "Using the *kan* trigram to fill the *li* trigram" or *Qukan tianli*.	65
4.1	Map of the middle and lower reaches of the Yangzi River.	79
4.2	The bronze temple on the summit of Mt Wudang.	90
4.3	A statue of Zhenwu inside the shrine on the summit of Mt Wudang.	99
4.4	Portrait of Emperor Yongle.	100
4.5	Portrait of Emperor Yongle, detail.	101

Tables

3.1	Common associations of the Five Phases	64
4.1	Private donations recorded at Mt Wudang during the Yuan Dynasty	88
4.2	Geographical distribution of the incense associations that made pilgrimages to Mt Wudang during the Ming dynasty	89

Abbreviations

ZHDZ *Zhonghua Daozang* 中華道藏, edited and punctuated by Zhang Jiyu 張繼禹 et al. (Beijing: Huaxia chubanshe and Zhongguo Daojiao xiehui, 2004). The code following ZHDZ refers to volume, page, and column numbers.
SKQS *Wenyuange Siku quanshu* 文淵閣四庫全書, online digital edition (Hong Kong: Dizhi wenhua shiye youxian gongsi, 2007).
SBCK *Sibu congkan* 四部叢刊, Electronic edition (Taipei: Transmission and Microinfo co., LTD., 2001).
TC   *The Taoist Canon: A Historical Companion to the Daozang*, ed. Kristofer Schipper and Verellen Franciscus (Chicago: University of Chicago Press, 2004). The number following TC indicate the sequential number assigned to the text in question in the companion.

Chronology

Spring and Autumn Period, 770 BCE–476 BCE
Warring States Period, 475 BCE–221 BCE
Qin Dynasty, 220 BCE–206 BCE
Han Dynasty, 202 BCE–CE 220
Three Kingdoms Period, CE 220–CE 280
Jin Dynasty, CE 265–CE 420
16 Kingdoms Period, CE 304–CE 439
Southern and Northern Dynasties, CE 420–CE 589
Sui Dynasty, CE 581–CE 618
Tang Dynasty, CE 618–CE 907
Five Dynasties and Ten Kingdoms Period, CE 907–CE 960
Song Dynasty, CE 960–CE 1279
Liao Dynasty, CE 907–CE 1125
Western Xia Dynasty, CE 1038–CE 1227
Jin (Jurchen) Dynasty, CE 1115–CE 1234
Yuan Dynasty, CE 1271–CE 1368
Ming Dynasty, CE 1368–CE 1644
Qing Dynasty, CE 1644–CE 1911

Acknowledgments

I am greatly indebted to Daniel L. Overmyer for his wisdom and support. He patiently indulged my working schedule as a graduate student but never compromised his high scholarly standards. Nam-lin Hur taught me everything I know about Japanese religion. I would also like to express my gratitude to my other teachers at University of British Columbia (UBC): Alexander Woodside, Harjot Oberoi, Catherine Swatek, Joshua Mostow, and Donald Baker. Diana Lary, then director of the Center for Chinese Research (CCR) at the UBC, provided me with a space at the CCR and helped me with numerous questions about Chinese history as well as life. Timothy Cheek, Louis Cha Professor at the CCR, shared me with his expertise in history, pedagogy, and joke-telling. I'd also like to thank my "academic siblings," Mary Yeung, Heng Ju, Philip Clart, Stephen Eskildsen, Mike Ralston, and Monika Dix. In different ways, they enriched my life as a graduate student.

Many people have read the whole or parts of the manuscript at different stages and have given me helpful criticism and needed encouragement: Stephen Bokenkamp, Hugh Clark, Eugene Cooper, Vincent Goossaert, Paul Katz, Terry Kleeman, Livia Kohn, John Lagerwey, Xun Liu, Thomas Michael, David Robinson, James Robson, and Wang Chien-ch'uan. Many others helped me to clear my ideas and pointed to the right direction: Poul Andersen, Marcia Butler, Philip Clart, Pierre-Henry de Bruyn, Jean DeBernardy, Thomas DuBois, Beata Grant, Shih-shan Susan Huang, Xiaofei Kang, Keith Knep, Elizabeth McAlister, Susan Naquin, Michael Puett, Paul Smith, Stephen Teiser, Barend ter Haar, Thomas Wilson, Janice D. Willis, Chün-fang Yü, and Kuang-hong Yü. Stephen Bokenkamp shared with me his extensive sources in Daoist studies. Without his generosity, this book would have taken much longer than it did. I would also like to express special gratitude to Russell Kirkland, who has been immensely supportive and encouraging.

I am fortunate to have become acquainted with Yang Lizhi and Mei Li, who kindly imparted to me their expertise on Mt Wudang and Zhenwu worship and showered me with great hospitality when I visited Mt Wudang. I'd also like to thank Chen Yongchao who hosts me every time I stop by Beijing. My colleagues at Rutgers University-Camden are the most collegial that one can expect. Edyth Kuciapa and William Wilson were of great help in producing the illustrations and maps. My publishers and editors, especially Leanne Hinves, Jillian Morrison, and Elizabeth Stone, are always patient with me and wonderfully helpful.

Acknowledgments

The Asian Library at the UBC under the directorship of Eleanor Yuan was a great resource for me as a graduate student. At Rutgers, I benefited from the Inter-library Loan section, especially through Mary Anne Nesbit, the specialist in religion, Vibiana Bowman, and the staff at the East Asian Library, especially Ying Wu, Li Sun, and Tao Yang. The staffs at Fu Si-nien Library and Ethnography Institute Library of Academia Sinica in Taiwan are remarkably knowledgeable, helpful, and patient. They made book hunting and document location as painless as possible. Chi-wah Chan , the Chinese Studies Librarian at University of Pennsylvania, helped me to obtain materials simply out of his marvelous collegiality.

The Chiang Ching-kuo Foundation, the China Times Foundation, and the Association of Asian Studies Small Travel Fund funded my research at the dissertation-writing stage. Rutgers University Research Council offered further funding for the research for revision and preparing the manuscript. I am grateful for their generous assistance.

My parents have been forever supportive, both morally and monetarily. My sister, Patty Chao Neath, has unquestioningly helped subsidize my studies. I'm not sure they entirely approve my choice of the academic path for life but they love me and thus support me to pursue the only thing I can do. Finally, if this book is at all readable, it is all thanks to Kevin Clark, my meticulous proofreader, critical reviewer, and better half. He has a saint's patience that I constantly test. I am a fortunate person and this book is a testimony of my good fortune.

***

Part of Chapter Three was published at as "Summoning the Thunder Generals: Internal Alchemy in Thunder Rites," in Livia Kohn and Robin Wong (eds.), *Daoist Inner Alchemy* (Magdalena, NM: Three Pines Press, 2009), pp. 108–124.

Introduction

On January 12, 1270,[1] in the reign of Khubilai (1215–1294; r. 1260–1294), khan of the Mongols and the ruler of northern China, an imperial ritual took place at the new political center of the empire, Dadu 大都, or Grand Capital (present-day Beijing).[2] The ceremony was requested by the khan's principal consort, Chabi, and consisted of presenting offerings to the river god on the banks of the Golden Water River (*Jinshui he* 金水河) running though the west of the city.[3] An altar was set up, the crowd assembled, and then, out of nowhere, a snake, a species that hibernates in winter, appeared in the river. This abnormal occurrence astonished everyone at the ceremony, including the imperial delegate. In response, he burned incense, presented a plate and made a kowtow to invite the snake to approach. The snake apparently understood the gesture, swam toward the crowd, landed on the plate, and turned its head around nodding, as if acknowledging the veneration. After roughly two hours, the snake departed. The next day, a similar manifestation occurred, but this time it was a turtle, another species that is supposed to be in hibernation. The turtle, too, was treated with great respect. Just like the snake, it appeared to enjoy the ritual and lingered around the site for a long while before disappearing into the water.

The appearance of two hibernal animals at the ceremony two days in a row was too much of an aberration to be taken lightheartedly for the imperial delegate. He dutifully reported the event to Empress Chabi, who had decreed the ritual. A long-time astute companion to Khubilai (Rossabi 1988: 16, 67–69; *Yuanshi* 114.2871–2), Chabi again demonstrated her political shrewdness. Instead of simply associating the turtle and snake with the river god of the Golden Water, she sought Chinese scholar-officials at the court to give their opinions. The courtiers, well versed in the classics, quickly reached the conclusion that the two creatures were no ordinary snake and turtle. Citing a classical Confucian apocrypha or *weishu* 緯書 (lit. "weft book," so named as they were complementary to the canonized classics, *jingshu* 經書 or "warp books"), they determined that the pair was really Xuanwu 玄武 ("Dark Martiality/Warrior") who was, according to their understanding, a divinity of the north. The north, based on the correlative cosmology of Five Phases (metal, wood, water, fire, earth), is associated with the cyclical cosmic phase of water. The manifestation of Xuanwu was a sign of the cosmic force of water in full play, asserted the scholars, and thus an omen for the Great Yuan to unite and rule the "realm under the heaven" since the Mongols as a people of the north possessed the virtue, or power, of water (*shuide* 水德).

Empress Chabi embraced the interpretation. She swiftly ordered and personally financed the construction of a temple in Xuanwu's honor. Within two months, the temple was completed. Then, Khubilai Khan learned about the episode and decreed the enlargement of the temple. By October 1270, a majestic temple complex was completed. The Khan granted it a name, the Illustrious Response Palace (Zhaoying gong 昭應宮) and commanded his court literati to produce two commendatory temple inscriptions.

The response of the Yuan monarchy to the turtle-and-snake apparition was enthusiastic, to say the least. Such enthusiasm went beyond a matter of religiosity.[4] The elaborate commemoration of the apparition cannot be comprehended without placing it within a particular historical event. Less than two years previously, in 1268, Khubilai had begun full-scale military operations against the Southern Song. This was his first war of expansion after ascending the throne eight years earlier, in 1260. In the Mongol warrior-ruler tradition, adding territory and resources to his domain constituted a crucial part of the success of a great khan. Yet the early years of Khubilai's reign had been marked by a power struggle with his brother, Arigh Boke (d. 1266), who challenged him for the khanate. Arigh surrendered in 1264 and conveniently died within two years. Even though Khubilai's position as the khan of khans was never again challenged by Mongol leaders, "an aura of illegitimacy continued to surround Khubilai," as Rossabi puts it (1988: 62). In the face of a frustrating silent skepticism, Khubilai resorted to the strategy of proving himself by conquering Song China, a task that his predecessor, Möngke Khan (r. 1251–1259), had died trying to accomplish.

Khubilai prepared for the invasion with an ambitious meticulousness. He even constructed a sizable fleet of skilled international sailors and officers for conducting the envisaged naval warfare (Rossabi 1988: 76–84). However, despite all efforts, he soon found the expedition bogged down in the siege of the strategically critical fortress city of Xiangyang 襄陽 (in Hubei) on the banks of the Han River (*Hanshui* 漢水). He summoned his most trusted Chinese general from semi-retirement to re-design the siege and added tens of thousands of new troops during the course of 1269 and early 1270; but Xiangyang still held out. With the city showing no signs of giving in, was his campaign also doomed, like that of his predecessor?

Then came the apparition of the turtle and snake in a winter river, a prophetic sign, according to Khubilai's Chinese court scholars, signifying that the cosmic force of water had risen to dominance. The Song dynasty had promoted itself as the holder of the virtue of fire (*huode* 火德) since its second ruler, Emperor Song Taizu (r. 960–976; *Songshi* 1.6). As the cosmos had moved on to the stage of water-dominance, the holders of the fire-virtue consequently lost their mandate of heaven.[5] The fate of the Song had been sealed. The resistance in Xiangyang was only a small setback to the irresistible and irreversible motion of the cosmos. Honoring Xuanwu by building a monumental temple publicized Khubilai's possession of the mandate of heaven and implicitly prophesized his success in a war that seemed to have reached a stalemate. Indeed, the temple steles produced by the scholar officials in commemorating the Illustrious Response Palace all asserted that the divine apparition was a sign that the new dynasty would soon rule the entire realm.

Once the temple was established, Empress Chabi selected Daoist clerics to manage it. The clerics, however, had their own theological interpretation of Xuanwu that was radically different from that of the court scholars. In accordance with their scriptural understanding, Xuanwu was an anthropomorphic god ranked initially as a general. General Xuanwu, often referred to as Zhenwu, did not take the form of snake and turtle in the Daoist view. The Daoists believe that the turtle and the snake were the general's emblems; they represented him but, in contrast to the court scholars' opinions, they did not constitute him in essence.

Different groups put forward their own interpretations of the symbolism of the divinity, and sought something specific in his worship which they could appreciate or benefit from. The monarchy appropriated the Xuanwu symbol as the sign of the mandate of heaven. To the practitioners of Daoist inner alchemy (*neidan* 内丹), a body of psycho-physical self-cultivation practices, the turtle and snake pair represented water and fire used to conduct internal refinement in meditation. Yet in folklore, the two creatures became demons to be subdued and recruited by Zhenwu; this interpretation was also accepted and included in more than one canonical Daoist text.[6] The different representations of the god's symbolism mutually influenced each other and produced one new image after another for him.

Before moving on to the next section, an explanation of the change from Xuanwu to Zhenwu is in order. In 1012, Zhenzong (r. 998–1022), the third emperor of the Northern Song (960–1127), had one of his many revelations. In this one, as recorded in both governmental and private documents, he met the founding patriarch of his clan, who was also one of the nine human-augustness (*renhuang* 人皇) of antiquity; his name was Zhao Xuanlang 趙玄朗.[7] The revelation, with all its political implications, was quickly propagated. Emperor Zhenzong issued a decree requiring that all deities whose names contained the character *xuan* be changed to *zhen* 真 in observing the tradition that monarchs' given names had to be avoided in writing and speaking in order to show respect.[8] Because of the edict, the god Xuanwu begat the god Zhenwu. In ritual manuals and temple inscriptions composed during the Song dynasty, the pivotal stages of the growth of his worship, the god was referred to as Zhenwu. After the demise of the Song and the end of its list of taboo name words, the ritual manuals rarely made the effort to change Zhenwu back to Xuanwu.[9] Therefore, this book employs the more widely used version, Zhenwu.

Multiple origins, mutations, and interpretations

This book is about a Chinese god and his worship in relation to the development of Chinese religion in general, and Daoism in particular during the Song–Yuan–Ming transition. Zhenwu is one of a handful of deities in modern China who can justly claim nationwide worship. Willem Grootaers and his team, who investigated 358 villages in northern China in the late 1940s, noted that there was nearly one Zhenwu temple in every two villages (Grootaers 1952: 163). Government surveys in Taiwan during the 1960s and 1970s showed that Zhenwu was one of the ten most popular deities in terms of temple dedication (Yü 1983). Although similar quantitative data are not available in other areas, a cursory search of gazetteers of imperial and republican times leaves no doubt that Zhenwu worship could be found in every corner of the empire. Behind the widespread popularity of the god lies a complicated history of godhead evolution.

Among the datable hagiographic records of Zhenwu, the earliest is the stone inscription carved in 1099 (second year of the Yuanfu reign of Emperor Song Zhezong) in central China, the *Scripture of Zhenwu of the North Told by the Heavenly Worthy of the Primordial Commencement* (*Yuanshi tianzun shuo Beifang Zhenwu jing* 元始天尊說北方真武經; hereafter the *Scripture of Zhenwu*; see figure I.1).[10] It relates what is arguably the most widespread version of Zhenwu's life since Song times:

> In the past, there were King Pure Joy (Jingle 淨樂) and Queen Virtue Triumph (Shansheng 善勝), who dreamed of swallowing sunlight and upon awakening became pregnant. The pregnancy was 14 months long. On the noon of the third day of the third month of the first year of Kaihuang 開皇,[11] corresponding with the year of *Jiachen* 甲辰, [a boy] was born in the palace. He was born with divine intelligence and grew brave and fierce. He refused to take the throne, concentrating only on self-cultivation in order to assist the Jade Emperor. He swore to eliminate the evil demons under heaven and to save and protect all beings. Day and night, he repeated this vow at the palace. The king could not stop him. Thus, the prince bid farewell to his parents, left home, and entered Mt Wudang to cultivate the Way for 42 years. After his cultivation was completed and the karmic fruit matured (*gongcheng guoman* 功成果滿), he ascended to heaven in broad daylight. The Jade Emperor, knowing the prince to be brave and fierce, ordered him to guard the north and granted him the position of Zhenwu (*tongshe Zhenwu zhi wei* 統攝真武之位) in order to eliminate the demons and sinister under heaven.
>
> 昔有淨樂國王,與善勝皇后,夢吞日光,覺而有娠。懷胎十四箇月, 於開皇元年甲辰之歲,三月建辰初三日午時,誕於王宮。生而 神靈,長而勇猛。不統王位,唯務修行,輔助玉帝,誓斷天下妖魔,救護 群品。日夜於王宮中發此誓願。父王不能禁制,遂捨家辭父母, 入武當山中修道。四十二年功成果滿,白日登天。玉帝聞其勇猛, 敕鎮北方,統攝真武之位,以斷天下妖邪。

Like all typical hagiography, the *Scripture of Zhenwu* then continued with the marvelous deeds of the apotheosized hero. It tells how the Heavenly Worthy of Primordial Commencement (*Yuanshi tianzun* 元始天尊), the highest authority in the Daoist pantheon, summoned General Zhenwu from his post in the north to subdue the demons harming the human world. Setting off on the task, Zhenwu "unbound his hair and stepped barefoot on a climbing snake and divine turtle of the eight trigrams," a standard iconographic image of Zhenwu. He then led 300,000

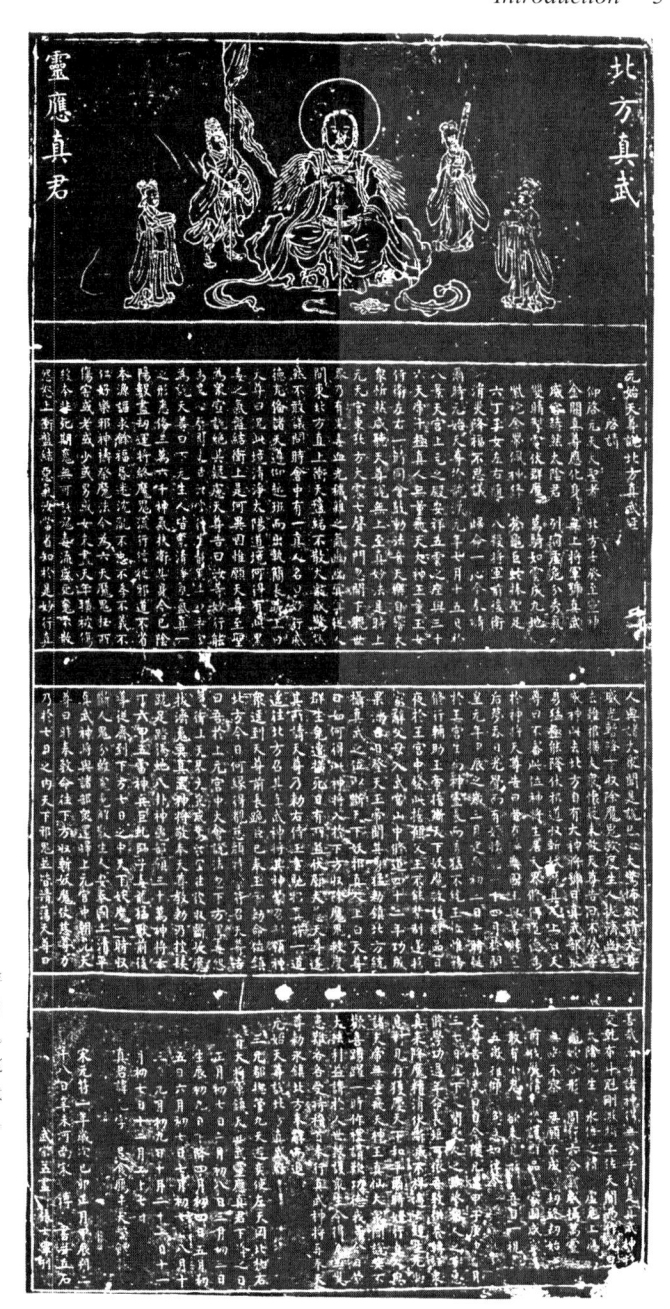

Figure I.1 A stone inscription of the *Scripture of Zhenwu* carved in 1099.
Source: Courtesy of the National Library of China.

soldiers, the divinities of the six *ding* 丁 and six *jia* 甲, soldiers of the Five Thunders, and a good number of fierce beasts to battle against the demons. Within seven days, he vanquished the enemies and returned to heaven in triumph. As a reward for his success, the Heavenly Worthy told the general that from then on he would go down to the human world to receive offerings and patrol the realm on appointed days. "The divine General Zhenwu then respectfully received the decrees of the Heavenly Worthy to be stationed in the north forever. [He] respectfully excused himself and withdrew [from the court]." 真武神將再奉天尊敕, 永鎮北方, 奉辭而退。

The life story of Zhenwu in the *Scripture of Zhenwu*, noted Hsü Tao-ling 許道齡 (1947), was influenced directly or indirectly by that of Shakyamuni. Furthermore, as Yoshihiro Nikaidō (1998: 64–5) demonstrates, the *Scripture of Zhenwu* was composed on the model of the opening section of *Wondrous Scripture of the North Emperor's Divine Incantations for Subduing Demons Set Forth by Heavenly Worthy of Primordial Commencement* (*Taishang Yuanshi Tianzun shuo Beidi fumo shenzhou miaojing* 太上元始天尊說北帝伏魔神咒妙經, TC 1412), a work venerating the North Emperor of Fengdu 酆都. This divine sovereign was the most prominent exorcist authority in medieval Daoism (Mollier 1997). Zhenwu, in the earlier stages of his career, served as an aide-de-camp of the North Emperor (see Chapter 1), thus explaining the textual imitation. Furthermore, the text gives Zhenwu a human origin and a connection to a specific place, Mt Wudang in central China. Utilizing this connection, the Daoist clerics on Mt Wudang added new facets of the image of Zhenwu, as Pierre-Henry de Bruyn (2004) argues.

During the Song–Yuan–Ming period (960–1644), the worship of Zhenwu grew steadily. He was venerated by the clergy and the laity, monarchs and commoners, literati and soldiers, and men and women across social strata. His devotees actively proselytized, providing and circulating information about his grace, sponsoring temple dedications, and organizing rituals or fairs in the god's honor. Rising from the rank of general in the late tenth century, he reached an exalted status in the Daoist divine hierarchy by the late Southern Song with the title of Supreme Emperor of the Dark Heaven, or *Xuantian shangdi* 玄天上帝 (*Dieshang ji* 13.1), a title later confirmed by the Yuan monarchy in 1304 (*Yuanshi* 21.456). Stories of his incarnations multiplied in print and oral form, and on stone and murals thanks to Daoist clerics, lay believers, and shrewd businessmen in commercial printing houses who could appreciate the potential profit from novelistic hagiographies. The depth and breadth of Zhenwu worship allow us to scrutinize the nexus and interaction between the state, local agents, the institution of religion, and the cultural industry itself. The cult furnishes a basis for comprehending the process of the formation of social order and cultural values in China. An examination highlights the active role of human agents in social integration and diversification.

Methods and sources

This study aims at a holistic understanding of Zhenwu worship in relation to the history and society of China. The question at the core of the book is how, in a given historical context, individuals and social institutions shape and reshape the religious world to which they profess devotion. To address the question, I have assembled a broad range of material including scriptures, liturgical manuals, hagiographic accounts, government documents, epigraphy, iconography, gazetteers, anecdotes, and popular literature. To circumvent the potential bias of the materials and those who compiled them, I do not treat them as factual sources, but as sources of perception. In fact, the bias of successive re-interpretations, when treated with awareness, reveals a great deal about the text-producers' mindset. It also allows us to see the intricate means by which various social groups contested with each other in appropriating cultural-religious symbols. By emphasizing a discursive interaction, this study explores the worship of Zhenwu as an ongoing negotiation between different conceptions of who the god is and what he could or should do.

The worship of gods is a "discourse" embodying both theory and practice, and encompassing both domination and contention. Cults devoted to the Empress of Heaven, Guan Yu (also known as Emperor Guan), Wenchang (commonly rendered as the God of Literature in English), the Lady of Linshui, Marshal Wen, Lü Dongbin Wutong/Wuxian, and fox spirits are some of the better-studied examples in the Chinese pantheon (see, for example, Watson 1985; Duara 1988; Kleeman 1993, 1994; Baptandier 1996, 2008; Katz 1995, 1999; Baldrian-Hussein 1986; von Glahn 1991; Cedzich 1995; Szonyi 1997; Kang 2006). The myths and symbols of divinities frequently evolve and mutate along the line of historical development. The shaping of a god's legend is a process of negotiation among different social groups competing in different social milieus. Various human agents invent, re-fuse, add, modify, and synthesize the meanings of religious symbols. Through a slow but persistent process, they renew the structure in which they act.

In analyzing the multivocal meaning of religious symbols, theorists of cultural anthropology have made important contributions. For this study, structuralism and practice theory are particularly useful. Structuralism, founded by Claude Lévi-Strauss, looks for a symbolic logic hidden under the myriad narratives and phenomena of human creations. In discussing mythology, for example, Lévi-Strauss famously claimed his works "show not how men think in myths, but how myths operate in men's minds without their being aware of the fact" (Lévi-Strauss 1969: 12). The human world operates both metaphysically and practically according to an underlying structure supported by a few simple principles which effectively classify cultural and social phenomena (Ortner 1984). The structuralist approach to religious phenomena offers a holistic interpretation that connects it to culture and society.

However, for a historian of religion, structuralism tends to neglect the particularity of the historical environment, since the cognitive response to any specific incident is dictated by a structure that transcends the surrounding reality. Human thinking becomes an "effort of, or a medium for, the pure play of structure" (Ortner 2006: 108). As analytic priority is given to the intrinsic structure of the human mind, the structuralist approach ignores or discounts practice and historical context. "The great challenge to an historical anthropology" as Marshall Sahlins once eloquently puts it, "is not merely to know how events are ordered by culture, but how, in that process, the culture is reordered. How does the reproduction of a structure become its transformation?" (Sahlins 1981: 8).

8 Introduction

Culture, or the system, "constructs people as particular kinds of social actors" while the latter "reproduce or transform" the system through practicing it (Ortner 2006: 129). In his study of the social relations of power and inequality, Pierre Bourdieu, who pioneered the practice theory, developed the concept of *habitus*, an internalized symbolic system of classification that is deeply buried in the human mind. This helps a given society to retain its structure. In a hierarchical society, for example, habitus works to maintain social hierarchy and class domination. The subjected class voluntarily accepts the dominance of "the system" without knowing it (Bourdieu 1977). Nevertheless, Bourdieu's habitus, different from Lévi-Strauss's "structure," is prone to improvisation by agency over time. In sum, practice theory, while appreciating the power of the structure, incorporates negotiation between the agency and the structure. Anthony Giddens pushes further the force of agency, and argues that individuals are never completely ignorant of the operation of "the system," including those who are under domination (Giddens 1979). James Scott demonstrates how the subordinated used their "hidden transcripts" as weapon of resistance (Scott 1992). Barend ter Haar, studying story-telling in pre-modern China, sheds light on how effectively non-literate common folk used oral communication in formulating an "autonomy of local people" (ter Haar 2006: 346). Thus, on the one hand, individuals act in accordance with a set of "organizational and evaluative schemes" that govern the world in which they live (Ortner, 1984: 148); on the other hand, they alter the vast invisible schemes through slow and persistent resistance. The total subordination to a cultural hegemony, in Antonio Gramsci's terminology, is thus more or less illusory.

In the case of Chinese religion, the literary elite, most of whom were trained to join the ruling class, typically spoke from the viewpoint of the dominating strata and dismissed the common folk's beliefs and practices as "vulgar" or "ignorant" and thus in need of transformation in accordance to the standards of the ruling elite. People at the bottom resisted this cultural hegemony not only through passive refusal but also by actively modifying the system. The conflict among different social strata and groups allows us to examine the power negotiations that shaped the religious landscape. It is in the criticism of learned men that we can find records about the illiterate masses. Written materials unveil ideas and activities beyond those of the groups to which the writers belonged. By looking for the "symbols and metaphors" in the narratives, we are able to find the structure that governs people's behavior and the evolution of that structure (von Glahn 2004: 18).

While anthropological theories have added deep insight into the analysis of human behavior patterns, excessive reliance on its methodology brings a risk of reductionism. Religion is not just a source of symbolic capital or a forum for power negotiation; it has its own inner logic. To shed light on the autonomous aspect of religion, this study devotes a substantial space to liturgy. The liturgical innovations of Song Daoism created a layered imagery of Zhenwu. Even though Daoist ritual knowledge is esoteric and known to the initiated only, the images of Zhenwu created in the Daoist ritual arena are not out of reach to ordinary people. Kristofer Schipper (1985) has pointed out that clerical Daoism (or "classical"

Daoism in his terminology), in spite of being "a literate, refined, elegant, and sophisticated expression of Chinese religion," never shied away from interaction with the common folk. Daoist priests were (and still are) in demand as providers of religious services, including mediating with the deities on behalf of the laity (Lagerwey 1987; Davis, 2001; Goossaert 2007). While Robert Hymes (2002) has convincingly argued that Daoist and lay perceptions of the divinities represent two separate models, fluidity between the two models is apparent, as this study will demonstrate. A liturgical study of Zhenwu worship deepens our understanding of the god's portrait in the mind of the common folks in particular, and the interaction between Daoism and popular religion in general.

The Song–Yuan–Ming period

Religion must be studied "in its social setting and noting the economic and political parameters to religious ideas and operations," asserts Raymond Firth (1996: 3). It has been argued that the period from around the end of the Northern Song period in 1127 to 1500 "constitutes an identifiable historical unit and a genuine historical transition," and the period has been described as the Song–Yuan–Ming transition (Smith 2003: 2). The religious landscape of the Song period in particular was characterized by a market-based system of ritual services extending from the priestly elite to the unlicensed, self-trained, semi-literate spirit mediums. In terms of Daoist religious history, the Song saw the incorporation of early medieval traditions, and tenth-century innovations, as well as continuing developments in sectarianism and monasticism. These developments would reach fruition in the Yuan and Ming (1368–1644) dynasties. The Song–Yuan–Ming period witnessed a trajectory of new ritual movements, the growth and re-invention of old sects, and the canonization of new ideas and practices.

The competition for ritual services during the Song was so advanced that it constituted a market. Unlicensed ritual specialists reduced their fees to attract bargain-hunting customers (Hymes 2002: 45). The competitive market further stimulated the development of novel ritual techniques and the master–disciple lineages centered around them. Such innovation was so threatening to traditionalist Daoists that they felt the need to condemn some of their colleagues for taking too many liberties in their techniques. Jin Yunzhong 金允中 (fl. 1224–1225), a self-described heir of the authentic rituals of the Lingbao 靈寶 school, relentlessly attacked the Tiantai 天台 lineage of the Lingbao school as well as its ritual codifier, Ning Benli 寧本立 (1101–1181), claiming the latter's liturgies to be nothing but distortions of tradition (Boltz 1987: 45–46). Huang Gongjin 黃公瑾 (fl. 1275), another Daoist master of the Southern Song, complained that "latter-day itinerant Ritual Officers (*faguan* 法官) contrived new rituals to entice the younger generation (*houjin* 後進) and increased talismans to fool the beginners."[12] The rivalry and acrimony reveal not only the seriousness of competition among the schools but also the active role of the ritual masters. They were tirelessly inventing new ritual programs or seeking to learn them from others to attract the ever-demanding customer base.

Experts on the psycho-physical exercise of inner alchemy (*neidan* 內丹), which obtained popularity by the early Song period, were also searching market towns and the countryside for worthy disciples.[13] The most successful ones among them were Wang Zhe 王喆 (1113–1170) and his apostles who established the Complete Perfection (*Quanzhen* 全真) school around 1170. In addition to its significance in inner alchemy, Complete Perfection is distinctive as a monastic order (Goossaert 1997). Its widespread network and exemplary practices promoted Daoist monasticism. The monkish priests on Mt Wudang (not necessarily Quanzhen friars) in turn were the key element in transforming the mountain into the pilgrimage center of Zhenwu worship in the fourteenth century. It was against such a background—the growing competition in the religious market, the creative ritual specialists, and the growing role of monasticism in Daoism—that the worship of Zhenwu became institutionalized in Daoism and in the Chinese religious landscape.

Terms

There are different words in Chinese to denote different religious buildings. Although there is a general terminology for naming temples, it is not always strictly followed. Furthermore, words often fail to reflect the actual religious practices that take place within the temple compounds. Given the syncretistic nature of Chinese religion in practice, the boundaries between different religions are often not strictly observed; it is no surprise to find the activities of one religion taking place in the temple of another religion. Nevertheless, for reasons of consistency, I adopt a set of straightforward rules in translating the name of temples into English: *si* 寺 as Buddhist monastery, *guan* 觀 as Daoist monastery, *an* 庵 as "cloister" (or "nunnery" when the context is clear), *yuan* 院 as "courtyard," *ci* 祠 as "shrine," *miao* 廟 as "temple" and *gong* 宮 as "palace." The word monastery used in this study contains no implication of an enclosed institution but simply characterizes a larger temple with either Buddhist or Daoist monks-priests in residence. Readers should keep in mind that the terminology will not always capture the scale or prestige of a temple accurately; smaller temples, for example, would choose grandiose names whenever they could to give themselves prestige.

For religious specialists, I follow the tradition of using "monk" and "nun" to refer to Buddhist clericks while rendering *daoshi* 道士 and *nüguan* 女官 as "priest" and "priestess." Of course, in reality, the distinction was more ambiguous; many Buddhist monks and nuns provided ritual services to the laity, much like priests and priestesses, while many Daoist priests and priestesses withdrew from society and sought refuge in their temples, much like monks and nuns. A more general term to refer to the ritual specialists was *fashi* 法師. *Fashi*, meaning literally "ritual (*fa*) master (*shi*)," is a term that has multiple connotations and can be used to address both Buddhist and Daoist clerics.[14] The term has always been used as a title of reverence for religious specialists. In today's Taiwan, for example, Buddhists still use it as a standard suffix after the names of monks and nuns. In the Daoist context, the ritual manuals of the new Daoist lineages typically refer to the initiated practitioners as *fashi* (also *faguan* 法官, "ritual officer"). *Fashi* in Song times and later was used in canonical and anecdotal material to address figures from eminent court Daoist masters to ritual practitioners who were not even licensed.[15] In a sense, it became a euphemism, a polite way to address a religious specialist.

Outline

Chapter 1 looks into the sources that initiated Zhenwu's godhead. Zhenwu was an exorcist divinity who first appears in the period of the Five Dynasties (907–960) and who had absorbed the astrological symbolism of classical times. The chapter starts with an exploration of the cosmological significance of the god's emblems—the turtle and snake—in relation to the Four Animals who are the zoomorphic representations of the four cardinal directions of the compass. The following section examines the origin of Zhenwu's exorcist power: he was a member in the Four Saints formulated in the late Five Dynasties as a new martial quartet serving under the traditional authority of exorcism in Daoism, the North Emperor (*beidi* 北帝), a title that Zhenwu would eventually assume.

Chapter 2 investigates devotional practice centered on Zhenwu during Song times (960–1279), the period when his worship took clear shape. This chapter asks how, when, and where the devotees worshipped him. The sources employed in this chapter are primarily government documents and scholar-officials' writings, supplemented with literature from the *Daoist Canon*. During Song times, the emperors and their capital cities hosted the most celebrated Zhenwu temples. Outside the capitals however, Daoist priests played a crucial role in temple construction; by the end of the Northern Song era, nevertheless, their efforts were matched by the scholar-official elite.

Chapter 3 examines Zhenwu worship within the internal dynamics of Daoism. Many Song-Yuan Daoist liturgical manuals, those of the Thunder Rites to be specific, instruct priests to "become" a deity when carrying out the ritual. Identity-transformation was perceived to have taken place not by divine possession but through the meditative liturgy, "transformation into the deity through inner refinement" (*bianshen neilian* 變神內煉). This trend of ritual development later underscored the ritual practitioners' dependence on their divine meditative partners, who were often referred to as ancestral teacher/master (*zushi* 祖師) or holy teacher/master (*shengshi* 聖師). Zhenwu was venerated as one of the godly tutelary masters in the new ritual lineages. From there, he swiftly climbed the hierarchical ladder from lineage ancestral master to "supreme emperor."

Chapter 4 introduces Mt Wudang, the pilgrimage center of Zhenwu worship since the later part of the twelfth century. By maintaining a network of holy sites on the mountain, the Daoist clerics of the Yuan period replaced the old mountain myths with Zhenwu legends. Pilgrims, while accepting the big picture clerics painted for the mountain, made use of their own traditions that were not always in accordance with those of the clerics. After catastrophic warfare at the end of the Yuan, the monarchs of the following Ming dynasty restored the ruined monasteries on the mountain as a way to seize control of the symbolic capital of Zhenwu. They then added another dimension to the mountain—the symbolism of state authority. The

12 *Introduction*

imbricated images of Mt Wudang, overlapping with and extending from each other, created the multivocal character of Zhenwu.

Chapter 5 concludes this study by analyzing the miracles attributed to Zhenwu from the Song to the Ming in order to capture how Zhenwu was perceived over time and across social strata. Zhenwu's original symbolism evolved into a more diverse one that encompassed new powers and characteristics. Once primarily an exorcist, he developed the ability to control weather, influence military operations, protect the community as a tutelary god, give sons, cure illnesses, and bring prosperity and posthumous salvation to the faithful. Zhenwu's various images projected themselves through numerous anecdotes related by gazetteers and literati-officials. New miracles were ascribed to him by ardent believers, and his persona expanded as he took on the form of a god for all time and for all people.

1 A god in formation

> Zhenwu was originally Xuanwu. To avoid the personal name of the [imperial] Holy Patriarch [which contains the word *xuan*,] he is therefore called Zhenwu. … The shapes of the constellations Xu and Wei [in the northern sky] are similar to the snake and the turtle, therefore the north is referred to as Xuanwu of the seven stars. … At present, people take Xuanwu to be a perfected saint and make [images of a] real turtle and snake beneath him. This is ridiculous enough. In addition, they added the perfected lords of Tianpeng, Tianyou, and Yisheng [with Zhenwu] to form the Four Saints.
>
> 真武本玄武, 避聖祖諱, 故曰真武 … 此本虛危星形似之故, 因而名北方為玄武七星 … 今乃以玄武為真聖而作真龜蛇於下, 已無義理, 而又增天蓬天猷及翊聖真君作四聖。
>
> Zhu Xi 朱熹, *Conversations of Master Zhu* (*Zhuzi yulei* 朱子語類 125.30b).

The turtle: a cosmological symbol

Traditionally, it was asserted that Zhenwu, as an anthropomorphic deity, was directly linked to, if not identical with, the main constellations in the northern sky, Xuanwu, that were depicted in the form of a turtle or a turtle encircled by a snake. Modern scholarship, until two decades ago, also embraced the theory that the veneration of Zhenwu in Song and later times was a direct evolution of a stellar cult of Xuanwu from classical times (for example, Hsü 1947; Huang Zhaohan 1988). New research, however, has begun to challenge this long held wisdom. Romeyn Taylor first describes the connection between the two as "tenuous" (1990: 154–155). Pierre-Henry de Bruyn (1997) asserted that only the shared name and emblems support the assumed mutation from one to the other.

Taylor and de Bruyn are correct in unveiling the objective truth of the origin of Zhenwu. However, regardless of how dubious the connection was, this assumed origin of Zhenwu has been accepted as an established fact in the minds of his devotees and critics alike. Zhu Xi's (1130–1200) disparaging comments, cited above, is an example. The belief of Zhenwu's identity as a cosmological symbol was the inspiration for the principal characteristics and interpretations of his godhead from Song times to the present. And his cosmological significance was most often theorized through his relation to the stellar Xuanwu. Understanding of the assumed astral origin of Zhenwu

14 *A god in formation*

therefore is indispensible in reconstructing the god's images and worship in the historical landscape.

The dark/black celestial turtle image

The term Xuanwu was coined by two characters: *xuan*, which denotes dark or deep, and *wu*, conventionally rendered into English as "martial" or "warrior." According to the eminent classicist Kong Yingda 孔穎達 (574–648), the turtle's hard shell resembled armor and thus symbolized the qualities of protection and defense (*Liji zhushu* 3.13b). The turtle therefore connoted the martial quality or *wu* 武. Most commentators on the classics, with one exception, associated Xuanwu with the turtle.

The term Xuanwu appeared in the Western Han (206 BCE CE 24) in the verse "Roaming Far Away" (*Yuanyou* 遠遊). Modern scholarship in general has determined the author to be Sima Xiangru 司馬相如 (179–117 BCE) or one of his contemporaries (Hawkes 1985: 191–192; Kroll: 1996; Mair 2001: 228), but traditionally the verse was credited to the legendary tragic litterateur Qu Yuan 屈原 (ca. 340–278 BCE) of the Warring States period (476–221 BCE). The poem demonstrates not only a high degree of literary skill but also erudition in mythological tradition in the account of an ecstatic journey to heaven. En route, the poet-protagonist was accompanied by a veritable entourage of mythical figures, including Xuanwu.

"Roaming Far Away" was published in the *Elegies of Chu* (*Chuci* 楚辭), an anthology of works from southern China compiled, edited, and annotated by Wang Yi 王逸 (ca. CE 89–158). Wang Yi maintained, in this particular context, that Xuanwu referred to the "great *yin* god" (*Taiyin shen* 太陰神), who was either the Moon or the Year Star (*suixing* 歲星).[1] However, when commenting on another piece in the *Elegies of Chu*, the "Nine Regrets" (*Jiuhuai* 九懷), which he attributed to Wang Bao 王褒 (fl. 74–49 BCE) of the Western Han, Wang Yi defined Xuanwu as "celestial turtle" (*tiangui* 天龜; see *Chuci zhangju* 15.7). Was Wang Yi a meticulous commentator who gave alternate meanings of Xuanwu based on usage during different time periods, and aware that the astral name was not used for the symbol of a turtle until the Western Han? After all, to Wang Yi's mind, "Roaming Far Away" was one of Qu Yuan's pieces written in the Warring States period while the "Nine Regrets" was a work composed two centuries later in the Western Han period.

By the Eastern Han, the Xuanwu symbol in visual representation appeared in two different patterns: a solitary turtle and a turtle encircled by a snake (see figure 1.1).[2] The insertion of a snake into the symbol corresponded with the contemporaneous perception that the snake was the turtle in the male form, a taxonomical theory that the authoritative lexicologist Xu Shen 許慎 (ca. CE 58–147) advanced in his monumental dictionary of CE 121.[3] According to Xu Shen, all turtles were female and all snakes were male. Or, to put in a different way, the turtle and snake are the same species; the former is female and the latter male. While the actual belief that the turtle and the snake were of the same species was abandoned long ago, the iconographic pattern of an entangled snake and turtle survives to the present day and has replaced the unitary image of the turtle.

Figure 1.1 A tile with the design of a turtle encircled by a snake, Eastern Han dynasty.
Source: © Wikimedia commons.

The celestial dark turtle was also the symbol by which the ancient Chinese depicted the constellations of the northern sky. In the "Monograph on Celestial Offices" (Tianguan shu 天官書) of the *Grand History* (*Shiji* 史記), Sima Qian 司馬遷 (ca. BCE 145–90) synthesized the astronomic–astrological scholarship known in his time and presented the first systematic description of the Chinese night sky. He recounted the constellations in terms of the classical astrological framework of five "palaces" (*gong* 宮): a Central Palace being surrounded by the East Palace of the Azure Dragon (*donggong canglong* 東宮蒼龍), the South Palace of the Vermilion Bird (*nangong zhuniao* 南宮朱鳥), the Western Palace of the Harmony Pond (*xigong xianchi* 西宮咸池), and Northern Palace of Xuanwu.[4] The two principal stellar patterns, or *xiu* 宿 (lit. lodgers),[5] which constituted the North Palace, were Xu 虛 and Wei 危. The *Book of Han* (*Hanshu* 漢書) remains faithful to the same structure in describing the nocturnal sky. This five-palace model was evidently the standard perception of the nocturnal firmament in China throughout the first century CE. Thus, in the beginning, Xuanwu was a creature of the immaterial world, with an astronomical connection and such human characteristics as the martial spirit which were embedded in its name.

The Four Animals

The *Record of Rites* (*Liji* 禮記), a Confucian classic compiled in the late Western Han period but consisting of materials from the Warring States period, provides another ideographical quartet that was similar but not identical to the astronomical symbols in the *Grand History* and the *Book of Han*: Xuanwu was teamed together with a vermilion bird, an azure dragon (referred to as *qinglong* 青龍), and a white tiger (*baihu* 白虎).[6] The symbols were painted on military banners, rear, left, right, and front, in order to organize military units. They were referred as the Four Animals (*sishou* 四獸) by the time of the Eastern Han.[7] The Xuanwu symbol further accumulated cosmological significance as the Four Animals made their way into the correlative cosmology of the Five Phases that prevailed in the Han political and intellectual milieu.

Chinese cosmology is based on "correlative thinking" (Graham 1989: 319–325; also see Puett 2002: 16–19, 145–200). Correlative cosmology connects human affairs with patterns in nature and combines them into one classification system. Elements grouped in the same category, whether phenomenal or non-phenomenal, are believed to correspond with one another faithfully and predictably in accordance with the principles of "cosmic resonance," or *ganying* 感應 (Henderson 1984: 20). As the *Huainan zi* 淮南子 of the second century BCE states "things within the same class mutually move each other" (*Huainan zi* 3.2a; Major 1993: 65 n.27). The most popular classification system of correlative cosmology since the Warring States period was the system of the five categories: water, fire, wood, metal, and earth.[8] After a long process of synthesis, this single all-encompassing classification system, generally referred to as the Five Phases (*wuxing* 五行), grouped practically every aspect of human civilization and natural phenomena. The Four Animals serving as directional indicators were naturally incorporated into the scheme. A fifth component, which varied in different sources, was added to complete the set of five, as showing in, for example, the *Huainan zi*:[9]

> The East is Wood. … Its animal is the azure dragon. … The South is Fire.… Its animal is the vermilion bird.… The Center is Earth.… Its animal is the yellow dragon. … The West is Metal.… Its animal is the white tiger. … The North is Water. Its animal is Xuanwu. Its musical note is *yu*. His days are *ren* and *gui*.
>
> 東方木也 … 其獸蒼龍，南方火也，… 其獸朱鳥，… 中央土也，其獸黃龍，… 西方金也，其獸白虎，… 北方水也，…，其獸玄武，其音羽，其日壬癸。

Xuanwu was the animal of the north assigned to the category of water, and accordingly was associated with other aspects in the water category, in the sense of mutual response or "resonance."

With their connection to the Five Phases cosmology, the Four Animals were used to create the cosmic frame of an orderly universe. In inferring the meaningfulness and organization of the sky, Zhang Heng 張衡 (CE 78–139) wrote in his "Spiritual Constitution of the Universe" (*Lingxian* 靈憲):

> The stars are formally generated in the earth and germinally formed in the sky. … The azure dragon twirls at the left, the white tiger fiercely occupies the right, the vermillion bird extends its wings in the front, the spiritual turtle (*linggui*) turns over its head at the back, and the yellow god Xuanyuan is at the central.
>
> 星也者，體生於地，精成於天 … 蒼龍連蜷於左，白虎猛據於右，朱雀奮翼於前，靈龜圈首於後，黃神軒轅於中．

Here, Zhang Heng used the Four Animals to represent the four sections surrounding the center division of the sky occupied by Xuanyuan 軒轅, whom Zhang Heng identified with the yellow god but is more commonly referred to as the Yellow Emperor (*Huangdi* 黃帝). Instead of using the four cardinal directions, Zhang used the right, left, front and rear, just like the paragraph in the *Book of Rites* cited above. The vast metaphysical sky became comprehensible and meaningful to humans only after it was organized or "civilized" by human power.

On a brick tomb in Yi'nan 沂南 dated between the second and third centuries, the Four Animals were engraved around a monstrous figure in chamber no. 1 (see figure 1.2), the front room immediately preceding the hallway open to the south. The monstrous figure, on the wall opposite the door, carries five weapons, identifying him as Chiyou 蚩尤 (*Shandong Yinan Han mu hua xiang shi*, 2001, p. 79 and illustrations nos. 12, 13, and 14). Above Chiyou's head is a vigorous bird with wings outstretched and below him is a turtle glancing at a snake coiled around it. A tiger and a dragon appear on the west and east walls next to Chiyou respectively. From Chiyou's viewpoint on the north wall, the dragon is on the left and the tiger on the right. The top always corresponds with the front, and the bottom with the rear. Chiyou, as modern scholars have argued, was a symbolic double of Xuanyuan, the Yellow Emperor (Lewis 1990: 185; Puett 1998). This brick engraving is virtually a graphic reproduction of the short paragraph from Zhang Heng's "Spiritual Constitution of the Universe" cited above.

Zhang Heng's verse and the Yi'nan tomb engraving are representations of the same idea but in different media, one literary and the other pictorial. They share the concept that an orientation frame is formed by the insertion of the Four Animals. Only after the frame is formed can the center be located. With the Four Animals as reference points, the focus point—the loci of the high deity—is created. Thus we find in the *Master who Embraces Simplicity* (*Baopu zi*) by Ge Hong 葛洪 (CE 283–343) that Lord Lao, the deified Laozi and the single highest divinity in Daoism until the Supreme Clarity revelations in CE 364, was surrounded by the Four Animals in multiple forms (*Baopu zi* 3.43a).

The cosmological significance of the Four Animals during the Han dynasty is further underscored by their incorporation into the TLV mirrors that were popular at the time (Lien-sheng Yang 1947; Cammann 1948). These mirrors are so named by modern scholars for the marks on the back that resemble the shapes of the letters T, L, and V. In addition to its so-named marks, the TLV mirror design often includes a square pattern in the middle and the Four Animals surrounding the square. The square symbolizes the earth, and the roundness of the mirror symbolizes the sky in accordance with the traditional concept of "round heaven and square earth." TLV mirrors were often found buried in coffins near the heads of the deceased. Scholars have long debated the design of such mirrors and the purpose of burying them with the deceased. Michael Loewe argues that the pattern is essentially a reproduction of the diviner's board (*shi* 式), which in turn was a reproduction of heaven and earth. By placing it in the coffin, the deceased was situated in the "most favorable position of the cosmos" (Loewe 1979: 61, 75–82). Mark Edward Lewis, although dismissing the idea of the diviner's board as the inspirational source, shares a common

18 *A god in formation*

Figure 1.2 The Four Animals in a tomb in Yi'nan, Shandong province. Eastern Han dynasty.
Source: Drawn by Edyth Kuciapa, based on *Shandong Yi'nan Huamu*.

consensus with Michael Loewe that these mirrors were meant to create an ideal micro-cosmos for the deceased: "The geometric simplicity with clearly enumerable dots and lines brought the entirety of existence within a space that could fit comfortably in a human hand and be taken in at a single glance. Consequently it could be manipulated for the benefit of the user, who could situate himself within the schema generated in the chart" (Lewis 2006: 27). The TLV mirror conferred on its owner the power to manipulate the cosmos by freezing time and space in a position most beneficial to the owner.

In light of the symbolic function of the mirrors, the incorporation of the Four Animals with the TLV pattern went beyond a simple decorative function. With their directional qualities, the Four Animals served as the framework for orientation, a function that conferred on them the symbolism of orderliness. Reproducing their images on man-made artifacts therefore brought heavenly orderliness to the earth. The inclusion of the Four Animals in the design enhanced the role of the TLV mirrors in pointing the way to a universe that was properly ordered.

A further example of the Four Animals' cosmological symbolism lies in the architectural principles behind the building of capitals and imperial palaces. The locus of the monarch's rule was expected to be a replication of the ideal pattern of heaven. The First Qin Emperor, for example, named his new palace the Apex Temple (*Jimiao* 極廟), referring to the Heavenly Apex (*tianji* 天極), that is, the central palace (*zhonggong* 中宮) of the heaven (*Shiji* 6.241–242; Lewis, 2006, 171; Wheatley 1971: 442). The central palace in classical astrology was regarded as the celestial counterpart of the imperial court, a concept inherited from the Han dynasty (*Shiji* 27.1289). In describing the Eternal Palace (Weiyang gong 未央宮), the principal imperial palatial compound of the Western Han, the *Yellow Chart of the Three Districts* (*Sanfu huangtu* 三輔黃圖) included an instructional explanation of the construction of the capital (3.3a):

> The azure dragon, white tiger, vermilion bird, and Xuanwu are the four numina in heaven used to locate the four directions. The kings who establish palaces, towers, halls, or pavilions should use [them] as the model.
>
> 蒼龍白虎朱雀玄武，天之四靈，以正四方。王者制宮闕殿閣取法焉。

The Four Animals provided the structural framework for creating an orderly cosmos ("put in order the four directions"), and in turn, were called upon to turn the palace into a replica of heaven in its ideal orderliness. It is thus not surprising to find that the names of imperial buildings and their decorations often reveal traces of the Four Animals. In the ruins of a Western Han sacrificial site near the capital, Chang'an 長安 (present-day Xian, Shaanxi), archeologists unearthed sets of roof tiles engraved with the Four Animals (Wang 1982: figs 33–36). The Four Animals were used to name the palatial gates in both Western and Eastern Han dynasties.[10] The great philosophical discourse from the Eastern Han, the *Comprehensive Discussions in the White Tiger Hall* (*Baihu tong* 白虎通), was so named because the conference that led to its production took place in the White Tiger Hall (Baihu guan 觀) in the imperial palace compound. Xuanwu and the Vermillion Bird were evidently used to name the north and south city-gates of the capital city of Jiankang 建康 (present-day Nanjing in Jiangsu) during the Six Dynasties.[11]

Throughout the Tang dynasty, we again find Xuanwu being used to name a northern palatial gate: the Xuanwu Gate of the Taiji Palace, where multiple

20 *A god in formation*

coup d'etats were hatched. Tang monarchs also invoked the Four Animals in constructing imperial burial sites. Qianling, the tomb of Emperor Tang Gaozong (r. 649–83) and Empress Wu (r. 690–705) possesses a funerary mound surrounded by four gates named after the Four Animals respectively (Steinhardt 1990: 18, fig. 17). After all, as palaces housing dead emperors, imperial necropolises, too, must reproduce the order of heaven on earth. An orderly space was a creation of human projection, invested with an intellectual construction of a symbolic nature.

Hsü Tao-lin, whose article pioneered the modern study of Zhenwu, cited the Xuanwu temple at the Xuanwu Gate of the Taiji Palace of the Tang court as evidence of the Xuanwu cult during the Tang dynasty and evidence that the cult itself was a remnant of the star worship of ancient times (Hsü 1947: 232, 240). This opinion has found widespread acceptance. However, I would suggest that the Xuanwu Gate was designed in accordance with the traditional architectural principles of replicating heaven in the ruler's palace, and the Xuanwu temple on top took its name from the gate. The temple itself was not a sanctuary for worshipping Xuanwu. Instead of signifying the practice of a constellation cult, the name of the Xuanwu gate was part of the vast cosmological scheme that attempted to manipulate the force of the cosmos.

The Four Animals, as symbolically important as they were, occupied no position in the Daoist pantheon of the Six Dynasties. As Hung-I Chuang points out, three different divine protocols took shape during this time period but none included the Four Animals or Xuanwu (Chuang 1994: 7). This absence suggests their obscure status.[12] Nevertheless, the Six Dynasties probably witnessed the beginning of the Four Animals' anthropomorphosis. A relief displaying a turtle entwined by a snake with a bust of a male in a civil official attire, found on the foot slab of a sarcophagus, was dated to the late Northern Wei (CE 386–534). Stephen Little (2000: 293) identifies this male figure as Xuanwu. If he is correct, the Four Animals had already acquired human properties (but had not yet lost their original animal form) by the beginning of the sixth century.

By the late Tang period we begin to find information on veneration of the Four Animals in a Daoist environment. The Daoist (*daoshi*) Chen Ruoyu 陳若愚 of the late ninth century produced a mural of the Four Animals in a Daoist temple in Chengdu, Sichuan. Huang Xiufu 黃休復 (fl. 1006) recorded the mural, which was still extant during his times, in his important contribution to Chinese art history, *Record of Famous Paintings in Yizhou* (*Yizhou minghua lu*, p. 198; also see *Tuhua jianwen zhi*, p. 472).

Xuanwu vs. the turtle: a clarification

While Xuanwu was closely identified with the turtle (or the turtle-snake pair), it would be a misleading simplification to say that Xuanwu was an alternative appellation of *gui* 龜 (the most common Chinese character for "turtle") as Yu Yan 俞琰 (1258–1314) claimed.[13] Two anecdotes that were in circulation by Tang times contained traces of the old Xuanwu in popular belief. The first story was supposed to have taken place in CE 484. A Daoist, visiting Mt Lu 廬山 in Jiangxi province, saw a coiled snake that resembled a pile of colorful satin. In a flash, it metamorphosed into a giant turtle. The Daoist later encountered an "old man of the mountain" (*shansou* 山叟) and asked him about what he had just seen. The old man answered that what he had seen was Xuanwu (*Youyang zazu* 酉陽雜俎, supplement, 3.8b). The other story tells of a boy who saw a turtle enveloped by a snake in a bamboo grove. He killed both creatures. Within ten days of the incident, several dozen of the boy's family members died one after another. The story ends with the comment: "Xuanwu is a deity" (*Xuanwu shen ye* 玄武神也; an alternative rendition would be: [It was] the god Xuanwu). This final remark betrayed a perceived connection between the killing of the turtle-snake pair and the death of the boy's family. The two stories attest to the mystical power attributed to Xuanwu, a supernatural being manifest in the form of a turtle-snake union.

The general: an exorcist symbol

Although Xuanwu the turtle went through a process of humanization prior to the tenth century, the anthropomorphic Xuanwu, or Zhenwu, derived his persona from a different source—Daoist exorcism. Zhenwu started his exorcist career as an aide-de-camp of the North Emperor, the sovereign of exorcism in Daoism. It is true that there is no concrete material prior to Song times that linked Zhenwu directly to the North Emperor. However, there was an indirect linkage: General Tianpeng 天蓬, a subordinate of the North Emperor and a fellow comrade-in-arms of Zhenwu. Exorcism in early Daoist practice, discussed below, was underlined by apocalypse and personified by the North Emperor and his right-hand man, General Tianpeng. As we explore Zhenwu's association with the latter during the late Five Dynasties, we will see that the worship of Zhenwu as a member of the Four Saints, headed by Tianpeng, in the administration of the North Emperor, was already in practice, at least among the elites in Fujian, by CE 975.

The North Emperor of the six heavens

The North Emperor appeared as a demon-demolisher during the Six Dynasties (CE 220–589). According to the *Declarations of the Perfected* (*Zhengao* 真誥; TC 1010), first written down in the mid-fourth century,[14] the North Emperor governed Mt Luofeng 羅酆, better known as Fengdu 酆都, located in the northernmost region of the universe.[15] This massive cosmic mountain was a land of the dead and its headquarters was located in six grotto-palaces referred to as the six heavens (Mollier 1997). The six heavens constituted a complex bureaucratic system that made judicatory decisions on new arrivals and accordingly assigned them positions and places within the realm. At the top of the officialdom was the North Emperor. The six heavens, as portrayed in the *Declarations of the Perfected*, might not be a desirable place but was certainly not hell on earth.

22 *A god in formation*

Nevertheless, the six heavens had an alternative connotation in Daoism that was associated with misery and wickedness. According to the teachings of the Celestial Masters school, established by Zhang Daoling 張道陵 (fl. CE 142) in the second century CE, the six heavens referred not to a specific location but to a particular *kalpa*, or cosmic era, that was winding down by Zhang Daoling's time. In the *Scripture of the Inner Explanations of the Three Heavens* (*Santian neijie jing* 三天內解經), a Celestial Masters school text from the fifth century, we find for the first time a well-developed theory about the apocalypse of the six heavens.[16] It goes as follows: By late Han times, the six-heaven *kalpa* had reached the final stages of its cycle and had gone stale. "Coming to the age of lower antiquity, the pneumas of the Dao thinned, so that perversity and evil arose in their turn. … [U]nder the rule of the Han house, all sorts of deviant forces flourished and the pneumas of the Six Heavens flared up. Three Ways[17] mingled and disease vapors ran amok. … The lives of heaven's people were thus cut short, and corpses of those who died suddenly were scattered about" (translated by Bokenkamp 1997, 212–213). Finally, the Most High (the deified Laozi) abrogated the authority of the *kalpa* of the six heavens and appointed Zhang Daoling to govern the next cosmos cycle, the three heavens. It is in this description that the six heavens were associated with the wicked spirits who created calamities and attacked humankind, causing humans to die before they had lived through their destined life spans. Before long, the Celestial Masters' interpretation merged with that of the Supreme Clarity, and the six heavens became a distant northern realm populated by malicious demon kings who commanded ghost troops. The North Emperor ruled over these demons and suffering souls. His administration was exalted enough to warrant the depiction of demon-controlling symbols, and his combatant generals took the form of the agents of exorcism.

The six heavens continued to serve as a theoretical basis in medieval Daoism for explaining the calamities of the world. A text from Tang times, *Scripture of the Golden Register for the Redemption of Sins and for Salvation, [including] the Nine True and Marvelous Precepts* (*Taishang jiuzhen miaojie jinlu duming bazui jing* 太上九真妙戒金籙度命拔罪經, CT 181), recognized the North Emperor of Fengdu (Fengdu beidi 酆都北帝) to be the head of the underworld (*mingsi* 冥司) where horrible tortures were inflicted on the deceased as posthumous punishment for their misdeeds in life.[18] This divine sovereign was supported by a large contingent of ghost officials (*guiguan* 鬼官) including some demonic figures such as "the arch-demons of the three realms and the 900 millions of ghost kings" (*sanjie damo, jiuyi guiwang* 三界大魔九億鬼王). When the Heavenly Worthy of the Primordial Commencement paid a visit to the underworld, the text relates, the North Emperor pleaded with him for redemptive measures on behalf of the suffering souls. The North Emperor's jurisdiction over the underworld, his authority over demonic kings (who by implication can overpower regular demons), and his compassion for the suffering souls of the deceased are ideal qualities that fulfilled the requirements for an exorcist authority.

The ritual movement centered on the North Emperor acquired substantial capital during the Tang dynasty. The erudite and prolific Daoist priest Du Guangting 杜光庭 (CE 850–933), who was revered in the courts of Emperor

Tang Xizong 僖宗 (r. 873–888) and the Shu 蜀 Kingdom (CE 907–925), recorded several "verified miracles" produced by the exorcist methods of Beidi in his *Evidential Miracles In Support of Daoism* (*Daojiao lingyan ji* 道教靈驗記 TC 590; hereafter, *Evidential Miracles*). One such story tells of a certain Fan Lingyan 樊令言 of Bianzhou 汴州, Henan, who married a woman with an unknown background (*Yunji qiqian* 121. 2674–2675).[19] He soon became sick, lustful (for the new wife), reclusive, short-tempered, and delirious. A Daoist priest recognized the signs as symptoms of demonic possession. He prescribed the performance of the North Emperor ritual (*Beidi daochang* 北帝道場) to vanquish the demons that were freeloading on Fan. The priest sent his acolyte (*tongzi* 童子, lit. lad) to go home with Fan to conduct the ritual. The novice selected a secure room in Fan's house and locked himself in. Fan's new wife angrily protested in vain. That night, a dozen or so divinities brought hawks and hounds from heaven. They went directly to the master chamber and killed Fan's new wife, along with her maids . All the corpses turned into foxes. Fan was dismayed and rushed to search for the acolyte in the locked room only to find that he had already gone (without unlocking the door). A note was left behind saying, "The Most High ordered the North Emperor's hawk-and-dog troops to execute the harmful fox spirits at Fan Lingyan's household, as the talisman ordered." This story illustrates the powers of exorcism that the North Emperor was perceived to possess. The final verse, furthermore, portrays the North Emperor as a vassal to Lord Lao, the Most High. Du Guangting, an authoritative figure in both clerical and political communities (Verellen 1989), sanctioned, preserved, and publicized the North Emperor's legacy.

The Tianpeng incantation and General Tianpeng

One of the most effective methods for adherents to invoke the North Emperor's powers of exorcism was to recite the "divine incantation of the North Emperor" (*Beidi zhi shenzhou* 北帝之神咒), according to the "North Emperor's methods for killing demons" (*Beidi shagui zhi fa* 北帝煞鬼之法) from the *Declarations of the Perfected* (*Zhengao* 10.10b). The incantation contains 36 stanzas starting with "Tianpeng Tianpeng" and thus was commonly referred as the Tianpeng incantation. Reciting it three times was supposed to be enough to kill any demons. As Isabelle Robinet points out, the Tianpeng incantation anthropomorphized into General (or Marshal) Tianpeng, the fierce demon-slayer and aide-de-camp of the North Emperor (Robinet 1997 [1992]: 37). By Tang times, General Tianpeng was portrayed as the right-hand man of the North Emperor (Liu 1987). The anthropomorphosis of the Tianpeng incantation did not stop here. A set of 36 talismans reportedly created in the eighth century portrayed every one of the incantation's 36 stanzas as an appellation of a particular individual or group of deities, all of whom were fierce fighters (*Secret Essential*, j.3, *ZHDZ* 30.332a–335a).

The talismans, along with the accompanied oral secret (*koujue* 口訣), were attributed to the Daoist master Deng Siguan 鄧思瓘 (CE 704–740), better known by his style name Ziyang 紫陽 or Purple Yang, who was active in the court of Emperor Tang Xuanzong between 736 and 740.[20] We are told that Deng practiced the "techniques of Fengdu" (*Fengdu zhi shu* 酆都之術) on Mt Magu 麻姑 and recited the Tianpeng incantation "unceasingly" (*Secret Essential*, j.3, *ZHDZ* 30.332a). Five years into his practice, on a tranquil night of an Upper Primordial Day (the 15th of the 1st month) under wide-open skies lit up by a full moon, Ziyang burned incense, pleaded to the perfected numinous ones to descend, and then proceeded to recite incantations. "Suddenly, a book descended from heaven. It was written in black ink on plain silk (*sujuan heiwen* 素絹黑文). Bright lights came out from it. It flew into the room and disappeared in a blink of an eye." Deng was puzzled and decided to seek the answer in meditation. In a vision, he saw a divine figure introducing himself as the emissary Six Ding of the North Heaven (*Beitian liuding shizhe* 北天六丁使者). The divine emissary explained that the book in question contained 36 talismans and was a gift from the Supreme Emperor (*Shangdi* 上帝). This was, according to our source, the origin of the "36 Talismans of Tianpeng." Such an account of divine transmission suggests that the talismans appeared during or after Deng Ziyang's lifetime, in the first half of the eighth century.

A story about reciting the Tianpeng incantation recorded by Du Guangting concerned a certain Wang Daoke 王道柯 who made a living by selling talismans and telling fortunes (*Yunji qiqian* 119.15). He habitually recited the Tianpeng incantation and therefore was protected by divine soldiers. Wang lived close to a White Horse General Temple (*Baima jiangjun miao* 白馬將軍廟) and often walked into the temple boldly reciting the Tianpeng incantation aloud to challenge the deities within. Then, one day he met a garlic vender on his way walking home and had a brush with death. The offensive smell of garlic kept the divine soldiers away and left Wang bereft of his usual protection. As the two men passed by the temple, the spirits residing there ambushed Wang. Nearly losing consciousness, Wang was dragged into the temple by several fox-spirits while the garlic vender left him behind. Thus, when Wang recited the Tianpeng incantation to invoke assistance, the divine soldiers returned and the foxes could not hurt him further. Finally, Wang managed to pull himself together and escape from the temple. After cleaning himself up at home, he regained his bravado and turned to the temple, yelling aloud:

> I am a disciple of the Most High. I know not only the Tianpeng incantation but also the *Scriptures of Dao*. The *Scripture* says: 'Heaven became clear by receiving the One; earth became tranquil by receiving the One; deities become numinous by receiving the One.'[21] If you were deities, you should assist the Dao to spread the teachings [of the One], why do you resent hearing the divine incantation? I know you are not the bright deity of the white horse but the demonic spirits of foxes who have taken refuge in a shrine to deceive the people. Today, I have decided to stay here to recite the incantation in order to alleviate harm from the people.

He then recited incantations for the entire night. On the next morning, five foxes were found dead in pools of blood in the back of the temple. Du Guangting concluded the story with his own comment: "General Tianpeng is the senior captain of the North Emperor who can subdue all ghosts and spirits. His powers are not limited to killing lesser demons like foxes." Du succinctly summarized Tianpeng's godhead as a formidable warrior vanquishing against demons.

Zhenwu as a comrade-in-arms with General Tianpeng

It is true that many Daoist liturgical manuals clearly depict Zhenwu as a subordinate member of the North Emperor's administration. However, these texts were not written down until Song times or later. Records prior to the Song dynasty directly linking Zhenwu to the North Emperor are scarce. Fortunately, we have one account, from Cheng Chengbian 程承辯 (fl. 938–965), a Daoist painter specializing in portraits, suggesting that Zhenwu and Tianpeng were fellow combatants. One of his representative works in an enclave in a Daoist abbey in Sichuan depicted Zhenwu in juxtaposition with Tianpeng (*Yizhou minghua lu* 198). Furthermore, he included two additional exorcist figures, the Black Killer and the Fire Flame (*Huoling* 火鈴); both the force of exorcism as well. Zhenwu's exorcist godhead is implicitly denoted by being positioned with other exorcist deities in this tenth-century sanctuary.

Zhenwu was also teamed with Tianpeng in the Four Saints (*sisheng* 四聖; see figures 1.3–1.4), in combination with Tianyou 天猷 and the Black Killer (Heisha 黑殺, also known as Yisheng 翊聖, or "Protector of Saintliness"), a topic that

Figure 1.3 The Four Saints, attributed to Wu Daozi (CE 680–740), but more likely from the thirteenth century.
Source: Courtesy of Daoist Iconography Project directed by Poul Andersen (http://manoa.hawaii.edu/daoist-iconography/dzm-big.html). The original album is in the collection of Cleveland Museum of Art.

26 *A god in formation*

Figure 1.4 The Four Saints, detail.

Edward Davis analyzed (2001: 74–79). In some Daoist liturgical manuals, the foursome had their own administrative office, the Mansion of the Four Saint of the North Apex (*Beiji sisheng fu* 北極四聖府).[22] While the extent editions of these liturgical manuals were not produced until the Southern Song period or later, there is evidence that the quartet was revered by lay people as Daoist deities at the beginning of Song times, if not earlier. Su Xiangxian 蘇象先 (fl. 1080–1127) recalled the family history told by his grandfather Su Song 蘇頌 (1020–1101), the renowned scholar-official and scientist of the Northern Song (*Chengxiang Weigong tanxun* 9.1a):

> My grandfather said: "When my great grandmother, Lady of Dai, married my great-grandfather, the images of the Four Saints of the North Dipper of the North Apex (*beiji beidou sisheng*) were included in her dowry. She worshipped them very meticulously. Since then, our family, on the 7th day of every month, must observe a vegetarian diet, display tea, wine, fruit, lanterns, and present paper money [to the Four Saints].

> 祖父云：吾曾祖母代國夫人歸曾祖時，資中裝有北極北斗四聖像，奉祀甚嚴。自是吾家每至上七日，必食素，設香茶酒果燈燭，奏冥幣焉。

The great-grandmother in the account is the mother of Su Zhongchang 蘇仲昌 (CE 975–?), née Zhang.[23] She came from a wealthy family in Quanzhou (southern Fujian) as Su Song told his grandson. Her large dowry contained, in addition to the images of the Four Saints, ten cases of books, an indicator of her family's elite status. Since Zhongchang was born in 975 (he was 16 *sui* in 990) and the Four Saints' images were part of Madam Zhang's (Lady of Dai) dowry, it is reasonable to assume that her devotion started during her youth in the early 970s or before. Vegetarian observance and offerings to the deities illuminated the Daoist nature of Madam Zhang's worship of Four Saints. In other words, the reverence for the Four Saints as Daoist deities was already reflected in domestic religious practices by the third quarter of the tenth century.

The adoration of the Four Saints continued to be popular at least until the Southern Song period. The temple fair of the Four Saints Daoist Monastery (Sisheng guan)[24] at the West Lake (Xihu 西湖) of Hangzhou, Zhejiang, attracted "men and women of the entire city."[25] In the meantime, Zhenwu, while remaining a member of the Four Saints, had also acquired a singular devotion addressed to him individually. This, however, is another chapter of his career.

The search for the origin of Zhenwu's godhead leads to two distinct precursors with the same name: One is the ancient cosmological symbol known as Xuanwu, which resembled a turtle alone or a turtle encircled by a snake, and the other is the demonifuge General Xuanwu (Zhenwu after CE 1012) operating under the Daoist exorcist authority, the North Emperor. As a cosmological symbol, Xuanwu denotes first and foremost the constellations of the northern quadrant sky, and accordingly the direction of north. Another three directional theriomorphic spirits (the Green Dragon, White Tiger, and Vermilion Bird), joined Xuanwu to form the Four Animals. The quartet was a set of symbols used to construct a meaningful space that human beings felt capable of manipulating. It formed an orientation framework that allowed the ancient Chinese to organize military troops, orient the cosmos, and develop astrology that brought humanity's fate to the universe surrounding them. With the Four Animals as reference, the four cardinal directions could be determined; with the latter as reference, the center then is located.

As one of the Four Animals, Xuanwu acquired a layer of cosmological symbolism that played an important part in Zhenwu's growing significance in the Daoist tradition of self-cultivation. The cosmological aspect not only illuminated the god with a classical aura so that his literati devotees could justify worshipping him, but also connected him to the all-inclusive categorization of the five-phase correlative cosmology. The latter was heavily invoked in the theory of inner alchemy (see Chapter Three), one of the most important developments of Daoism in the second millennium. In addition, the cosmological symbolism was also crucial for political legitimization; and thus Zhenwu's significance in the state pantheon increased. As we will see in the following chapters, both religious and secular dynamics were involved in the shaping and reshaping of his godhead.

The anthropomorphic origin of Zhenwu lay in the demon fighter General Xuanwu serving the North Emperor, the old symbol of exorcism in Daoism. General Xuanwu could be found in juxtaposition with Tianpeng, the first lieutenant of the North Emperor, in Daoist temples and domestic households during the second half of the tenth century. Drawing his authority from the North Emperor, Xuanwu the exorcist general assimilated Xuanwu the cosmological symbol. From this point on, his godhead rapidly developed and mutated. Eventually he became a god of multiple facets that symbolized the interests of the various groups in society.

2 A god in full

This chapter analyzes the early stages of the growth of Zhenwu worship during the Song period (960–1279). The god's debut in the Daoist pantheon in the mid-tenth century brought him to the attention of the public; within a century, individual temples and affiliated chapels dedicated to him could be found in the capital, in inland areas, and along the frontier. Practices in veneration of Zhenwu became well developed during Song times. Devotees enshrined his images at home and in temple, held congregational gatherings, and observed the calendar and dietary restrictions prescribed in the name of the god. They also organized the ritual of Offering (*jiao* 醮) and parades to celebrate the god's birthday. By reconstructing the various rituals and activities of Zhenwu worship, this chapter demonstrates that Zhenwu already commanded empire-wide worship at this time.

Temple dedication

Sanctuaries dedicated to gods often constitute a votive commitment. Making and fulfilling vows constitute a direct engagement between devotees and the divine, even though sometimes a pragmatic reciprocal exchange is implied. For the average worshipper, temple building, while involving local politics and various personal self-interests, is essentially an expression of devotion. Knowledge about the spread of the temples and how they spread helps us to measure the strength of veneration of the divinity in discussion.

Many religious sources and gazetteers identified Zhenwu temples as having been built in the Tang period or even earlier, but the basis of their claims is legendary.[1] The Clean Cloud Hall (Jiyun dian 霽雲殿) in Quanzhou, southern Fujian, has a slightly more credible claim; it was ostensibly constructed during the Tianfu era (936–942) of the Jin of the Five Dynasties period and refurbished during the Kaibao era (968–976) in Song Taizu's (r. 960–976) reign, according to a local gazetteer (*Anhai zhi* 7.579). The source, compiled between the seventeenth and eighteenth centuries, is rather late, and the description of the temple's founding is suspiciously similar to that of countless other temples. Yet the existence of a Zhenwu temple in southern Fujian at that time is plausible. After all, as discussed in the previous chapter, the worship of the Four Saints, which included Zhenwu, was active in the area during the last quarter of the tenth century.

30 *A god in full*

The early stages

The first Zhenwu temple with a reliable pedigree was the Zhenwu guan (Daoist monastery) built in the early Song period in the eastern city of Jiankang 建康, present-day Nanjing. A Southern Song gazetteer states in an assertive tone: "The Zhenwu Daoist Monastery was built in the second year of the Taiping Xingguo era [CE 977] of our dynasty (*guochao* 國朝)" (*Jingding Jiankang zhi*: 44.16a). While the source is not exactly contemporaneous, the author, Zhou Yinghe 周應合 (1213–1280), was known for his meticulous verification of details when he worked on this gazetteer.

Also at the end of the tenth century, in the central-west part of the Song empire, a side chapel dedicated to Zhenwu could be found in Palace of Great Peace of the Supreme Clarity (Shangqing Taiping gong 上清太平宮) at Mt Zhongnan 終南 in Shaanxi. This abbey, sponsored by Emperor Song Taizong, was occupied by Daoist clerics. Its founding abbot, Zhang Shouzhen 張守真 (?–d.996), was an ordained Daoist cleric who received revelations from the Black Killer to whom the abbey was dedicated.[2] (The Black Killer, as we recall, was one of the Four Saints that also included Zhenwu.) The Palace of Great Peace of the Supreme Clarity was completed by CE 980 (*Jinshi lüe*, 246). Along the vertical axis of the compound there were four halls dedicated, from front to the rear, to the Jade Emperor, Purple Tenuity (the North Emperor), the Seven Primordial Ones, and finally the Black Killer (*Yunji qiqian* 103.2224). On the eastern and western sides of the vertical axis were two wings of four side-halls each. The front hall of the west wing was dedicated to Zhenwu and the front side of the east wing to Tianpeng. In the symmetric design Zhang Shouzhen used the revelations of the Black Killer to dictate the design of the abbey (*Yunjin qiqian* 103.2222), and the inclusion of a Zhenwu hall was without doubt his doing. Zhang actually once announced that he received a revelation in which the Black Killer referred to himself along with Zhenwu and Tianpeng as the "three great generals of heaven" (*Yang Wengong Tanyuan* 112).

More than three decades later and 200 miles further west of Mt Zhongnan, another Zhenwu chapel was established by Daoist priests inside a state-sponsored Daoist temple. In 1013, Kong Daofu 孔道輔 (987–1039), a young *jinshi* degree-holder (in 1012), took on his first government position in Ningzhou, located in today's northwest province of Gansu, practically the westernmost frontier of the Song empire.[3] At the time, Daoist priests of the county's Celestial Celebration Monastery (Tianqing guan 天慶觀)[4] were erecting a statue of Zhenwu. As they were setting up the statue, a snake appeared and lingered. The event was duly reported to the magistrate, who decided to come to the chapel to pay his respects. He took along with him his subordinates, including Kong Daofu. Nevertheless, Kong, differing with his superior, perceived the snake to be demonic (*yao* 妖) and hit it in front of everyone. This became such a celebrated event in Kong's political career that several prominent Song scholar-officials, including Grand Councilor Wang Anshi 王安石 (1021–1086), wrote to praise him. Thanks to Kong's disrespectful action, an early record of a Zhenwu chapel was documented. By the early eleventh century, Zhenwu worship was evident in the eastern end of the empire as well as in the west.[5]

Another prominent Daoist abbey, the Great Purity Palace (Taiqing gong 太清宮) located in Bo county, Anhui province, which was the believed birthplace of Laozi to whom the temple was dedicated, also hosted a chapel for Zhenwu by the early eleventh century. In 1014, Emperor Song Zhenzong (r. 997–1022) came to the Great Purity Palace to pay homage to Laozi. The lengthy ceremony included presenting offerings in Zhenwu's own hall (*bendian* 本殿; *Xu Zizhi tonjian changbian* 82.3a). In addition, the emperor composed three eulogies to Laozi, Laozi's mother, and Zhenwu respectively. As a matter of fact, Zhenwu has often been identified as the 82nd reincarnation of Laozi (*Xuantian dasheng*, j. 1, ZHDZ 30.525-b; *Daofa huiyuan*, j.154, ZHDZ 37.389a). The distinction Zhenwu received during the royal visit to Laozi's temple gives a tantalizing glimpse of a special relationship between the two divine figures and suggests that the conception of Zhenwu as a manifestation of Laozi might already have developed by the turn of the eleventh century.

The Auspicious Fountain—Sweet Spring Monastery

While Daoist clerics clearly played an important role in setting up side chapels for Zhenwu, it was through the agency of the military of the early Song that he first entered the limelight of the national stage. In 1017 (Tianxi 1 of Zhenzong's reign), the soldiers of the Gongsheng 拱聖 Regiment, an elite cavalry unit based south of Kaifeng,[6] saw a turtle and a snake near their barracks. They consequently built a small shrine for Zhenwu at the spot.[7] Later that year, a spring appeared next to the shrine, and people who had been sick were said to have recovered after drinking from the spring. The water then came to be known as "holy water" (*shengshui* 聖水) and quickly drew large crowds—not only soldiers but also ordinary city dwellers—to the shrine. The spring generated such a public sensation that within a few months the Capital Security Office (*Huangcheng si* 皇城司) had to report the phenomena to the emperor.

In response to the report, Emperor Zhenzong appropriated the shrine. He ordered the construction of a new Zhenwu temple at the location to replace the original one. Wang Qinruo 王欽若 (962–1025), grand councilor at the time (*Songshi* 210.5444), was appointed to supervise the project. Six months after the commencement of the project, a new but still modest temple of three halls was built. The emperor named it Auspicious Fountain Monastery (Xiangyuan guan 祥源觀) and composed a eulogy in honoring Zhenwu. The god's image was enshrined in the main hall in the center of the complex, between the emperor's eulogy in the east hall and the "auspicious fountain" itself in the west.[8]

Two years later, after having suffered eight months of sickness, Zhenzong ordered an extension to the Auspicious Fountain Monastery. This seemed to do the trick. Within a month, he recovered enough to make his first public appearance in nearly a year.[9] The extension turned into a major imperial project: the main beam-setting ceremony brought together a crowd of prominent guests including the future Emperor Renzong, at the time Crown Prince. In terms of scale, the temple was a massive complex of more than 600 pillars. It caught fire in the fourth month of 1054 during Renzong's reign. Restoration quickly took place and was completed by the 12th month of the next year. Renzong renamed the restored temple Sweet Spring (Liquan 醴泉) Monastery.[10]

The Auspicious Fountain—Sweet Spring Monastery was a state agency from the beginning. Its chief superintendent (*da gouguan* 大勾管) was on the state's payroll (*Songshi* 172.4144), and the title of custodian-commissioner (*shi* 使) of the Auspicious Fountain Monastery—later of the Sweet Spring—was an honorific position in central government. At least five out of the seven Northern Song emperors after the temple's establishment graced it with their presence, and both Renzong and his successor, Yingzong (r. 1064–1067), went to the abbey to pray for rain during times of drought.[11]

There were a number of Zhenwu temples in the Kaifeng area during the Northern Song -that left next to no trace in history. We know of their existence, ironically, because of their destruction. In 1111, Emperor Huizong decreed the demolition of unregistered temples in Kaifeng prefecture (*Song huiyao*, li, 20.14b–15a.771). The edict further instructed the prefect:

> Relocate images in those shrines to [registered] Buddhist, Daoist, or to the deities' own temples; for example, move Zhenwu's images to the branch temple(s) of the Sweet Fountain (Liquan xiaguan 醴泉下觀) and the earth gods' images to the temple of *Chenghuang* (城隍). Temples for Wutong, General Stone (Shi) and Daji were abolished in the course of illicit cults. Also, forbid soldiers and civilians to build shrines of any size without authorization (*shanli* 擅立).
>
> 遷其像入寺觀及本廟, 如真武像遷醴泉下觀, 土地像遷城隍廟之類。 五通, 石將軍, 妲己三廟, 以淫祠廢. 仍禁軍民擅立大小祠廟。

The document informs us, first, of the existence of branch temple(s) of the imperial Sweet Spring Daoist Monastery that otherwise went unmentioned in government or anecdotal records. Second, the document clearly spells out that while some of the destroyed temples were dedicated to "excessive cults" (*yinci* 淫祠), others enshrined state-approved divinities. The temple buildings were destroyed because they were unauthorized; that is, they were not registered with the Ministry of Rites. The fact that Zhenwu, along with the earth gods, was singled out for mention suggests that there were more than a few isolated cases of unauthorized temples enshrining him that were located in public areas.

A brief remark about Song laws on building temples is in place here. The Song government made constant efforts to regulate the sites of public worship. Temples, whether Buddhist, Daoist, or of local cults, were supposed to be registered with the local government and receive a name plaque (*ming'e* 名額)— a term which also means "quota"—from the Bureau of Sacrifices (*cibu* 祠部) of the Ministry of Rites (*libu* 禮部) at the central court; otherwise, they risked being torn down. Song statute law specified that whoever built a temple containing more than 100 bays but failed to register with the government was liable to prosecution for violation of the law (*weizhi* 違制) and the temple would be immediately demolished.[12]

Continuing spread

Temple worship of Zhenwu continued to spread to inland and peripheral China during the second half of the Northern Song period. More importantly, from this point on, surviving temple steles provide us with information about the collaboration between Daoist abbots and lay patrons in the community. In 1047, the Divine Crane Daoist Monastery in Goushi, in Henan, had a new abbey from Kaifeng and a new restoration project.[13] A commemorative stele erected in 1051 listed the names of the donors (both male and female) and specified how their donations were used. The abbot and the "lamp oil offering society" (dengyou jiaoshe 燈油醮社) along with other benefactors, financed the establishment of a Zhenwu Hall (Jinshi lüe, 271–272).

The Zhenwu Hall at the Pure Void Daoist Monastery (Qingxu guan 清虛觀) in Pingyao 平遙, southern Shanxi, is another example of the collective effort of the clergy and laity (Jinshi lüe, 296–297). The Pure Void Daoist Monastery, originally built in the late seventh century, had fallen to near destruction during the early Song. Then, some time before 1092 (the seventh year of the Yuanyou era), a certain Daoist priest called Wu Taiwen 武太文 took the abbotship. Abbot Wu set his heart on restoring the temple; every penny of the income from the abbey's farming lands was used on the restoration, according to the temple stele. The development took time and eventually abbot Wu solicited a major patron, a member of the local elite named Pei Shuzhi 裴述之, a jinshi degree-holder himself. From then on, progress picked up. When the renovation was completed, the temple boasted not only a refurbished grand main hall for Heavenly Worthy of Primordial Commencement but also four new lesser halls (xiaodian 小殿), including the one dedicated to Zhenwu.[14]

If patrons with resources could be found, side chapels could develop into individual temples. The Bowing to the Apex Daoist Monastery (Gongji guan 拱極觀) originated precisely this way. In 1107 (Daguan 1), a court official surnamed Wang went to Huayin 華陰, Shaanxi, under orders from the emperor to refurbish the Western Peak Temple. During his stay, Wang resided in the Zhenwu hall of the temple. He prayed to Zhenwu and vowed to build a bigger new chapel for the god after completing the refurbishment to "publicize the extraordinary efficaciousness, and manifest the benevolence" of the god. Wang carried out his mission and did not forget to fulfill his vow. He built a new compound, properly called Zhenwu Daoist Courtyard, outside the east wall of the Western Peak temple and arranged for a Daoist priest, Lei Daozhi 雷道之, to take charge. Priest Lei continued to develop the Zhenwu Daoist Courtyard into a large edifice of 100 bays. In 1125 (Xuanhe 7), it received a new name from the court, Bowing to the Apex Abbey, with Lei as the first abbot (Jinshi lüe, 342–343).

Zhenwu temples also grew on the periphery of the empire. The fortress city of Dashun 大順 (in eastern Gansu) at the western border with the kingdom of Xi Xia, also benefited from a Zhenwu temple. The fortress was built in 1042 by Fan Zhongyan 范仲淹 (989–1052) on the site of a military outpost,[15] and in 1075 (Xining 8), Emperor Shenzong honored its Zhenwu temple with a new name (Song huiyao, li, 21.63a).[16] Thus, within 33 years of its establishment, Dashun already boasted a Zhenwu temple significant enough to warrant the state's investiture. Another Zhenwu temple in the west was recorded in the early twelfth century next

34 *A god in full*

to an important source of salt, Lake Xie (Xiechi 解池), in Shaanxi (*Song huiyao*, li, 20.56c.792). Eventually, the Zhenwu cult would travel even further west, to the land of the enemy of the Song, the kingdom of the Xi Xia (see below, page 39).

Motivations of temple building for Zhenwu

Temples are the result of collaborative efforts, and different participants often have different motives in joining the enterprise. The 1115 commemorative stele inscription of the Zhenwu Hall in Jizhou 濟州, Shandong, reads (*Lejing ji* 6.1a–3b):

> Prominent households and rich families could afford setting aside compartments that are carefully equipped and decorated, purified by incense, and thoroughly cleansed, to welcome the god's arrival. In humble tenements, with worn-out drapes and shabby rooms, with fathers and sons yelling at each other, with blood and other kinds of pollution never cleansed, [the residents] desiring to see the cloud flags and hear the wind horses [accompanying the god] could only look searchingly at the vast nine heavens tens of thousands of miles wide [since Zhenwu would never come to such a polluted place]; how is it possible for them to locate him? ... The Celestial Celebration Monastery [of Jizhou] had had no chapel to the Perfected Lord [i.e. Zhenwu]. Court gentleman consultant (*fengyi lang* 奉議郎) Chen Gu 陳穀, his excellence, talked to Daoist priest Shi Zhizhen 史知真, saying: "[Zhenwu is] an awesome deity of heaven and ranked in the Yellow Register (*huanglu* 黃籙). You know how to recite his scriptures daily [but] fail to ask for his blessing for the people, you are indeed the one to blame among Daoist priests. I am willing to use 300,000 of my salary to make a statue of the Perfected [i.e. Zhenwu] and install it at the side of the Three Pure Ones to alert and inspire. As for organizing the materials, summoning laborers, raising a foundation on which to build the construction, those are your responsibilities." Zhizhen accepted these words. He visited people in the district (*liren* 里人). A certain Xue Zhu 薛洙 from Hedong, who was a son of an established family (*shijia zi* 世家子), responded in joy, saying: "this is my wish." Together they spread the word among the good people. They accumulated 1.3 million cash.

> 大家富室猶能虛館寓，嚴器飾，薰被汎掃，以迎其來。下里寒陋，敗帷破屋，父子喧呼，腥穢不除，欲望雲旗，聞風馬，九天寥寥，區域萬里，果何在也。…大慶觀舊無真君祠，奉議郎陳公穀語道士史知真曰，天之威神位在黃籙。汝知日誦其經，不能為人請福，亦黃冠之罪人也。余願以月俸三十萬造真像，寄位三清之側，以示警發。度材聚工，峙基結宇，汝之責也。知真領其語。因謁諸里人。有河東薛洙者，士族子也，歡然應之曰，此吾志耳。相與風曉善類，積錢一百三十萬。

This quotation presents three different understandings of the need to build a public devotional center for Zhenwu. First, as the author lamented, Zhenwu devotees in poor households had no chance to "meet" the god in person at home because they lacked rooms free of disturbance and the pollution of the profane. Yet the poor were eager to encounter the god; they craned their heads searching the sky for a trace of his "cloud flags and wind horse," but in vain. By implication, the erection of a Zhenwu shrine would satisfy such desires for those who could not afford to set up private sanctuaries for the god. Chen Gu, the scholar-official who proposed the project, expressed a more or less different motivation. He pointed out to the priest Shi that the latter should have requested blessing from the god, and then he put forward his plan to carry out the project. Chen's purpose was obviously to obtain blessing, for himself in particular and for others as well. Xue Zhu responded enthusiastically because he was a long-term devotee and probably had been waiting for such an invitation all along.

The Daoist Courtyard of the Beneficent God or *Fushen daoyuan* 福神道院 (hereafter the Fushen Courtyard) built in 1130 in Xianyou 仙遊 (southern Fujian), was another example of the multiple motivations in building a Zhenwu temple, even though the project was primarily sponsored by one individual. The Fushen Courtyard was dedicated to Zhenwu, as attested in local history (*Xianyou xianzhi* 17.2), but according to the temple's commemorative inscription of 1243, it also honored and enshrined the founder's deceased father.[17]

The founder of the Fushen Courtyard was Fu Qianshou 傅謙受 (fl. 1130), a native son of Xianyou and a lower-ranking local itinerant scholar-official. When serving in Kuocang, Zhejian, Fu Qianshou met a Daoist cleric, Mei Xiaodong 梅霄洞, known for his skill in the occult ritual of prophesying by observing the *qi* (*Xianyou xianzhi* 45.3). Fu was impressed by Mei and brought Mei along with him when he made the journey home from Kuocang. Traveling by the river route, they encountered a storm. Priest Mei immediately carried out the Daoist ritual of *budou* (Pacing the Dipper) to save the boat. Fu still fell in the water, but when he looked up, he saw "the banners of the correct god of the north" (*beifang zhengshen zhi zhi* 北方正神之幟) on the riverbank (*Quxuan ji* 5.26a). He then knew that the god was there to bring about his rescue, "correct god of the north" was no other than Zhenwu. Fu Qianshou returned to Xianyou, built the Fushen Courtyard with his own income, enshrined Zhenwu there, and installed Priest Mei as the first abbot. While the temple was no doubt Fu's repayment for Zhenwu's protection during the shipwreck, the fact that Mei and his disciples became the abbots in succession suggests Mei's influence in Fu's interpretation of his vision. The collaboration between Fu Qianshou and Priest Mei was further demonstrated in a founding legend of the Fushen Courtyard. The temple record recounts (*Quxuan ji* 5. 27):

> At a time when the casting the of the bell [for the temple] could not be completed for months; Madam neé Chen,[18] threw her hairpin into the furnace and the bell then was finished.[19] After completion, however, the bell did not produce a sound when struck. Mei hit it with a sword and produced a sound shaking the sky. Until today, the marks made by the hairpin and the sword are slightly visible above the [patterns of] the squatting bear and coiling dragon (*dunxiong panlong* 蹲熊盤龍).
>
> 鑄鐘纍月不就，陳夫人投金釵於爐而鐘成。 叩之無聲，梅揮劍擊之，聲始大震。 至今一釵一劍之痕，隐隐浮於蹲熊盤龍之上。

Fu Qianshou's second motivation for building the temple was to conduct ancestor rituals in homage to his late father, Fu Ji 傅楫 (1042–1102; *jinshi* 1067). Fu Ji was the first in his sub-clan to rise to elite status; and his political career climaxed with service as a tutor for Prince Duan 端, the future Emperor Huizong.[20] When Fu Ji died in 1102, Huizong designated a Buddhist temple in Yixing, Jiangsu, to conduct his former teacher's mortuary and memorial service.[21] Fu Ji's tomb was never relocated to his hometown. His two elder sons, along with their families, also moved to Yixing and settled down. Fu Qianshou, the third and youngest son of Fu Ji, remained in his native town, and decided he needed a proper place to display the regular offerings for his father's ghost. This was the other purpose that Fu Qianshou built the temple.

The Fushen Daoist Courtyard, under the abbotship of Priest Mei's disciples and with the support of the descendants of Fu Qianshou, became a community temple. Locals came to pray for recovery from sickness, and when there was too much or not enough rain. By the 1250s, it had undergone a through renovation and extension to include a chapel for the East Peak, whose lord was one of the most popular deities of Song times. The Fushen Daoist Courtyard exemplified the transformation of a Zhenwu temple from an embodiment of personal devotion connected with Daoist clergy to a landmark serving the public good.

Few commemorative temples have records providing multiple voices like the two above. In most cases, one particular motivation was emphasized. While such phenomena were no doubt the result of selected, if not biased, memory, the selectiveness tells us which elements were more meaningful to the minds of the legend-shapers.

Ritual specialists who invoked Zhenwu, whether ordained or not, often inspired their adherents to construct temples dedicated to the god and headed by the specialists themselves. One story in Hong Mai's 洪邁 (1123–1202) *The Records of the Listener* (*Yijian zhi*)—a treasure house of Song anecdotes—tells the story of a man called Liu Daochang 劉道昌 from Yuchang 豫昌, Jiangxi, a local bully born to a military family.[22] We are told that he received a scroll of talismans and incantations (*fuzhou* 符咒) from a Daoist priest (*daoshi*) in a dream. When he woke up, the text was in his sleeve (*zai xiu jian* 在袖間). Liu returned home and, for reasons unexplained, "painted a portrait of Zhenwu for worship" (*hui shi Zhenwu xiang* 繪事真武像). He proceeded to begin "treating illnesses and performing the ritual of Offering" (*zhibing xingjiao* 治病行醮). The charms he wrote were simple, according to Hong Mai, but they were efficacious in treating whatever they were intended for. Villagers held him in such esteem that they constructed a Zhenwu Hall (*tang*) for him to reside in (*ju* 居). Liu was not a Daoist cleric, but he certainly tried to present his rituals as if they were derived from Daoist tradition. This complex dynamic between ordained Daoists and village ritual masters is still in place today (Schipper 1985). Ritual specialists such as Liu inspired their clients to build shrines dedicated to Zhenwu, and this became an ongoing tradition (Chao 2002).

The Qingzhen guan 清真觀 (Pure and Perfect Daoist Monastery) in Kunshan 崑山, Jiangsu province, was developed from the Zhenwu Daoist Courtyard (*daoyuan*) built in 1172 by priest Zhai Shouzhen 翟守真, a native of Tiantai, Zhejiang.[23] Two years later, a group of local lay people filed an application with the government to allow the Zhenwu Daoist Courtyard to fill the quota opened up by the abandonment of an old temple, the Pure and Perfect Daoist Monastery.[24] Permission was granted and the temple accordingly adopted the new name of Pure and Perfect, under the abbotship of

Zhai. After Zhai passed away, his disciples succeeded him, one after another. They continued to expand the temple in scale, and maintained a good relationship with the local elite. The temple survived the Song dynasty, burned down during the Yuan–Ming transition in the fourteenth century, and was rebuilt during the early Ming period. It remained a temple dedicated to Zhenwu and became famous in the Kunshan area.

Zhenwu temples, like many sacred sites, were often surrounded by an aura of mystery. The Aiding Sage Palace (Yousheng gong 佑聖宮) in Huzhou (Zhejiang) built between 1131 and 1162 was a good example. A local gazetteer briefly related that the temple originated from a cloister (*an* 庵) of the Daoist priest Shen Wuai 沈無礙, style name (*hao* 號) Chongzhen 崇真 (*Wuxing beizhi* 14.21a). Shen saw Zhenwu in revelation and erected a stele carved with the image that he observed. Later, a snake and a turtle—the emblems of Zhenwu—appeared following each other in the stream in front of the cloister. "From then on" (*zishi* 自是), the Blessing Saint Palace was established. The *Yijian zhi* gave a similar account, but with distinct variations (*Yijian*, zhiding, 3.989):

> At the beginning of the Shaoxing era (1131–1162), in the western part of Bianshan, Huzhou county, there was a Daoist cleric (*daoren*) named Shen Chongzhen who had acquired (*de* 得) an icon of the Numinously Responsive Zhenwu. For this reason, he built a cloister (*an*) there to enshrine it. He also used charm-water to treat haunting ghosts and cure illnesses (*zhisui liaobing* 治祟療病), outstandingly efficacious. Thus, the people customarily called him the perfected one (*zhenren* 真人). Later, he built an additional hall, and bought a license of ordination to be a [registered] Daoist priest (*daoshi*). His disciples and followers were about several dozens.
>
> One day there were four rays of red light rising behind his hall, but nothing could be seen upon close examination. After ten days, priest Shen tried to dig a hole in the earth where the light came out, and discovered a blue stone (*qingshi* 青石). It was 30 feet (*sanzhang* 三丈) long and more than one feet (*chixu* 尺許) wide, carved with a pair of an entwined turtle and a snake (*tianguan dizhou* 天關地軸). A bright radiance surrounded the stone for two days. For that reason, he built a sanctuary [for the stele]. Thereafter, men and women's devotion and respect doubled. The priest Shen and the devotees together adopted the name-placard of the abandoned Primordial Summit Daoist Monastery in a remote countryside to denote their temple. Prime Minister Shen Shouyu 沈守約 was head of government administration at the time and recommended that the emperor grant the temple the name of Yousheng Palace. [Priest] Shen had died by this time; it was said that his second-generation disciple was the current abbot.

紹興初，湖州卞山之西，有沈崇真道人者，得真武靈應聖像，因結庵於彼奉事之，仍持符水治祟療病，效驗殊異，而民俗皆呼為真人。後增建一堂，買度牒為道士，其徒從之者數十輩。忽有紅光四道，起於堂後，近視則無所睹。沈旬日試於光處掘地，獲得青石，長三丈，闊尺許，上刻天關地軸相交紐，兩日光彩浮動，遂砌一龕。自是士女敬信，益倍昔時，共為移遠鄉廢元

38 *A god in full*

峰觀額以標其宇。沈守約丞相當國，奏賜額曰佑聖宮。崇真既沒，今闕孫住持。

In the gazetteer version, the legendary Zhenwu image enshrined there and the apparition of the snake and the turtle were the cynosure. In Hong Mai's narrative, it was the mystical discovery of the stele depicting a snake and a turtle that was the critical factor in augmenting the reputation of the priest and his temple. The two narrations varied noticeably in the details; they most likely derived from different sources. Yet both sources gave prominent places to the mystical images. It was the miraculous icon, either Zhenwu himself or that of his emblems, that certified the temple's legitimacy.

The Efficaciously Responsive Daoist Monastery (Lingying guan 靈應觀) in Chengdu, Sichuan, was intended to serve as the place where city dwellers could pray to the god for favors (*Heshan ji* 38.10a–11a; *Jinshi lüe* 374). A temple inscription says, "Chengdu, as a metropolis of the southwest, has no particular shrine [for Zhenwu]. When faced with floods and drought, there is no place to pray for blessing and ward off disasters." Therefore, some time between 1195 and 1200 (the Qingyuan era), a "tribute gentleman" (*gongshi* 貢士) and a Daoist priest together initiated the temple project.[25] The inscription notes that after the temple was completed, "whenever there was an epidemic, prayers were made to him; [for] timely rain and timely clear skies, prayers were made to him. Indeed, [Zhenwu] is never unresponsive to prayers for blessing and for averting calamities." The locals then petitioned on behalf of the temple for a title. In 1205, the court granted the temple the title of Numinous Response.

Finally, Zhenwu temples could emerge from a gradual development of private congregational meeting places, as did the Mysterious Primordial Daoist Courtyard (Xuanyuan daoyuan 玄元道院) in Huating county 華亭 in present-day Shanghai area. "In the Xianchun era (1265–1274), migrants (*yugong* 寓公) to the county pooled money to build it, and the image of the emperor-lord Xuanwu (Xuanwu dijun 玄武帝君) was enshrined within."[26] The immigrants invited a Daoist priest, a certain Chen Renshou 陳仁壽, to manage the rituals. Priest Chen led both the émigré and native elite (*junshi* 郡士) to read scriptures together. The building did not have a formal name; it was known as the "Daoist courtyard in the south of the city" (Chengnan daoyuan 城南道院) because of its geographical location and religious affiliation. The lack of a formal name for the temple suggests it was not registered with the government as a site of public worship. Instead, it was a private club for a scripture recitation society. After Abbot Chen retired, his disciple, Chen Lanyin 蘭隱, took over. Abbot Lanyin died at some point between 1308 and 1311 and was succeeded by his disciple, Wu Qingyi 吳清逸. It was during Qingyi's lifetime that the place finally obtained its current name, an indication of its conversion into a public devotional space.

Devotional practices

It was a common practice for Zhenwu devotees to enshrine the god's image in their homes. Sima Kou 司馬寇 of Ruzhou 汝州 (Henan), a popular religious painter at the end of the Northern Song, was known for his awe-inspiring Zhenwu portraits, which were in high demand among scholar-officials for the purpose of veneration in their residences (*Huaji* 6.77). Mao Xuan 毛璿, a native of Quzhou 衢州, Zhejiang, and a student in government school during the final decades of the Northern Song, had a Zhenwu image in the main hall of his family home.[27] Wu Guancheng 吳觀成, acting magistrate of Fuyang 富陽, Zhejiang, during the Fang La 方臘 insurgency (1120–1122) "burned incense to Zhenwu" constantly (*Chunzhu jiwen* 2:17). Hong Hao 洪皓 (1088–1155; *jinshi* 1115), a native of Boyang, Jiangxi, and the father in the famous father-son literati triad known as the "three Hongs," worshipped Zhenwu at home from his days as a junior official if not before.[28] Ye Fang 葉昉 (*jinshi* 1169) of Wu 婺 (Jiangxi) gave a Zhenwu portrait to his nephew, who hung it on his home altar in veneration (*Yijian zhi, zhijing* 3.905). Wang Deguang 王德廣 a native of Jiaodong 膠東, Shandong, observed Zhenwu worship diligently from his youth and had a sanctuary for the god in his home shrine (*Yijian, zhi kuei*, 2.1232). A story from the Chunxi era (1174–1189) told us a village boy in Wujiang 吳江, Jiangsu, was rescued by a divine man in golden armor and the boy's family immediately interpreted the miracle to be a blessing from Zhenwu whom they "had worshipped with extreme assiduity" (*sushi Zhenwu shenjin* 素事真武甚謹) (*Kuiche zhi* 2.9).

The practice of venerating Zhenwu's image penetrated the ethnic boundaries of the empire by the Southern Song. The Jurchen encouraged their soldiers to worship Zhenwu (*Shanxi tongzhi* 28.27b . There is also evidence to suggest that the Tanguts began to accept the god. A painting on a silk scroll, dating from at least the early thirteenth century, was unearthed from the remains of the Tangut city of Khara Khoto (Black Water) in the kingdom of the Xi Xia.[29] In the center of the painting, a large man in black sits barefoot on a stone with loosened hair and sword in hand. In front of him on the ground is a turtle encircled by a snake. The painting constitutes the standard elements of Zhenwu iconography. On the lower right-hand corner, a man in military attire with non-Han features (straight nose and deep eyes) kneels facing Zhenwu. He is disproportionately small in comparison with Zhenwu. The painting appears to be the type of devotional artwork that customarily included donors who commissioned the paintings in the composition.

In records compiled by the laity, the description of Zhenwu worship rituals is rather opaque. The collections use fixed expressions such as "industriously attending to the incense" or "burning incense every day and night without fail." Concrete details about the veneration ritual can only be found in Daoist texts that took the form of both instructions for worship and accounts of individual practices. One story collected in a Zhenwu hagiography, *Record of the Epiphany of the Supreme Emperor of the Dark Heaven* (*Xuantian shangdi qisheng lu* 玄天上帝啓聖錄; hereafter *Qisheng lu*), tells of a low degree-holder (*xiucai* 秀才 or "cultivated talent") Chen of Langzhou 閬州 (Sichuan) who failed the provincial level civil service examination three times (*Qisheng lu*, j. 2, in ZHDZ 30.644b-c). A Daoist priest from Mt Qingcheng 青城山 (near Chengdu in Sichuan) counseled Chen that his failure was caused by his karma (*yeyuan* 業緣) and prescribed venerating Zhenwu as the remedy. It was particularly important to make offerings on days with double dates when Zhenwu was scheduled to descend from heaven, the priest emphasized. He carefully described the rituals for making these special offerings. Chen quickly had a Zhenwu portrait painted on clean silk. On the fifth day of the fifth month, a "double date," he set up an altar outdoors during the hours of 7:00–9:00 p.m. (the hour of *xu* 戌). Facing north, Chen knelt on the ground and bowed 100 times to the north.

Another entry in the *Qisheng lu*, entitled "presenting the ritual," relates the instructions for making offerings to Zhenwu according to the teachings of a Daoist priest of the Supreme Clarity from Mt. Tai. On days when Zhenwu was scheduled to descend from the heavenly realm, one should present a bowl of water from a well with a branch of a willow tree (*yangliu zhi* 楊柳枝), lanterns (or candles), date soup, tea, and incense (*Qisheng lu*, j. 2, ZHDZ 30.645c). There is no meat; fruit and vegetables, excluding plums and pomegranates, constituted the food offerings. The offerings were displayed at the altar until 11:00 p.m. The devotees, in the meantime, burned sticks of incense, golden mock money, a paper horse, and a memo of their wishes to Zhenwu. The instructions took particular note of the serious injunction against animal sacrifice. Not only was meat excluded from the offerings, so was musk, incense obtained from a gland of deer. In addition, the paper horse offering was not supposed to be painted in color, because the pigments often contained *niujiao* 牛膠, a thickening agent made from oxen. The meticulous care taken to avoid animal products in the offerings corresponds with Zhenwu's Daoist godhead. In the Daoist kitchen, offerings of flesh were condemned, and killing was abhorrent (Kleeman 1994: 201–202; 2004: 154).

Dietary restrictions

A noteworthy aspect of private piety was the observance of dietary restrictions in Zhenwu worship. Vincent Goossaert's study of the cultural restrictions on beef consumption in late imperial China shows that the food taboo, with its rules of sacrifice and purity, can promote social differentiation in groups (Goossaert 2005). The forbidden food "operated as a social marker" that distinguished those who observe the rules from those who did not.

The 1099 stele of the *Scripture of Zhenwu*, discussed in the introductory chapter of this book, included a list of taboo foods in the appendix, including a warning against wild geese, beef, dogs, turtles, carp, and garlic (*Jinshi lüe* 308). The *Qisheng lu* includes a number of stories illustrating the divine retribution administered by Zhenwu to those who violated the food taboo on top of other ethical issues. A woman of Xizhou 隰州 county, Shanxi, surnamed Zhu, used her dowry money to commission a Zhenwu portrait and invited a Daoist priest to consecrate it by intoning scriptures (*Qisheng lu*, j. 2, ZHDZ 30.650c). The priest also instructed her in such devotional practices as burning paper horses and golden mock money during the god's monthly day of descent. She was advised to hire Daoist priests on such days to recite scriptures if she could afford it. The priest further laid down a list of ethics and taboos, including food forbidden from consumption: dogs, turtles, eels, garlic, and Chinese leeks (*jiu* 韭). She followed the instructions carefully for the rest of her life.

Zhu lived a long life, followed by a peaceful death. Her husband, on the other hand, served as a contrary example in this allegory, representing those who violated the food taboo. The husband's favorite food was eels and he indulged himself in consuming them. In the end, he suffered a painful sickness followed by a horrible death: a tumor on his head burst open. Blood and tissue came out in three-inch-long clusters resembling the conger eels he had eaten. The way in which his life ended was clearly the result of violating the food taboo

The divine retribution the husband received may seem unduly cruel for a poor choice of cuisine. Yet dietary behavior is often a crucial part of the code of ethics in religious communities, as, for instance, with kosher food in Judaism and vegetarianism in Chinese Buddhism. In religious allegories, consumption of prohibited food was commonly portrayed as an ethical transgression against the religious community or proof that the believer had renounced the community. Those who defied dietary restrictions violated one of the community's basic behavioral laws. The harsh punishment that the husband received reflected the moral torment that he inflicted on himself and on the community. The observance of the food taboo was not simply an expression of individual piety but a means of keeping the community cohesive. In other words, the Zhenwu devotional movement had reached the stage where it had developed an identity as a group of mutual interests and ethics.

Dietary observance was a mark of distinction that could distinguish Zhenwu believers from non-believers. An anecdote from the Southern Song told of just such a case (*Xishang futan*, shang, 17b). It was at the banquet given by Jia Sidao 賈似道 (1213–1275), the powerful grand chancellor during the reign of Emperors Lizong (r. 1224–1264) and Duzong (1265–1274). A guest who came to see Jia to plea for a position of magistrate refused to eat when turtle soup was served. He explained that, as a worshipper of Zhenwu, the turtle was a forbidden food to him. Jia was offended and ridiculed the guest. Others at the banquet, taking their cue from their host, also jumped in to mock the Zhenwu devotee. The man was not only greatly embarrassed but also lost the promotion which he had sought from Jia. The culinary choices made by devotees distinguished them from others at social occasions and reinforced their self-identity.

Congregational gatherings

During Song times, it was common among Daoist laity to have a monthly meeting to recite scriptures at private homes.[30] A certain Chen Yenzhao 陳彥昭 in Haiyu 海虞 (present-say Changshu 常熟, Jiangsu) during the Northern–Southern Song transition "respectfully served Xuanwu [i.e. Zhenwu] and repeatedly received auspicious signs and extraordinary responses from the god" (*Jinshi lüe* 343). Every month, people in his neighborhood gathered to recite scriptures of the Numinous Treasure (*Lingbao jing*), usually meeting at Chen's place. Chen eventually constructed a "scripture hall of Numinous Treasure" for their meeting and Zhenwu's statue was enshrined in the center of the hall, an indicator that Zhenwu was the devotional focus. Chen Yenzhao's group was unlikely to have been the first Zhenwu veneration association. The erection of the 1099 stele of the *Scripture of*

42 *A god in full*

Zhenwu points to the existence of a scripture-oriented devotional congregation (with their scripture, calendar, and precepts) at that time. Zhenwu veneration societies that focused on scripture recitation continued to flourish, as we noted in the case of the Mysterious Primordial Daoist Courtyard discussed above.

Some Zhenwu congregations not only constructed meeting places but also took steps to achieve financial independence by purchasing lands as a financial resource. In southern China in the fourteenth century, a certain Zhang Boxiang 張伯祥 intended to do just this. He sent to his fellow sutra-reciting devotees an announcement (*Guichao gao* 10.36):

> I will build a Daoist hall of Zhenwu for our party's (*wudang* 吾黨) monthly meetings and for cultivation in purity. For constructing the hall and the statues, [I] shall try my best to do it myself. As for establishing the farmland for the Hall, I would dare to summon the effort of everyone, if only you gentlemen would accept this.
>
> 某將建真武道堂為吾黨月會清修之地。築室塑像勉當獨為，預置齋田敢衷眾力。惟諸君領之。

Veneration calendar

A calendar, as Clifford Geertz observed, "cuts time up into bounded units not in order to count and total them but to describe and characterize them, to formulate their differential social, intellectual, and religious significance" (1973: 391). The days that Zhenwu scheduled to descend from heaven punctuated the life rhythm of his devotees and formed a liturgical calendar for them. Li Zhaoqi 李昭玘 (d. 1126; *jinshi* between 1086 and 1093) in his "Record of the Zhenwu Hall in Jizhou 濟州真武殿記" (*Lejing ji* 6.1a–3b) recalled:

> On each of the deity's descending days, titled noblemen, relatives of harem-women, scholar-officials at the court, and commoners of wards fasted behind closed doors and [then] rushed through the street, shoulder to shoulder, carriage wheels bumping carriage wheels, to fight their way through the gate [of the Auspicious Fountain Daoist Monastery]. It was like this all the time.
>
> 凡神降之日，公侯貴人，宮闈戚里，朝士大夫，閭巷庶人，屏居齋戒，奔走衢路，摩肩擊轂，爭門而入，歲以為常。

"Descending days" are those on which Zhenwu was believed to come down to earth from heaven. According to some scriptures, when in the human realm, the god patrols the world and also takes note of virtuous behavior. These days are the best time to make ritual offerings to him. The above description of eager worshippers racing to the abbey and competing with each other while observing the Zhenwu liturgical calendar undoubtedly derived from the author's own eyewitness, a Zhenwu devotee himself who lived in Kaifeng for several years.

There is some dispute regarding the dates of the god's "descending days." The 1099 *Scripture of Zhenwu* stele alone contains two different sets. The text of the scripture reads (*Jinshi lüe* 307–308):

A god in full 43

> The Heavenly Worthy told Zhenwu, saying: "From now on, on the days of *jiazi* 甲子 (1st day of the 60-day cycle), *gengshen* 庚申 (the 57th day of the 60-day cycle) and the 7th, 17th, and 27th days of every month, you may descend to the human realm and receive the sacrifices at the offering rituals of people."

The appendix to the scripture on the stele, however, maintains a different schedule (the number before the slash refers to the month and the number after the slash refers to the day of a month): 1/7, 2/8, 3/3, 3/9, 4/4, 5/5, 6/7, 7/7, 8/13, 9/9, 10/21, 11/7, 12/27. According to this list, the god descends only once a month in addition to his birthday.

The *Qisheng lu* also contains three different sets of descending days. The first set is recounted in the legend about Zhenwu's reincarnation as a certain Pei Zhongfang 裴仲方, a made-up figure in the court of Empress Wu (r. 690–705) (*Qisheng lu* 2, in ZHDZ 30.644a). When called to return to the heavenly realm, he told his grieving parents that he would come to visit them once a month to see to their needs and receive offerings. He then proceeded to reveal the days on which he would return to the human realm; they were exactly same as the dates in the appendix—not the text—of the 1099 stele, except for omitting the third day of the third month, Zhenwu's birthday. (This was probably omitted on the grounds that a special offering on his birthday was taken for granted.) A couple of pages later, however, in a different entry, the *Qisheng lu* records a Daoist priest from Mt Tai, located in the eastern part of the empire, telling that Zhenwu descended to the earth once a month in addition to the days of *gengshen*, *jiazi*, the "three primordial" (1/15, 7/15, 10/15), and the "five *la*" (1/1, 5/5, 7/7, 10/1, 12/8) (*Qisheng lu*, j.2, ZHDZ 30.645c), which were all traditional Daoist holidays. The third version of the descending days in the *Qisheng lu*, given by a Daoist priest from Mt Qingcheng, Sichuan, is the double dates (5/5, for example).

The different liturgical calendars suggest, first, a geographical difference (Henan and Shaanxi in the west vs. Mt Tai at the east). In addition, there was a level of independence among the lay devotees regarding their devotional practices. Daoist clerics clearly tried to incorporate their traditional holidays (the days of *gengshen*, three primordial and five *la*) into the rising cult of Zhenwu. In the case of the 1099 stele, however, the devotees who erected the stele insisted on their own opinion about the god's descending days despite the clear list in the scripture. The calendar these men followed was the same as the one credited to Pei Zhongfang, also a layperson. Pei's calendar was authenticated by the claim that he was an incarnation of Zhenwu. The laity's calendar (once a month) is much simpler than the clerical version (three times a month in addition to other Daoist holidays). Here we see a negotiation on devotional practices between the institutional authority of the clergy and scriptures on the one hand and the laity's autonomy legitimized by direct divine revelation on the other.

Birthday and other celebrations

Zhenwu's birthday was naturally the highpoint and the main festival in the calendar. The clergy took the lead in celebrating Zhenwu's birthday, as can be seen in the

44 *A god in full*

setting of an allegory critical of the ritual release of captured animals (*fangsheng* 放生, *lit.* "release the living beings"). At the Extending Auspiciousness Palace (Yanxiang gong 延祥宮) in Tanzhou, Hunan, says the story, the temple clergy routinely organized temple-goers to carry out "release of living beings" on Zhenwu's birthday. They bought birds and aquatic creatures prior to the ritual and kept them captive in the temple grounds (*Qisheng lu*, j.8, *ZHDZ* 30.690b). On Zhenwu's birthday, all participants, led by the abbot and accompanied by music, paraded through the town to the riverside and ceremoniously released the creatures. Afterwards, they returned to the monastery and the abbot gave a lecture expounding on a Zhenwu scriptural text.[31] The story then moves on to its main purpose, deploring the hypocrisy of *fangsheng* through the mouth of Zhenwu who manifests himself in the form of a Daoist priest. The polemic on the merits and demerits of the "release of the living beings" has been an enduring one (Smith 1999). Nevertheless, the parable is not cited here for its intended moral lesson but for its background description of the observance of Zhenwu's birthday during Song times: a collective celebration centered in a temple under clerical leadership.

The temple celebration of Zhenwu's birthday was a major event in the religious calendar of Hangzhou during the Southern Song. The epicenter of the festivities in the capital was the Aiding Saint Monastery converted from an old residence of Emperor Xiaozong. The imperial court also assigned Daoist priests to carry out the ritual of Offering at the temple on the god's birthday. Meanwhile, individual devotees came to pay respect by burning incense, and devotional societies put on displays of offerings at the abbey. Wu Zimu 吳自牧 (fl. 1270) provided a compact narrative in his *Mengliang lu* 夢梁錄 written during the last decades of the thirteenth century (*Mengliang lu* 19.9b):

> On the birthday and the descending days of the Aiding Saint of the North Apex [i.e. Zhenwu], the elite, common people and Daoist priests organized gatherings at temples or in the courtyards of homes. On his birthday, [priests of] the Aiding Sage Daoist Monastery carried out the ritual of Offering in obedience to the imperial decree. [Both] elites and commoners lit incense sticks. Military units [*zhai* 寨, *lit.* bases] that had built [worship] halls for the god held gatherings [honoring him]. In addition, different guilds formed societies (*she* 社) to make offerings.
>
> 北極佑聖真君聖降及誕辰，士庶與羽流建會於宮觀或於舍庭。誕辰日，佑聖觀奉上旨建醮，士庶炷香紛然。諸寨建立聖殿者，俱有聖會，諸行亦有獻供之社。[32]

Wu's rather succinct description of the Zhenwu birthday celebration is supplemented by other accounts. In his nostalgic memoir of life in Hangzhou, Zhou Mi 周密 (1232–1298) looked back on the festival of King Zhang, another popular god during Song times (Hansen 1990: 140, 148–159). On the day of the celebration, participating societies put on shows that highlighted their best talents and skills. The food offerings to King Zhang included fine cuisine and rarely found delicacies, decorated with exquisitely carved vegetables as well as jewelry; each dish was priceless in cash terms. In making his concluding remarks, Zhou Mi told readers that the celebrations for Zhenwu on the third day of the third month were just as impressive as those for King Zhang (*Wulin jiushi* 3.10b–11a).

Grand temple festivals undoubtedly attracted large crowds. Street entertainers flocked to the Aiding Saint Daoist Monastery on Zhenwu's birthday to cash in on the crowds attending the temple fair (and in return attracted more crowds wishing to attend the fair). When Zhou Mi wrote about the temple fair of the Aiding Saint Daoist Monastery, he particularly recalled the "stunts on the bird-pole" (*quegan zhi xi* 雀竿之戲), a pole 100 feet high on which performers carried out numerous acrobatic maneuvers. The audience, described Zhou Mi, broke out into a sweat upon watching the dangerous tricks (*Wulin jiushi* 3.11a). Zhenwu's birthday at the Aiding Saint Monastery was no less than a carnival of faith.

Zhenwu temples also held celebrations on traditional holidays universally observed by the Chinese, such as the Lantern Festival on the fifteenth day of the first month, the climax of the New Year period. For example, the Auspicious Spring Monastery's extravaganza on this day was such a grand affair that Emperor Huizong graced it with his presence (*Songshi* 113. 2699).

Zhenwu reached the full dimension of his godhead during the Song dynasty. At the beginning of the dynasty in the mid-tenth century, there was little contemporaneous evidence of the reverence of an anthropomorphic Zhenwu. By the late thirteenth century, however, Zhenwu enjoyed popularity and had developed into a god in full. He could count adherents across the country and across social strata, and his shrines dotted every corner of Song China. His devotees observed dietary restrictions as part of their behavioral code and perceived the violation of such restrictions as an abjuration of their ethical principles. Their culinary choices, fortified by a sense of ethical fulfillment, gave them strength and distinction.

The other crucial element in shaping the sense of identity of Zhenwu believers was the religious calendar. Being a Daoist god, Zhenwu held offices in the heavenly court instead of inhabiting the human realm. He descended to the earth for regular inspection and to receive offerings. Observance of Zhenwu's descending days constituted the most important ingredients in his liturgical calendar. On these days, devotees upheld a fast (*zhaijie* 齋戒) and made ritual offerings to the god. His birthday, which was also one of the descending days, was particularly celebrated, especially at temples dedicated to him. Sharing a calendar special to the group solidifies sentiments of group membership, as Eviatar Zerubavel argues (1981: 70, 83–95).

With their dietary observations and liturgical calendar, Zhenwu worshippers arguably developed a strong self-awareness. This awareness did not necessarily stop them from worshipping other gods; Zhenwu was not a jealous god. They prayed to as many deities as they could find, like most of their fellow Chinese, but when their prayers were answered, it would be Zhenwu to whom they most likely credited the miracles. A god who is credited for performing miracles is a god who is perceived as responsive or *ling*. *Ling* is the primary criteria for the popularity of a divinity in China, a fact noted by many scholars (for example, Hansen 1990;

Feuchtwang 2001). The dietary restrictions and liturgical calendar therefore were contributive factors in the rapid expansion of Zhenwu worship.

Gratitude for Zhenwu's responsiveness was a common reason for devotees to dedicate temples and statues to him (which in turn increased the god's reputation of being *ling*). The god's Daoist godhead added yet another dimension to the temple building. It was perceived that Zhenwu, like all self-respecting Daoist divinities, demanded a space that was separate from mundane interruption and pollution. Maintaining a secluded shrine at home, however, was beyond the means of common people, and a public worshipping center became necessary. Finally, Zhenwu's prominent role in exorcist rituals made him a popular patron saint among ritual specialists, both ordained Daoist priests and village shamans. When these charismatic religious figures won devotion from their clients, the devotion was naturally transferred to Zhenwu. As pious followers raised alms to build temples for their religious masters to head, naturally, Zhenwu took over as the main deity of the temples.

As seen in the archival and epigraphic material, independent temples or affiliated shrines for Zhenwu veneration activities appeared in metropolitan cities such as Kaifeng and Nanjing by the early eleventh century as well as in frontier towns in present-day Gansu. Over the course of the eleventh century, new sanctuaries for Zhenwu continued to be added to the Chinese landscape. A temple inscription from 1115 indicated that even in the remote countryside (*fangzhou xiaoyi* 方州小邑), one could find Zhenwu temples (*Lejing ji* 6.1a). They were likely funded by non-government agents, since, as the author lamented, they were often under poor maintenance.

Indeed, the spread of Zhenwu temples was due less to imperial patronage than to the piety of individuals, both ritual specialists and ordinary people (scholar-officials and commoners). It is true that the Song court built two majestic temples for Zhenwu, but there were only two, and imperial patronage could barely account for the popularity of a god. It was the collaborative effort of the local elite and commoners under the initiative of the Daoist clergy that was responsible for creating Zhenwu temples. While temples embodied collaborative efforts of various social groups, Daoist clerics deserved the largest credit for the widespread installation of those dedicated to Zhenwu during Song times. Nevertheless, this is not to suggest that lay believers were flocks of meek sheep with Daoist priests as their shepherds. The negotiation of authority between laity and clergy is clear in the designing of Zhenwu's descending days. Both parties tried to install their versions. While the former held on to historical and institutional authority, the latter appealed to a direct revelation from the divinity without the mediation of the clergy.

The cult of Zhenwu grew up in the cultural and religious milieu of Song times. Song people lived in an environment of unprecedented commercialization and social change. It was during the Song era that Daoism experienced its "renaissance," using Michel Strickmann's terminology (1979), which witnessed various new ritual movements surfacing from within to cope with the challenges from without. Zhenwu figured prominently in this background and became one of the main deities that ritual specialists invoked and venerated. It was these new ritual schools that would bring Zhenwu into the center of the Daoist pantheon.

3 A god in transition

A Daoist priest (*daoshi*) named Zhao Zujian 趙祖堅, the *Record of the Listener* tells us, practiced therapeutic exorcism by the ritual program called Five Thunders. During the exorcist procedure, he summoned spirits for an interrogation in which he would make the spirit possess his assistant in order to facilitate communication. One day during the ritual, his young assistant unexpectedly jumped up and, in a roaring voice, announced himself to be the late tenth-century Daoist master Tan Zixiao 譚紫霄 coming to help Zhao to advance in the Five Thunders ritual. But first he needed to know what knowledge Zhao had already acquired. Zhao replied, "Only the four talismans that were transmitted to this world by Zhenwu" (*Yijianzhi yi* 5.831–832; Davis 2001: 80–82). Zhao's answer marks Zhenwu as an essential source of the Thunder Rites, one of the most important ritual movements in post-Tang Daoism.

This chapter examines the new Daoist rituals that gave Zhenwu a pivotal role. As an anthropomorphic god, Zhenwu entered the Daoist pantheon late but reached a high position relatively quickly. A new style of liturgical meditation, "transformation into the deity through inner refinement" (*bianshen neilian* 變神內煉), promoted by the new ritual lineages surfacing in the early twelfth century, held the key to Zhenwu's story of success. In the course of time, he grew into a meditation partner, a lineage master, and a patron in the heavenly court for Daoist ritual specialists. By the fourteenth century, in some ritual programs he has even become the ultimate source of authority and was given the title of emperor (*di*). From an attendant general to a supreme monarch, Zhenwu had come a long way in the Daoist pantheon.

Pantheon rejuvenation

The Five Thunders ritual systems mentioned in the anecdote above belongs to a vast body of ritual theories and practices in Daoism known as *leifa* 雷法 or Thunder Rites that surfaced in the early twelfth century. Facilitated by complex meditative methods as well as invocations, talismans, and *mudra*s (symbolic hand gestures), the Thunder Rites were developed to harness the thunder force to serve the Way. Interpretations of the thunder force, even among Daoists, varied widely from the pure cosmic *qi* to violent spirits of half-man half-beast monsters, and everything in between (Skar 1996–7: 178; Reiter 2007). The bottom line is that they embodied

48 *A god in transition*

the vigor of thunder and could be domesticated through the Daoist divine bureaucratic system. Their recruitment in the Daoist pantheon attested to Daoist efforts in incorporating popular cults in Song times, a development that characterized the ritual evolution of modern Daoism (Schipper and Verellen 2004: 635; Robinet 1997: 178–179).

Thunder deities: the early development (pre-tenth century)

The Chinese have long appreciated the power of thunder. Sima Qian 司馬遷 (145?–86 BCE) observed that thunder animates the cosmos just as the bell and drum initiate the symphony (*Shiji* 24.1195–1196). The Thunder Lord (*leigong* 雷公), along with the divinities of wind, rain, and agriculture, had a designated place on the outer altar of the state pantheon during the Eastern Han period (*Hou Hanshu* 97.3106). In the ritual innovations of Emperor Tang Xuanzong 玄宗 (r. 712–756), the divinity of thunder, referred to as Thunder Master (*leishi* 雷師), was promoted to the second level of the three-tier state sacrificial protocol (Xiong 1996). Until the end of imperial times, thunder received imperial sacrifices and homage as middle-ranking gods (*Qingshi gao* 82.2492). In the orderly state pantheon, thunder is domesticated through impersonation and hierarchy.

In mythology and folklore, on the other hand, thunder deities were represented as mythical creatures, if not monsters. Written records from the end of the first century BCE described the look of thunder gods in brief: "There were thunder gods (*leishen* 雷神) in the thunder swamp who are of dragon bodies and human heads" (*Shanhai jing* 13.1b).[1] The fourth-century *Record of An Inquest into the Spirit-Realm* (*Soushen ji* 搜神記 12.5a) illustrated local belief in Fufeng (near Xi'an, southern Shaanxi province) that the thunder god resembled a monkey. This iconography survived for a long time and spread far. *The Journey to the West* (*Xiyou ji* 西遊記) completed by Wu Cheng'en 吳承恩 (ca. 1500–1582), a native of the coastal province of Jiangsu, often poked fun at the protagonist Monkey King being misidentified as *leigong*, or thunder lord, by confused villagers. This comical routine underlies the fact that the monkey was a well accepted depiction of the thunder deity in eastern China as well during Ming times.

The simian iconography, however, competed with other facets of thunder gods. The *Extensive Records of the Taiping Era* (*Taiping guangji* 太平廣記), a collection of pre-tenth-century anecdotes, devotes three entire chapters to thunder. One of the accounts relates that in Leizhou (Guangdong province) people drew images of thunder gods for worship, and the gods were portrayed as having pigs' heads (*Taiping guangji* 394.8b). In the story of the battle of Chen Luanfeng 陳鸞鳳 with a thunder god, the latter was described as "resembling a bear-pig (*xiongzhu* 熊豬) with hairy horns and dark-blue featherless wings."[2] This description brings to mind *brachyphylla*, the species of bat with a pig-nosed hairy face and big pointed ears found in Central and South America. Could the *brachyphylla* by a rare chance have come to southern China and inspired the Cantonese depiction of the thunder god? Pig-headed thunder gods lingered on in Daoist Thunder Rites as attested in the *Daofa huiyuan* (j. 90, ZHDZ 36.572). Furthermore, on a seventeenth-century

A god in transition 49

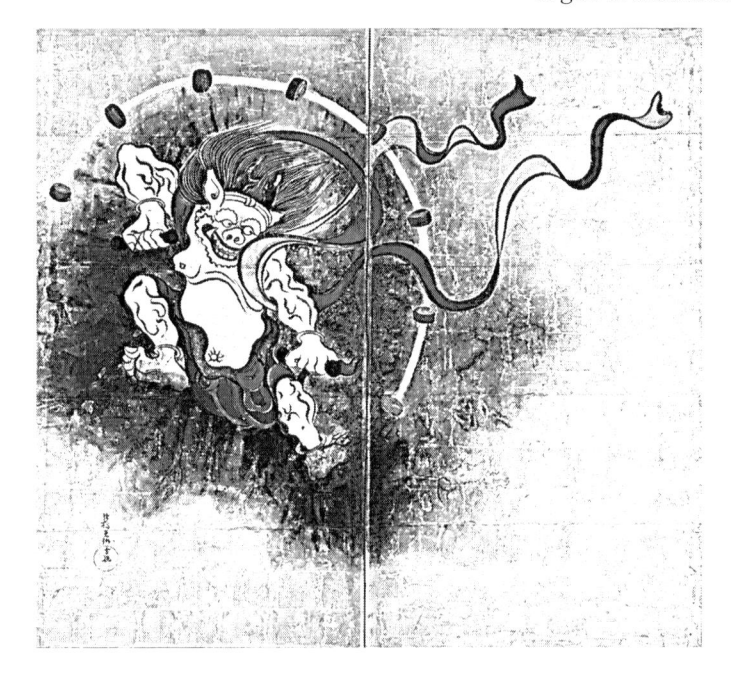

Figure 3.1 Thunder God by the Japanese artist Tawaraya Sōtatsu, fl. early seventeenth century.
Source: © Wikimedia commons.

Figure 3.2 Thunder God, detail.

Japanese screen, we also find the thunder god being given a snout and big ears (figures 3.1 and 3.2). Another common depiction of thunder deities employs beaks, claws, and feathered wings, still used in modern Taiwanese Daoist ritual scenarios (Meulenbeld 2006: 71). The length and breadth of thunder deity iconography resulted in numerous animalistic depictions. In Daoist liturgical manuals, we can find still more variations of the images of thunder deities.

Daoist recruitment of the thunder forces

Efforts to recruit thunder deities into the Daoist pantheon began in the eighth century CE at the latest. The *Scripture of Jade Purity of the Great Dao of the Most High* (*Taishang Dadao yuqing jing* 太上大道玉清經; TC 1312), produced before 753 (Lagerwey 2004: 527), contains short narratives about the thunder lord (*leigong*) enforcing the law of the Dao by obliterating the transgressors. The scriptural text also indicates that students of the Dao could deploy (*shi* 使) thunder deities (*leishen*) to demolish the "spirit of wood" (*mujing* 木精).[3] At roughly the same time, thunder deities were recruited in Daoist ritual programs of Retreat (*zhai* 齋) as a police force to punish transgressors. Wang Fajin 王法進 (d. 752), a Daoist initiate from northeast Sichuan, received such a ritual program in a revelation.[4] It was in the middle of a famine, we are told, when Wang encountered three divine envoys in her courtyard. They announced that the Supreme Emperor (*Shangdi* 上帝) had sent for her, so they had came to escort her to the celestial court. Before realizing it, she found herself levitated into the sky. The Supreme Emperor received Wang and bestowed on her the program of the "method of the Pure Retreat of Lingbao to declare penitence to heaven and earth" (*Lingbao qingzhai gaoxie tiandi fa* 靈寶清齋告謝天地法). He also warned Wang that the famine was a punishment for the wastefulness of mankind. People on the earth must repent sincerely by carrying out the ritual of the Pure Retreat (*qingzhai* 清齋) and then pray to heaven for a good harvest in the spring, and give thanks for the harvest in the autumn. The ritual should be carried out in an elevated location such as that of a tranquil mountain (*youshan gaojing zhi chu* 幽山高靜之處). Wang then was escorted back home. It turned out that she had been asleep for three months. Her return to consciousness in a normal condition after a long coma arguably authenticated her revelation. Before long the ritual became popular, and eventually was referred to as either *Qingzhai* or *Tiangong zhai* 天公齋 (Retreat of Heavenly Lord/Fair Heaven; see the discussion below). The participants had to be not only pure in mind but meticulous regarding the ritual requirements. Otherwise, rainstorms would demolish the altar and "the quick and roaring thunderbolts would destroy the utensils."

Tiangong is conventionally rendered as "the lord (*gong*) of heaven (*tian*)." However, a text directly related to Wang Fajin and her ritual program found in the *Daoist Canon* volunteers a unique interpretation of *tiangong* as an abbreviation of "the way of heaven (*tian*) is fair (*gong*) without preference" (*Tiangong zhe, tiandao gongping wusi ye* 天公者，天道公平無私也).[5] This obscure interpretation plays with the multiple meanings of the Chinese character *gong*, which can mean both "lord" and "fair." This Daoist reading of the title suggests the intent to switch the meaning of *tiangong* worship from adulation of a particular divine individual (as popular religious rituals do) to veneration of the cosmos, which is what a Daoist ritual of Offering should be. Wang Fajin's story, argues Kristofer Schipper (1993), is an example of Daoism working in common with the traditional popular cult of earth and harvest. The dehumanized re-interpretation of *tiangong*, I would suggest, further underscores the Daoist effort in redefining popular religious practices to make them fit into the Daoist theological system. Wang Fajin's *Tiangong* Retreat was a Daoist ritual program and it deployed thunder as the punitive force over transgressors.

More details about the *Tiangong* Retreat and the thunder deities were recorded by a scholar-official in the tenth century, Sun Guangxian 孫光憲 (ca. 900–968), also a native of Sichuan. Sun tells us that people in east Sichuan often built *Tiangong* altars on the summits or in pristine places and held the *Tiangong* retreat to pray for rain or good weather.[6] The protocols and liturgies practiced "were bequeathed by the Supreme Emperor (*shangdi*) during the reign of Kaiyuan (714–741)." During the ritual period, participants were forbidden to consume meat and alcohol; transgressors "were often struck dead by thunder." Sun then relates an anecdote in which Wang Yao 王堯 (fl. 847–859), a native of Xinfan 新繁 (near Chengdu, Sichuan), paid a visit to his countryside estate and attended a pork banquet in his honor. At the table, he noted that a guest who enjoyed the pork had just returned from the *Tiangong* Retreat. Wang asked him: "Aren't you afraid of the thunderclaps?" The guest replied casually that it was not a concern because "Thunder and I are brothers." Bewildered, Wang poked further. The man explained, "I have obtained the Register of Thunder (*leigong lu* 雷公錄) and hold the same *zhi* 職 (official position) as Thunder does." It is clearly spelled out here that the thunder lords working in the *Tiangong* Retreat were registered as bureaucratic employees. Bureaucratization, as Edward Davis argues, is one of the characteristic developments that distanced Daoist Thunder Rites from their non-Daoist predecessors (Davis 2001: 26). The *Tiangong* Retreat described here evidently consisted of a Daoist ritual program of deploying thunder.

Although Sun Guangxian did not mention Wang Fajin by name, the *Tiangong* Retreat in his account is unmistakably the same ritual that Wang transmitted. In addition to the identical names, they both commenced around the same time (during the reign of Emperor Xuanzong), were attributed to the same source (the Supreme Emperor), were popular in the same region (Sichuan) for the same purpose (to engender proper weather), and were carried out in the same type of venues (high and pure locations). Combining the two accounts, we can confirm the existence of a Daoist communal ritual program that enlisted thunder deities as part of its bureaucratic system.

Sun Guangxian next reported that a certain Daoist priest (*daoshi*) Li in Jiangling (west Hubei) also possessed an identical Register of Lord Thunder. However, Sun continued, the Register of Lord Thunder was among "one hundred and two ritual methods" outside the recognized "correct rituals" and was banned by Celestial Masters. Sun's observation went beyond a layman's impressionistic remarks. During his time, a popular Daoist exorcist order became known for practicing an unorthodox "rite of thunder lord."[7] Those who were initiated into the order would receive, among other texts, a single-chapter manuscript called *Ritual of the Thunder Lords of the Northern Emperor* (*Beidi Leigong fa* yi juan 北帝雷公法一卷), according to a tenth-century handbook on the ranks and protocols of Daoist clergy (*daoshi* 道士 and *nüguan* 女官). Nevertheless, the text informs us, the order in question was outside the seven established ranks of ordained Daoists.

If, during the mid-tenth century, the deployment of thunder deities in Daoist rituals was still controversial and limited to certain orders, by the beginning of the twelfth century the ritual landscape had changed considerably. In the final decades of the Northern Song dynasty, Thunder Rites took a central position on the imperial religious stage and rose to great significance. Lin Lingsu 林靈素 (ca. 1074–1119), the religious adviser who wielded much influence at the court between 1116 and 1119, was renowned for deploying the ritual of Five Thunders to summon rainfall.[8] The Celestial Masters school by then had also changed its earlier attitude of rejection and embraced the Thunder Rites. Zhang Jixian 張繼先 (1092–1126), the 30th generation Celestial Master, even designed a number programs for it (Ren *et al*. 1999: 738; Skar 2000: 433). Several ritual compendia compiled at the end of the twelfth or early thirteenth centuries were marked by the prevalence of Thunder Rites. Daoist masters no less prestigious than Wang Wenqing 王文卿 (1093–1153) and Bai Yuchan 白玉蟾 (1194–1229), among others, wrote treatises elaborating on the theories and praxis of Thunder Rites. By the end of the twelfth century, the Thunder Rites had become a generic practice that was accepted by every major school, new or old, of Daoism.

The method of "transformation into the divinity through inner refinement"

The Daoist Thunder Rites serve mainly to manipulate the weather favorably and to pacify or demolish harmful spirits. Since demons and vengeful ghosts were thought to cause illness in Daoist pathology (Strickmann 2002), the ritual was also used as a therapeutic remedy. Cases in which Thunder Rite masters successfully treated demonic possession (i.e. psychotic disorder) or literally blew up temples of rival deities with thunderous bursts of flames can be found in both Daoist and non-Daoist sources. Modern scholars have offered rational explanations for such miraculous ritual powers, including the theatrical effects that the ritual could produce on patients' psychological condition (Davis 2001: 107–114) and Daoists' knowledge of the science of gunpowder (Boltz 1993: 285–286). However, to the writers and compilers of Thunder Rites literature, the efficacy of their ritual derived from the fact that it was carried out by the thunder deities under the command of initiated Daoists.

For Daoist practitioners, therefore, the key to an efficacious Thunder Rites performance is the success in summoning and deploying the thunder deities. Always armed with weapons and often dressed in armor, the thunder deities are militant in nature and are assigned ranks such as those of general and marshal in the Daoist bureaucratic paradigm. Their fieriness is threatening enough to require

A god in transition 53

taking precautions when summoning them.⁹ Furthermore, they are reputed as unruly. Statutes in Thunder Rites specify punishments for thunder deities who fail to respond to the ritual masters' calls.¹⁰ The punitive aspect of these penal codes reflect Daoist masters' concerns about their needs for control over thunder subordinates. Consequently, various techniques were generated to ensure the latter's obedience, and one of them is the subject of this section: the liturgical meditation of "transformation into the divinities through inner refinement" (*bianshen neilian* 變神內煉), often abbreviated as *bianlian* "transformation—refinement" or simply as *bianshen*.

To avoid confusion, it should be noted immediately that the term *bianshen* was already in use in pre-Song Daoist liturgical manuals. The old *bianshen* ritual was a preparatory step that a priest used to metamorphose his or her body into the cosmos before making audience at the heavenly court.¹¹ The new *bianshen* exercise aimed at transforming (*bian*) the priest temporarily into a particular deity (*shen*) in order to appropriate the power of the deity in question. In the following discussion, when the word *bianshen* is used, it refers to this new style of liturgical meditation.

Transforming into Zhenwu

The "transformation into the divinity" is a meditative liturgy through which Daoist priests subordinated their identities to that of the individual deities commanding the thunder generals. Zhenwu is one of these high authorities, as attested in the mid-fourteenth-century compendium of the Thunder Rites, the *Retrieved Pearls from the Sea of Rituals* (*Fahai yizhu* 法海遺珠). The manuscript is titled "Model Rites for Submission, Dispatch, Fusing, and Refinement" (Zou chuan hun lian fashi 奏傳混鍊法式). It says:¹²

> Form your hands into the hand gesture of transformation into the divinity (*bianshen jue*), then place them next to your waist. First visualize yourself as a withered log of wood. The two hands form the sign of *wu* (*wu wen* 午文) [by joining the thumbs to the tips of the middle fingers] (figure 3.3), inhale the *qi* of the south, and merge it with that of the heart to form the perfect fire. Next, flick your thumbs from the tip of your middle fingers to set the log afire from the bottom. At once, the flame rises up. Now form the sign of *si* (*si wen* 巳文) [by putting your thumbs on the tips of your index fingers] to generate the wind of the *xun* 巽 [trigram] to blow away the ashes; leave no traces.
>
> [Following this,] visualize an infant growing larger in your cinnabar field. [See him] with loose hair and barefoot, clad in a black robe and golden armor, looking like the Perfected Warrior. Beneath his feet, there is a dark-green turtle exhaling *qi* which merges with that of the kidneys ([original footnote]: place [your thumb on] *zi* (the bottom of the ring finger), [visualize] the head of the turtle moving); there is also a red snake exhaling *qi* that merges with the *qi*

54 *A god in transition*

of the heart ([original footnote]: place [your thumb on] *wu* [the bottom of the index finger], [visualize] the head of the snake moving).

兩手握變神訣，叉腰。先存身為枯木，以兩手掐午文，吸南炁一口，與心炁合為真火。兩手剔午，發火下木根，一時燒上。次掐巳文，發巽風，吹散灰塵，別無纖翳。存丹田內一嬰兒漸大，披髮跣足，皂袍金甲，如真武相，足下有蒼龜吐炁，與腎炁合，(掐子，龜頭動)。有赤蛇吐炁，與心炁合 (掐午，蛇頭動).

Thus, in meditation, the material body is refined by the "perfect fire" (*zhenhuo* 真火) and the cosmic wind (Xun is the symbol of wind in the Eight Trigrams of the *Book of Change*). As the *mudra*, or "hand gesture," that begins the instruction declares,

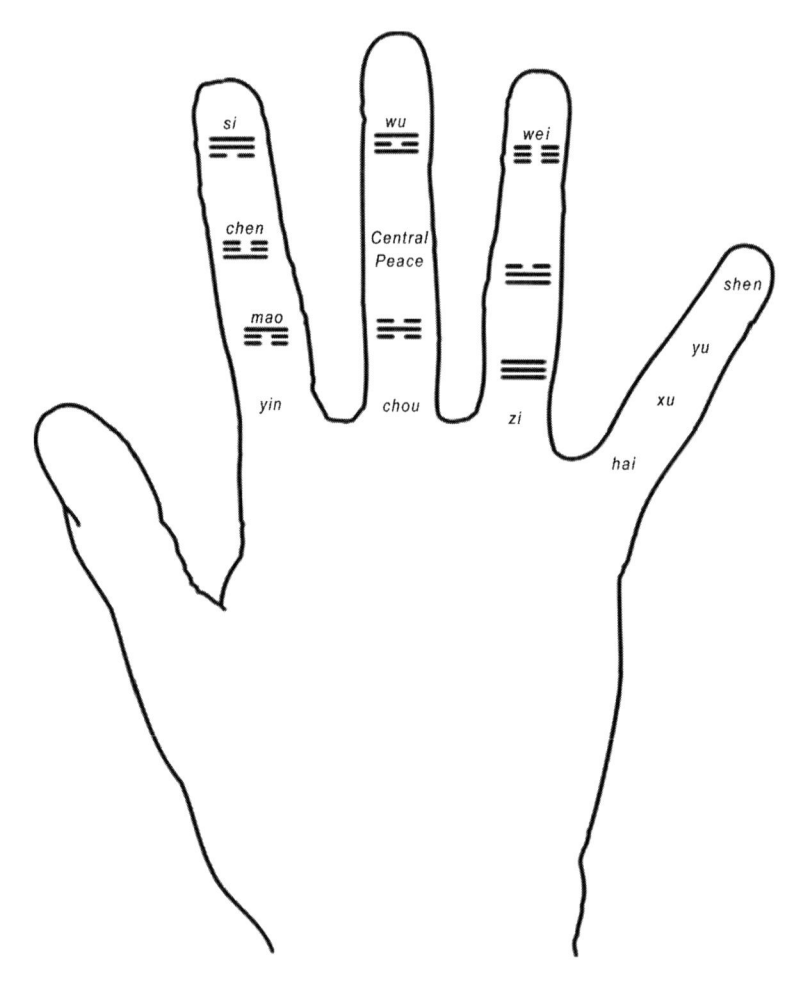

Figure 3.3 The 12 "earthly branches" and eight trigrams on a hand.
Source: Drawn by Edyth Kuciapa.

A god in transition 55

this visualization aims at transforming the practitioner into the divinity. Indeed, after reducing the old body to ashes and blowing the ashes away, the practitioner conceives and generates a pure spiritual body, the "infant" (*yinger* 嬰兒), in the "cinnabar field." The inner-body infant then grows into Zhenwu, with whom the practitioner merges with the help of the god's emblematic animals, turtle and snake. In the temporary apotheosis, the adept proceeds to wield the miraculous powers promised by the Thunder Rites.

It is true that the practice of transforming oneself into a particular deity during a ritual was not without criticism within Daoism. Nevertheless, a cursory search of the liturgical manuals in the Daoist Canon leaves no doubt about the prevalence of such methods and how well they were received among many reputable Daoist masters. One of the most popular and influential new ritual schools of Song times, the Celestial Heart School, expressly promoted the method of *bianshen* in their ritual compendiums.

In the Celestial Heart school

The Correct Rites of the Celestial Heart, which was popular across the territory and social strata of China from the twelfth century, was the first ritual movement compromising the Thunder Rites at its core. Its own genealogical lore traces the revelation of the Celestial Heart texts and oral secrets (*jue* 訣) to two men: Tan Zixiao (fl. 935– after 994), whom we met at the opening of this chapter, and Rao Dongtian 饒洞天 (fl. 994).[13] Tan Zixiao was a highly regarded Daoist priest at the court of the Min kingdom (based in the province of Fujian on the southeast coast) between 935 and 939. The court's chief religious advisor unearthed a batch of unknown talismans and showed them to Tan, who determined them to be part of the ritual program called Correct Rites of Celestial Heart. After the Min kingdom fell in 944, Tan fled to Mt Lu in northern Jiangxi. There, he became a much sought-after teacher with more than 100 students, among whom was Rao Dongtian, a native of central Jiangxi. Rao had a revelation that led him to discover a case of texts on the mountain, entitled "the secret formulas of the Celestial Heart" (Tianxin mishi 天心祕式). The booklets, however, were incomprehensible to him. Then he had a second revelation informing him that Tan Zixiao held the key to these mysterious writings. Rao went to see Tan for instruction—and the rest was history. Both Tan and Rao were honored in the Celestial Heart school for generations to come as "transmitters of the teaching" or *chuanjiao* 傳教 (*Secret Essential*, j.2, ZHDZ 30.319a). Nevertheless, it was Rao rather than his mentor Tan who was recorded as the "first-generation patriarch" (*chuzu* 初祖) in the lineage's genealogy.[14]

The early forms of the Celestial Heart tradition are preserved in two compendia compiled two centuries after Tan and Rao: the *Secret Essentials of the Most High Principle Zhenren Assisting the Country and Saving the People* (*Taishang shuo zhuguo jiumin zongzhen miyao* 太上助國救民總真祕要 TC 1227; hereafter, *Secret Essential*) compiled by Yuan Miaozong 元妙宗 (fl. 1086–1116) in 1116 and the *Correct Method of the Celestial Heart of the Supreme Clarity* (*Shangqing*

56 *A god in transition*

Figure 3.4 Zhenwu talisman from the *Secret Essential* j. 2.

tianxin zhengfa 上清天心正法; CT 566; hereafter the *Correct Method*) by Deng Yougong 鄧有功 around the same period.[15] Both texts agree that three talismans (*fu*) are fundamental to the Tianxin ritual system and one of them carries the name and authority of Zhenwu (see figures 3.4 and 3.5).[16] It is called the Zhenwu Fu in the *Secret Essential*,[17] and the Xuanwu-Heisha Fu in the *Correct Method of the Celestial Heart*.[18] Xuanwu was the old name of Zhenwu before 1012 (see the Introduction). "Upon drawing the [Xuanwu-Heisha] talisman," the *Correct Method* instructs, "transform into the divinity" (*bianshen*).[19] The instruction then proceeds to depict a portrait of Zhenwu:

> One hundred feet tall, with disheveled hair in golden armor he steps on the numinous turtle of five colors which is also known as the turtle of the eight trigrams [encircled by a] leaping snake. One [of his] hands forms the 'seal of pacifying demons' ([original note:] i.e. the Zhenwu seal). Lightening comes out from his eyes. The other hand holds a sword as he stands still.
>
> 身長百尺，散髮，金鑠甲冑，足踏五炁靈龜，又名螣蛇八卦之龜。手結伏魔印，即真武印。眼出電光，按劍而立。(*Shangqing tianxin zhengfa* j.3, ZHDZ 30.253a).

This depiction further confirms that the Xuanwu in the Xuanwu-Heisha talisman is indeed the General Zhenwu with whom we are familiar.

Celestial Heart masters made house calls to treat victims of diabolic possession (*huanxie ren* 患邪人), during which they would often transform themselves into Zhenwu. According to the *Secret Essential* (j.7, in ZHDZ 30.358c):

> the Ritual Master mentioned above arrives at the patient's home, enters the door, walks several steps, visualizes (*cun* 存) oneself (*shen* 身) to be (*wei* 為) Zhenwu with loosen hair brandishing a sword. The four envoys on duty, the Heavenly Pass and the Earthly Pivotal (i.e. the turtle and the snake) as well as the pageantry follow behind. Form the [*mudra* of] Brush Seal with your left

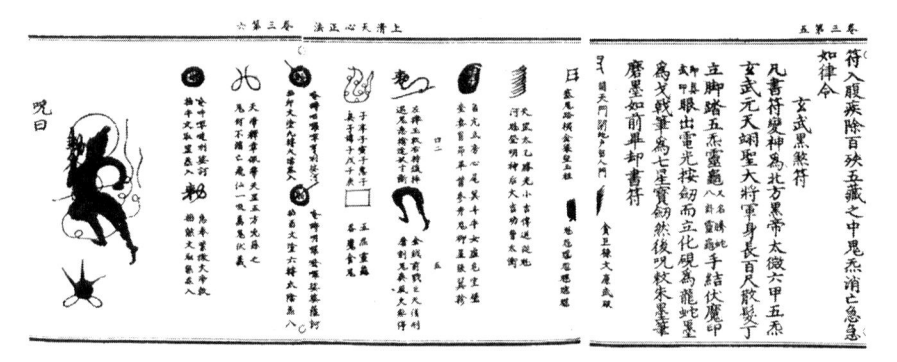

Figure 3.5 Xuanwu-Heisha talisman from the *Shangqing tianxin zhengfa* j. 3.

hand, recite in silence the incantation three times. Reach the main hall of the household of the patient, sit down, give the order to bring the victim of diabolic possession, and conduct interrogation carefully.

右法師至患者家門，行數步，存身為真武披髮仗劍，四值使者，天關地軸，儀仗隨從。以左手結斗印，默念法三遍。至患人家廳上坐，令驅患邪人出來，勘問，子[sic.]細施行。

Again, once the meditative transformation is completed, the priest "turns into" Zhenwu. At his disposal is an entourage of aides-de-camp. The Summon and Investigation ritual of therapeutic exorcism is then ready to proceed. In addition to spirits who possessed victims, the ritual master can summon all the relevant spirits including the local Earth God who was supposed to keep an eye on neighborhood security. The latter's response to the subpoena must be prompt since it was not issued by man but by god.

When in combat with *shanxiao* 山魈 (*lit.* mountain goblin), the mythical one-legged demons,[20] the *Correct Method* instructs, the ritual masters also should transform themselves into Zhenwu (j.5 in ZHDZ 30.267a):

Whenever you want to control *shanxiao* … when you first set out on your quest, first cleanse yourself and attend an audience with the Highest Emperor in silent [meditation] to respectfully make your case [for performing the exorcism]. Visualize the Northern Emperor leaving his stellar palace, ascending to the [audience] hall, and taking his seat. The emperor next summons Zhenwu along with other [deities] and orders them to take control of the source of wickedness in the Three Worlds.

Next, envision Zhenwu coming directly to the front of the [altar] table with the decree. Stand up. [Carry out] "transformation into the deity" and become the grand general Zhenwu himself—with loosened hair and bare feet, holding the sword of samādhi fire in the right hand and forming a *mudra* with the left hand, while standing on the turtle and snake. After concluding "transformation into the deity through inner refinement", walk the stellar net of the Three Terraces and the Dipper. Once that is complete, invoke the officials and generals of all the bureaus of the Southern Court, visualizing them one by one.

凡欲追治山魈 … 臨去治日，先淨身，默朝上帝，奏陳因依，存見北帝自星宮中升殿而坐，召真武等，令攝三界邪源。復想真武領敕命下界，直至案前。起身，變神為真武大將，披髮跣足，右手仗三昧火劍，左手叉印，足踏玄武。變神內煉迄，次步三台七星罡，一一了畢，呼召南院諸司官將，一一存。

The ritual master thus first acquires divine authorization from the Northern Emperor.[21] Although Daoist priests already possessed the authority to command by virtue of ordination, the situation was similar to that of a general in command of troops who still needs to acquire approval from his superiors before launching a battle. Then, Zhenwu, with the Northern Emperor's decree, descends to the human realm to take charge of pacifying the wicked. The god moves directly to the front of the altar table, that is, the very spot where the ritual master is lying prostrate. The ritual master now stands up and begins the next step of meditation to "become" (*wei* 為) the god. Only after completing this transformation does the master begin to summon the officers and generals of the Celestial Pivotal Court (Tianshu yuan 天樞院) of the South Apex.[22] The figure at the altar who sends for the divine thunder generals is, therefore, no longer the priest. This new "self" generated by the procedure of deity-transformation is, as far as the ritual is considered, Zhenwu himself.

Here we see a Daoist ritual manual requiring the priests to subjugate their identities to that of the divinity summoning thunder generals. This, as Judith Boltz points out, is "in some ways reminiscent of their [Daoist priests'] shamanic counterparts" (Boltz 1983: 25). Boltz's observation, without passing judgment, confirms the criticism made by the eminent twelfth-century Daoist Wang Wenqing, a Thunder Rite master himself. Wang denounced "visualizing (*cun*) oneself as the Celestial Master or the Dark Emperor [i.e. Zhenwu]" as one of the "bewitching and false" (*yaowang* 妖妄) practices.[23] Wang's admonishment might sound harsh but not groundless within the context of classical Daoist theology. Since the early stages of the religion, Daoists proclaimed that only "vulgar deities" routinely manifest themselves through the "vulgar rites" of possession. Daoist deities, on the contrary, were not supposed to possess humans at least in theory. "The Jade Regulation of Heavenly Altar of the Most High [Lord Lao]" (Taishang tiantan yuge 太上天壇玉格), for example, specifically warned: "All supreme perfected ones, celestial transcendent ones, and divine generals do not possess (*fu* 附) living persons' bodies. If there are ones that often possess humans to speak, they are definitely sinister demons outside the Way and wrongful ghosts. … Gentlemen who practice rituals must carefully pursue this." (經云: 一切上真天仙神將，不附生人之體，若輒附人語者，決是邪魔外道，不正之鬼。… 行法之士當審察之。 *Daofa huiyuan* 250, *j.xia*, ZHDZ 38.400b).

It is true that induced possession was part of the Daoist clerics' ritual repertory. In the ritual of Summon and Investigation, for example, they employed assistants to be the mouthpieces through whom the trouble-making spirits could verbally communicate with the priests (Davis 2001: 87–114). Yet it was not the priests themselves but the assistants—sometimes the neighborhood spirit mediums, sometimes ordinary youngsters—who were possessed. Then as now, ordained Daoists consciously distinguish themselves from neighborhood spirit mediums. They have always described themselves as the "dignitaries of the Dao," the delegates of the heavenly court on earth. They are not vessels but colleagues of the divinities. Daoist gods and their priests eat, drink, converse, and excurse together; sometimes they even get romantically involved with each other, but possession is out of the question.

Therefore, it is understandable that Daoist masters who embraced the techniques of becoming gods had to re-theorize the practice of temporary identity-change to make sure it had absolutely nothing to do with divine possession. They appealed, as Schipper points out, "to the inner ritual of meditation" (Schipper 1993: 34), and exhausted the available sources in Daoism, old and new, and probably sources outside Daoism as well. Finally, they created the meditative techniques that facilitated an identity-transformation without falling into the trap of divine possession.

The technique

Deng Yougong, the late twelfth-century Celestial Heart master discussed earlier, explained the innovative meditative technique in his monumental *Correct Method*, under the heading of "method of grand transformation of spirits through refinement and metamorphosis" (*lianhu da bianshen fa* 鍊化大變神法; see *Shangqing tianxin zhengfa* j. 2, in ZHDZ 30.248b:

> As for Ritual Officials who have not practiced for long time, how can they obtain the affinity between the divinity and the human? They have to obtain the way of refinement, metamorphosis, and transformation into the divinity. ... Now, [I] pass it down to later generations. In following and practicing the [instruction], there will be not one failure in ten thousand times. The ritual officials who want to practice, have to burn the incense and wave their hands above the incense [for purification]. Form [the sign of] *mao*[24] with the left hand and [the *mudra* of] sword with the right hand, recite the "incantation of cleansing heaven and earth" three times. Inhale the *qi* of east, blow it on the body to make it clear and clean.
>
> Next, visualize (*cun* 存) your body as a withered tree (*kushu* 枯樹). Then form the sign of *wu* with the left hand, and the form the *mudra* of *dou* with the right hand. Place your hands on the waist, use the *wu* sign of your left hand to light the fire of heart [*wu* associates with fire], bursting from the chest all the way to the top of the head. Inhale the *qi* of the south, blow at the left, visualize the flame burning the body, bright, clear, and clean. The left hand

forms the *mudra* of seal, the right hand the *zi* sign.[25] From the "palace of kidney" [the organ associated with water], guide the water of the Yellow River. Guide it upwards from the low [where the kidneys are located] and pour it over the entire body. Inhale the water-*qi* of the north, blow on the right, visualize the ashes being washed away. Only the *qi* of perfection remains. Shinning as a bright pearl, it gradually grows bigger.

Form the *mudra* of bush with two hands. Recite the grand incantation of deity transformation: "My body is not an ordinary body/My head is like black clouds/My hair is like wild stars/My left eye is like the sun/my right eye is like the moon/My nose is like a fire-bell/My ears are like golden gongs/My upper lip is the Rain Master/My lower lip is the Earl of Winds …. Hastily, hastily (let it be so), as commanded with the force of law."[26] Recite the incantation three times. Inhale the *qi* of north, form the bush *mudra* at the chest and move upward to pass the forehead. Break the bush *mudra* into two halves to cover the left and right sides. Visualize yourself (*zishen* 自身) gradually turning into the shape of an infant (*ying'er* 嬰兒) being surrounded by a halo of red radiance like a wheel. … Crush the radiant aureole. Visualize the self [i.e. the infant] becoming the Celestial Master, Tianpeng, or Zhenwu at your wish.

鍊化大變神法: 凡法官行持歲月未深，安得神人契合？須得鍊化變神之道 …。今特傳之於後，依斯行之， 萬不失一。 凡法官欲行持，須香上度手過，左卯右劍，念淨天地呪三遍，吸東炁一口，吹身，令清淨。次存本身如枯樹。次左午文，右斗訣，叉腰，將左午文引心火，自心前燒至頂門。吸南炁同[sic., should be "一口"]，吹於左，存火燒身，光明瑩潔。左手結印，右手子文，自腎宮引黃河水，自下引上，澆灌一身。吸北方炁一口，吹於右，存灰燼蕩盡。只存一真之炁，瑩若明珠，漸漸增長，兩手斗印，念變神大呪："吾身非凡身頭如黑雲，髮如亂星。 左目如日，右目如月，鼻如火鈴，耳如金鐘。 上唇雨師， 下唇風伯。……"念呪三遍，吸北炁一口，雙手斗訣，自心前移上，拂過額上。 撒開斗印，剝於左右，存自身漸成嬰兒狀，有紅光一團圍遶，如坐車輪中。… 拍破光暈，自身存為天師，或天蓬，真武任意。

As Deng Yougong made clear at the beginning of his instruction, the method was designed to help "ritual officers" (*faguan* 法官) that had learned but not yet mastered deploying divinities on their own. In order to carry out the ritual to its expected efficacy, the inexperienced ritual specialists united themselves with a deity through a sequence of inner refinement. The underlining idea, as Poul Andersen explains, was to impersonate the "prototype of the ritual practitioner" in order to assume the power and authority attached to that identity. The impersonated figures were often "seen to be the active force operating in and giving effect to the method in question" (Andersen 1995: 197).

The sources

Despite being designed for untried experts, the "method of grand transformation of spirits through refinement and metamorphosis" is notably complex because it derived from multiple sources. Indeed, as novel as the ritual was when it surfaced in Song times, it was not exactly conjured from thin air. Its elements are covered in four Daoist sources: the classical Daoist thought of Warring States period, the Supreme Clarity (*Shangqing*) visualization practices, the incantation originated in the Celestial Masters school, and the inner alchemy vocabulary and imagery. In addition, the inspiration for assuming a god's identity to appropriate his power through meditation was most likely derived from tantric Buddhism. The following pages discuss these elements one by one.

To begin with, the images of dry wood (*kumu* 枯木 or *kushu* 枯樹) and ashes acknowledge a connection to the *Zhuangzi* of classical times. "Can you really make the body like a withered tree and the mind like dead ashes?" This is the question that opens one of the most studied pieces in Chinese literature history, the eloquent "Discussion on Making All Things Equal" (*Qiwu lun* 齊物論) by Zhuangzi. The question was not directly answered here, but a few chapters later, in "Fit for Emperors and Kings" (*Ying diwang* 應帝王), Zhuangzi told a story that suggests the answer is positive (*The Complete Works of Chuang-tzu*: 94–95). In this story, the Daoist thinker Liezi 列子 reported his astonishment to his teacher, Huzi 壺子, that a shaman (*shenwu* 神巫) had the ability to accurately predict a person's death down to the day. Huzi scowled at his student for being amazed by unworthy tricks. To show his student just how inferior life-prediction skills were in comparison with his (Huzi's) way (*dao*), Huzi required a session with the shaman. The shaman came, made the observation, and pulled Liezi aside to announce his prediction that Huzi was dying because there was no sign of life within the man. "I saw something very strange" the shaman said, "something like wet ashes (*shihui* 溼灰)." When Liezi passed on the prediction in tears, Huzi dismissed it not without a sense of triumph. He explained that he, Huzi, "appeared to him [the shaman] with the Pattern of Earth," and thus the latter saw wet ash-like earth. Huzi, a master of the Way, embodied the belief of the possibility to induce an inward metamorphosis through visualization.

In another chapter of the *Zhuangzi*, "Tian Zifang 田子方," another story was told, one of Confucius meeting Laozi. The latter sat in such perfect stillness that "he no longer seemed human. Confucius at first stood back and waited, but after a while introduced himself, saying: 'Dare I believe my eyes? A moment ago, master, your body seemed dried out as dead wood, as if you had abandoned all things and left the world of men for solitude.' Laozi replied: 'I let my heart revel [in the realm] where [all] things had their beginning'" (translated by Schipper 1993: 113). Here, the *Zhuangzi* actually conveys the idea that meditation can produce physical transformation. The possibility of meditative metamorphosis was endorsed in one of the most important Daoist classics, so long as one grasped the method. The next question is obvious: What was the method? Here it is time to look into the Supreme Clarity tradition.

The Supreme Clarity school, founded in the fourth century, advanced the idea of burning one's material body in meditation as a method of self-refinement. In discussing ways of obtaining immortality, the Supreme Clarity texts relate the cause of death and its antidotes. Death takes the form of knots in the human body. The knots of death are congenital at the embryonic stage. Removing them is one of the main requirements for reaching immortality. In the practices of Supreme Clarity, there are multiple meditative exercises designed to *jiejie* 解結, or "unravel the knots" (Robinet 1993: 139–143). One is for the practitioner to visualize the emperor lord (*dijun* 帝君) holding three strands of red silk rope in his hands, each tied into eight knots with 24 in total, representing the major obstacles or "major knots" (*dajia* 大結) in one's body.[27] Then he passes on the ropes to the Three Ladies of Simplicity (*Sansu* 三素) who together embody the Feminine One (*ciyi* 雌一). The three ladies, with help of three sets of the Perfected Ones of Eight Inner Landscapes (*bajing zhenren* 八景真人), unravel the knots. After the knots are removed, the silk ropes burst into flames, burning the practitioner's body to such a degree that it looks like a red-hot coal. The fire removes the 120 "thin knots" (*xijie* 細結) of mortality that penetrate the muscles, blood, and joints. Once all the particles of death are cleansed, the practitioner is ready to move forward for immortality and transcendence. Another method of removing the knots focuses on an exercise of mutual nourishment between the practitioner and the deities, but in the end the divinities also set fire to burn away the knots of death.[28] The underlining concept appears to be that fire detoxifies the body by burning out harmful elements, and the practitioner is thus prepared to return to the primary, unpolluted status.

Now, let us resume Deng Yougong's instruction. Returning to original purity has prepared the practitioner for the next step—the transformation that was to be initiated by reciting the "grand incantation of transformation into the divinities." The incantation was adopted from yet another early Daoist tradition, the Celestial Masters school. The *Master Red Pine's*, one of the most important pre-Song Celestial Masters liturgical manuals, introduces to us the incantation that complements the therapeutic exorcist talismans as follows: "The head is the thunder lord, the hair is a black cloud, the top of the head is a bright star ... the eyes are the sun and the moon, the nose is the fierce tiger, the upper lip is the wind lord, the lower lip is the rain master ...."[29] The overlap between this incantation and the one in Deng's Method is clear. Nevertheless, in the *Master Red Pine's*, the incantation was used to start the process by which the practitioner's body becomes "cosmic" (Andersen 1995: 195), while in Deng's manual, in contrast, the incantation was to generate the inner infant who would develop into a particular deity.

The inner infant generated through *bianshen*, as Deng described it, emerged from uniting the *qi* of the practitioner with that of the cosmic and corporal deities. The fusion of the practitioner's *qi* with the cosmic *qi* brings us back to, again, the Supreme Clarity tradition. The Supreme Clarity meditation method of "fusion of female and male" instructs the practitioner to visualize sitting in one's own head together with 14 deities, five female and nine male all in the shape of newborn babies in naked (*luoshen wuyi* 裸身無衣).[30] Each blows white *qi* from their mouths. These *qi* jointly form a cocoon covering the practitioner. This continues for a long while. Then the 14 divinities and the practitioner together vaporize into one aura of white *qi* like a sun. At this time, the practitioner loses consciousness (*huanghuang huhu* 惚惚恍恍) and feels the material body ceasing to exist (*zhao wufu yishen* 兆無復一身). The white *qi* then glows and generates a pair of infants, one male one female. These are the embodiment of the Sun and Moon. They chant a hymn respectively announcing that the practitioner, referred to as "host" (*zhuren* 主人), will be listed on the register of the divinities. The meditation then ends. The practitioner returns to consciousness and recovers sensual feeling (*zhaonaishizijue* 兆乃始自覺).

Another example of Supreme Clarity meditation that focuses on uniting the *qi* is the Whirlwind (*huifeng* 徊風) method.[31] The adept visualizes the "hundred deities" (*baishen* 百神) turning into one orb of white *qi* entering his mouth, filling the body and coming out from the "jade stem" (the penis), from the hands and feet and then rejoining into a white cloud. This white cloud turns purple, entering and flowing out the body all over again. After the purple *qi* has condensed into clouds, the adept then blows a *qi* of wind to produce a whirlwind that harnesses and transforms the purple cloud into a "perfected one" (*zhenren* 真人), male, like a new born baby with a body length of four inches. He is the Worthy Lord of the Imperial One of the Grand Grotto (Dadong diyi zunjun 大洞帝一尊君).[32]

It is true that the imagery of an embryo in the inner body as the real self precedes the Supreme Clarity school (Pregadio 2006: 138–139). The *Xiang'er Commentary to the Laozi* (*Laozi Xianger zhu* 老子想爾注) of the late second or early third century mentions that some of the followers of the *Dao* upheld the belief of "nourishing the [transcendent] embryo (*peitai* 胚胎) and refining the physical form should be like making clay into pottery."[33] The early medieval *Central Scripture of Lord of the Most High Laozi* (*Taishang Laojun zhongjing* 太上老君中經, TC 1168)[34] presents an inner body pantheon in which an infant deity, called *chizi* (*lit*. red child)[35] resides in the stomach. *Chizi*, referred to as "self" (*wu* 吾) in the *Central Scripture*, is nourished and instructed by its divine parents dwelling together in the inner body.[36] Neither the *Xiang'er Commentary* nor the *Central Scripture*, however, mentions practices of conceiving or generating an inner embryo. As a matter of fact, the *Central Scripture* clearly states that *chizi* is innate; all human beings have it. It is only in the Supreme Clarity tradition that we find the practitioner must generate interior infant deities in meditation by manipulating *qi*.

While Supreme Clarity visualization underlies the inner-refinement technique of the *bianshen* meditation, astute readers must have spotted a very different framework in the latter. First, unlike in the Supreme Clarity tradition where the inner body embryos were actualized to carry out the refinement; the embryo generated in the *bianshen* meditation in contrast was the result of the refinement that would replace the practitioner's mundane body at conducting ritual. Second, the *bianshen* meditation deploys multiple sets of symbols assimilated under the rubric of the Five Phrases correlative cosmology. This classical Chinese worldview classifies every existence in the universe into five categories—metal, wood, water, fire, and earth—and believes that items in the same category have a special association with each other. Table 3.1 is a chart of some of the basic associations:

64 *A god in transition*

Table 3.1 Common associations of the Five Phases

Phases	Metal	Wood	Water	Fire	Earth
Directions	West	East	North	South	Center
Colors	White	Green/Blue	Black	Red	Yellow
Organs	Lungs	Liver	Kidney	Heart	Spleen

As in both "Model Rites for Submission, Dispatch, Fusing, and Refinement" and "Method of Grand Transformation of Spirits through Refinement and Metamorphosis" cited above, the "fire" comes out from the heart is enhanced by the *qi* of the south. Heart and south are subsumed under the category of fire in the Five Phases system. When the help of the turtle and snake was enlisted in the *qi* manipulation exercise, the turtle's *qi* was matched with that of the kidney and the snake's *qi* was with that of the heart. This arrangement corresponds with the classification system of correlative cosmology in which the turtle and the kidney both fall in the category of water while the snake and the heart belong to the category of fire.

Both points—cultivating an inner infant to replace the material body and integrating correlative cosmology with self-cultivation meditative exercise—are the characteristic traits of *neidan* meditation. *Neidan*, or inner alchemy, as a body of advanced psycho-physiological exercise, grew into a distinct class of theories and praxis during the late Tang and Five Dynasties after a long history of development (Baldrian-Hussein 1989–90; Robinet 1989; Pregadio 2006). It was in the inner alchemy texts that cosmology was fused with breathing exercises. This meditative breathing exercise ideally culminates in generating the internal elixir which—as many texts explicitly describe and visually depict—grows into the form of a human infant. The elixir-infant, or embryo of sainthood (*shengtai* 聖胎), will eventually replace the practitioner's physical body.[37] Furthermore, in the coded language of inner alchemy, the turtle and the snake are the symbols of the trigrams of *kan* 坎 ☵ (water) and *li* 離 ☲ (fire) respectively. The merging of the *qi* of the turtle and the snake described in the "Model Rites for Submission, Dispatch, Fusing, and Refinement" therefore parallels the inner alchemy jargon *qukan tianli* 取坎填離 or "taking [the middle line of] *kan* to fill the [broken middle line of] *li*" (see figure 3.6).[38] Exchanging the middle lines of the trigrams *kan* and *li* produces a metaphor indicating the practice of "refining essence into pneuma" (*lianjing huaqi* 鍊精化氣), the first stage of the *neidan* practice. The overlap between *neidan* and the *bianshen* is obvious in terms of imagery and vocabulary.

While multiple strands of Daoism gave rise to the *bianshen* ritual, none advocated appropriating power of the divinity to whom they became. Their aim was permanent transformation into transcendence, not provisional apotheosis. On the other hand, the idea of the initiated uniting with a divinity in order to utilize the latter's divine authority when carrying out rituals is only too familiar to students of Tantrism.[39] It is one of the distinct and fundamental traits of Tantra that a ritual specialist assimilates himself to a divine figure or principle (such as Shiva, Vishnu, the Buddha, the "body of the [Buddha's] dharma," etc.) as a means to engender a miraculous power. In discussing the introduction of Tantrism into China, Michel

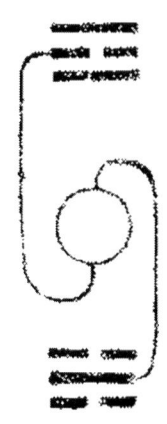

Figure 3.6 Chart for "Using the *kan* trigram to fill the *li* trigram" or *Qukan tianli*. The trigram on top is *li* (representing fire) and the trigram at the bottom is *kan* (representing water). This Inner Alchemy jargon *qukan tianli* literally means "taking the *kan* to fill the *li*", which indicates exchanging the inner lines of the two trigrams. The principle of refinement through water and fire is thus implied.

Strickmann highlighted the mid-fifth-century *Book of Consecration* (*Guanding jing*, T. 1331), a Chinese apocrypha of Tantric Buddhism, writing (Strickmann 2002: 201):

> This text instructs the healer, who is about to use his wooden seal to cure a patient, first to visualize his own body as the body of the Buddha, with the thirty-two primary and eighty secondary signs of buddhahood. Only then, when he has effectively turned himself into the Buddha through meditation, can he effect the miracle of healing. This is the basic premise that underlay the entire Tantric revolution and that distinguished it from the Vedic and post-Vedic phases of Indian ritual on which it freely drew.

Thus, as early as the fifth century, Chinese Buddhists had already come to terms with the Tantric concept of divine unity through meditation. During the next several centuries, more elaborate theories and rituals of Tantric Buddhism were introduced into China in general and Daoism in particular. Although Tantra declined in the monarch's court after the eighth century, its practices continued to pervade Chinese ritual landscape in Song times and later, including the Thunder Rites movement (Orzech 1989: 87–114; Davis 2001: 115–52). The Incantation of the Bush Mother (Doumu 斗姆) often found in Thunder Rite manuals, for example, was transplanted from the Tantric incantation of Marīci (Mozhilitian 摩支利天 in Chinese; see Li 2003: 446–447). Daoist ritual masters might very well also borrowed the identity-transformation concept from Tantric Buddhism.

Contextualization

In the Song dynasty, Daoism experienced a "renaissance," using Strickmann's terminology. This renaissance, however, did not come into existence without

66 *A god in transition*

growing pains. Some of the greatest developments resulted from the emancipation of the local cults (Schipper and Verellen 2004: 635). Since the early stages of Daoism in the fourth to sixth centuries, as Rolf Stein (1979) points out, Daoists expressly dismissed the objects of popular cults as "vulgar deities" (*sushen* 俗神). The eminent Daoist master Lu Xiujing 陸修靜 (406–477) famously scoffed at local deities as "dead generals of defeated troops." On the other hand, Stein continued, the Daoist religion constantly absorbed elements from popular religion," whose followers therefore "found elements there [Daoism] to which they were accustomed" (Stein 1979: 59). Thus, from the beginning, Daoist masters drew on a dual-strategy of rejection and assimilation in reaction to popular religion. They constantly and consistently criticized local cults while relegating popular deities to the Daoist divine protocol whenever possible and envisioning them as enforcers of the Dao.

During Tang times, Daoism slowly began to develop a partnership with cults of apotheosized local saints or cultural heroes but it was not until the Southern Song period that local deities finally could be fully incorporated into the Daoist pantheon (Schipper 1993). The Northern Song was the time when this recruitment intensified. This intensification can only be understood in the context of the bigger picture. In the 1070s, the Northern Song state implemented a sweeping reform program called the New Policy (*xinfa* 新法) and aggressively extended its influence over local social life. The practice of granting titles was a standard tactic to seize control of popular worship, and the numbers of local deities who received imperial recognition soared (Hansen 1990: 81, 176–177). Local deities so rewarded automatically assumed noble status and worthiness even if they had a dubious past. Daoists could not readily dismiss the state-endorsed gods as illicit; the tactic of assimilation was far more pragmatic.

Popular deities, however, entered the Daoist pantheon with a certain amount of baggage; they brought with them their way of manifestation through their priests—commonly known as *wu* 巫 among other local variations. *Wu*, typically rendered into English as neighborhood shamans or spirit mediums, subject their identities to those of spirits as a way to conduct communication between the human and divine realms. They enter states of altered consciousness and visibly change their manner of speaking and acting, a phenomenon that modern scholars refer to as trance or ecstasy. Believers, on the other hand, take the altered persona as signs of a god's manifestation via taking over the body of the "servant." The latter becomes the god so long as the possession lasts. This practice of temporary apotheosis entered Daoism along with the popular cults, and Daoist priests picked it up. Yet possession was incompatible with Daoist doctrines as discussed above; the priests had to generate a new methodology to explain how they transformed themselves into a god. The masters of the new ritual movements then developed the *bianshen* exercise to "naturalize" the practice of identity-change in accordance with Daoist theology.

The aim of *bianshen* was to grow a spiritual embryo in one's inner body in order to carry out the ritual to its full efficacy. The embryo would grow into the deity whose authority the priest would appropriate and whose identity the priest would assume during ritual performances. The embryo is full of potential—not unlike the embryonic stem cell in modern medicine expectations: it can grow into a number of divinities, according to the visualization, incantation, and hand seal used during the meditation. In formulating the *bianshen* ritual, Daoist masters adapted a classical Celestial Master incantation and combined it with the inner refinement visualization techniques derived from the early Supreme Clarity. The result was a liturgy that promoted an intimate partnership in meditation (though not necessarily an equal relationship) between the initiated practitioner and the deity who administered the ritual program. The new *bianshen* ritual facilitated a new perception of the relationship between ordained Daoists and the divinities. It was influential in remolding the Daoist pantheon and enriching Daoist theology in general and elevating Zhenwu in the Daoist protocol in particular.

At the time of his debut in the Daoist pantheon in the tenth century, Zhenwu was a militant figure serving under the exorcist North Emperor combating enemies of Daoism. He was far from the pure and sublime ideal of Daoist deities. Nevertheless, the new ritual schools, starting with the Celestial Heart, advised their initiated to assume Zhenwu's identity in carrying out exorcist rituals through the newly developed meditative liturgy of *bianshen neilian*. In addition, Zhenwu's emblems, the turtle and the snake, were constantly utilized in inner alchemy, which underlies the theoretical framework of *bianshen neilian*. Thus, as the new ritual schools engaged in liturgical innovation, Zhenwu became a symbol and source of ritual power with whom many Daoists constantly meditated. Their relationship with Zhenwu resembles that between Tantric practitioners and their divine lineage masters. In fact, lineage master was exactly the role that Zhenwu would soon assume in the ritual manuals codified in the late thirteenth and early fourteenth centuries.

My lord, my teacher: the master–disciple bond in the bureaucratic model

Zhenwu was referred to as *zushi* 祖師 (ancestral master/teacher) or *shengshi* (holy master/teacher) in a number of Thunder Rite liturgical manuals. His "descendant" disciples requested his intervention to harness disobedient thunder deities. Such requests were made through *jiashu* 家書, or letters home, a personal communication between the cleric and the divine.[40] A good example of such practices can be found in the *Secret Methods of the Divine Fire of the Pure Tenuity Heaven* (*Qingwei shenlie mifa* 清微神烈祕法, TC 222). First composed in the late thirteenth century,[41] the *Secret Methods of the Divine Fire* introduced methods deploying thunder generals Gou and Bi as the commanders-in-chief.[42] At rain-praying ceremonies, for example, the ritual masters first sent for the two generals who then would take charge of (*tongshe* 統攝) divine creatures to "carry out the order of the talismans, generate clouds, and bequeath the rain" (*chengfeng fuming, shiyu xingyun* 承奉符命，施雨興雲; ZHDZ 31.43b). However, Generals Gou and Bi, as unruly as thunder deities were expected to be, did not necessarily comply with the ritual master. When this happens, instructs the *Secret Methods of the Divine Fire*, the ritual master dispatches a second set of talismans and writs with stronger rhetoric to summon the two generals. If they fail to obey the order again, then another set of even stronger commands should be sent. If, after seven dispatches, there is still no sign of rain, the ritual master should, in addition to petitioning to the Jade Emperor (*zou Yudi* 奏玉帝), "submit a letter home to reach the Dark Emperor" (*baijiashu da Xuandi* 拜家書達玄帝). The Dark Emperor is a commonly used title of reverence for Zhenwu.[43] After dispatching the letter home by burning it, the practitioner should make a prayer as follows (ZHDZ 31.45c):

> Your subject, surnamed X, reports to the ancestral master (*zushi*) on high, your holiness: Your subject, I, on behalf of X of X place for X matters earlier issued talismans and commands repeatedly. I summoned the thunder deities by writ and briefed the heavenly court in detail to ask for rain. The dispatches are not yet going through. Your subject, I, have no other choice but to respectfully follow what was taught by my teacher to request commander X and envoy of talisman X of the Heaven of Pure Tenuity to promptly make a plea to the high above. I respectfully hope that my compassionate teacher, you, will approve the plea from me, the obtuse one, and grant a decree commanding the officials and generals to fully display their awesome efficiency.

> 具位臣姓某上啓祖師聖位。臣據某處某人，為某事，昨已累行符命，檄召雷神，及具奏聞天廷，請降雨澤。去後尚未感通。臣情不獲已，恭依師授，告行清微某令某符使，速令上達。恭望師慈，俯從愚懇，特賜旨命官將大顯威靈。

Here, the ritual practitioner addresses Zhenwu as the ancestral master (*zushi*) and expects him to grant preferential treatment by wielding his authority to force the thunder deities to undertake their tasks. Zhenwu was perceived as a powerful patron in the court, and his patronage was grounded implicitly on the bond between the master and the disciple.

The ritual program in the *Secret Methods of the Divine Fire* belongs to one of the new ritual movements that surfaced during the Southern Song, the Pure Tenuity (*Qingwei* 清微) school. According to its own accounts, the school was founded by a woman called Zu Shu 祖舒 (fl. 889–904) in Guangxi province in southern China at the end of the Tang dynasty (*Qingwei xianpu*, TC 171, ZHDZ 31.5b–6c). She left no written works, and codification of the Pure Tenuity ritual in written form did not begin until the second half of the thirteenth century. In one version of the school's genealogy, matriarch Zu's teaching passed from individual to individual through a series of four generations of heiresses followed by another four generations of heirs. They too left only scarce traces. Then, the lineage's legacy passed on to Huang Shunshen 黃舜申 (1224–after 1268) who brought Pure Tenuity teachings to distinction (*Daomen shigui*, ZHDZ 42.642b). As asserted by the 43rd generation Celestial Master Zhang Yuchu 張宇初

(1361–1410), who himself was also an initiated Qingwei, it was Huang who "propagated" (yan 衍) the Pure Tenuity ritual system. One of Huang's disciples brought the Pure Tenuity tradition to Mt Wudang, the headquarters of Zhenwu worship (see Chapter Four), and passed it on to Zhang Shouqing 張守清 (1254–1336), who further disseminated the Divine Fire ritual program among the Daoist cleric circle.

Zhang Shouqing was renowned during his lifetime. He was summoned to the Grand Capital by the Mongolian monarchy to bring an end to droughts two years in a row (*Xuelou ji* 5.21b). On both occasions, the rain came immediately after he conducted the rituals. The South Cliff Daoist Monastery (later South Cliff Palace) on Mt Wudang that he headed hosted over a thousand of "learners of the Way" who studied with him. Zhang's primary curriculum was the Divine Fire ritual, according Zhao Yizhen 趙宜真 (d. 1382), a leader of the succeeding generation of Daoists and an initiate of the Pure Tenuity school.[44] Zhang's teaching, observed Zhao Yizhen, reached as far as "the seas at the four ends [of the world]." The Divine Fire ritual program and consequently the veneration of Zhenwu as an ancestral master spread in tandem with Zhang's teaching.

Source of Zhenwu's power: imperial metaphor

Thus, it was the master–disciple bond that gave the ritual specialists the privilege of accessing Zhenwu's authority. Yet what was the source of Zhenwu's authority and power? Or, to be more precise, how was his power projected? Of course, his image as a masculine general waving a sword makes a forceful presence in its own right; the incantation found on the stele of CE 1099 (see Introduction) notes that the "light coming out from his [Zhenwu's] eyes pacifies various demons" (*Jinshi lüe* 306). However, as depicted in liturgical manuals, his power does not derive from his imposing presence; instead, it came from the authority attached to his position. In the citation of *Secret Methods of the Divine Fire* quoted above, for example, Zhenwu, with a title of *di* (emperor), was asked to decree (*sizhi* 賜旨)—an imperial courtly metaphor—the unruly generals to follow the priests' order. He was not expected to flex his muscles. It was through a bureaucratic framework, in the sense of a formal communication through a chain of authority, that Zhenwu's authority was formulated. Thus, while access to Zhenwu's power by private patronage was rationalized through a master–disciple bond, his actual power was carried out within a bureaucratic framework. The blending of the ancestor master's patronage into the classical bureaucratic model of Daoist liturgy is well demonstrated in the liturgical manual "Numinous Writs for Urgent Submission to the Dark Heaven" (Xuantian jizou lingwen 玄天急奏靈文).

This manual is found in the *Retrieved Pearls of the Sea of Rituals*, compiled in the late fourteenth or the early fifteenth century (*Fahai yizhu* j.20, in ZHDZ 41.487c–491a). In most parts of "Numinous Writs," Zhenwu is referred to by his exalted title, Xuantian shangdi 玄天上帝, or Supreme Emperor of the Dark Heaven. In instructing the appropriate format for submitting petitions to him, however, the manual recommends the appellation of "the perfect lord Zhenwu, the holy teacher

70 *A god in transition*

of the dark heaven at the north apex" (Beiji Xuantian shengshi Zhenwu zhenjun 北極玄天聖師真武真君). The practitioners are recommended to approach Supreme Emperor Zhenwu as the teacher Zhenwu. To submit the petition, the manual instructs the practitioner to conduct a visionary journey:[45]

> Visualize a circle of red radiance in the heart. The left hand forms a bush *mudra* and flick [the fingers to dispatch the *mudra*]. Then visualize the red radiance going upward, following the *mudra*, directly to the heavenly gate, moving off so far away as tens of thousands of miles. Visualize four generals standing in front respectfully hold the petition in hand and your spirit (*zhaoshen* 兆神) leads the generals under commend follow behind the red radiance. After a long while, see a long bridge, illuminated with flickering light. [Cross the bridge?] After a long while, [you will see] a tower of twelve stories. Climb to its top. Next, a red bridge [comes into sight]. Cross it and go all the way to the Jade Gate of Central Heaven covered by purple clouds. The generals and officers stayed outside the gate. You and the four [envoys] on duty enter. Once through the gate, turn left and go into the Bureau of the Aiding Saint (Yousheng fu 佑聖府) which is heavily guarded by numerous deities. Visualize the four envoys on duty giving the petition to the official in charge of petitions. Go to the hall, bow down on your knees nine times, get up, enter the hall from the left side to make your petition in front of the desk, and kneel straight. Visualize the perfected official submitting the petition and the Dark Emperor complying. Bow. Withdraw from the hall via the right side. Exit the hall, bow nine times, thank the favors and exit the Mansion. The four [envoys] on-duty leading in the front and the generals and officials following behind, exit the jade gate. Return via the same route. In a half-conscience state, you came back to the altar. Bring the red radiance back to the heart.

> 存心中紅光一團。左手剔斗一座，即存紅光上出，隨訣彈，直接天門萬里，極遠。存四將居前捧章，兆神部領眾將隨紅光而去。良久，見一長橋，上有光芒烜赫。良久，升上十二重樓，再歷絳橋而上，直至中天玉闕。有紫雲垂廕。將吏侍闕外，兆與四直入闕內。望左邊橫轉，入佑聖府門闕威嚴，萬神環衛。存四直使者付章奏與典奏真官，至殿下九拜，起，居自左街登殿，于案前奏事，長跪，存真官呈章玄帝允奏，就拜。自右街降，至殿下。九拜，謝恩，出府門外。有四直前引，官將後隨，出玉闕外，循故道而回，恍惚至壇前，收紅光入心。

The imperial bureaucratic metaphor presented in this instruction is unmistakable. A written petition (*zhang* 章) from the ritual practitioner was submitted to Zhenwu with court etiquette in a ceremonial audience attended by sundry officials. He reads and grants the petitions. The ritual specialist, with delegated power, then is authorized to continue to carry out the tasks he was hired to perform.

To students of Daoism, the meditative journey described above cannot be more familiar. It is the standard procedure of submitting petition to the heavenly court,

A god in transition 71

which is one of the oldest liturgies in Daoism. Nevertheless, it also reveals a fundamental change. When comparing it with the petition-submission routine described in the early fifth-century *Taizhen ke* 太真科 (*Protocols of the Great Perfected*) preserved in the *Red Pine Master's Petition Almanac*, there is an alarming variation:[46]

> The [*Great Perfection*] *Protocols* says: … Then prostrate yourself in front of the [altar] table. Visualize red *qi* coming out from your heart and ascending to heaven.[47] … Upon reaching the purple clouds, you see the 18-foot heavenly gate. Your attendant guards all have to stay here except General Zhou and the envoys-functionaries on duty. [Follow the lead of] the petition-submitting jade lad who carries the petition in his hand through the gate. Turn west and pay your respects to the ritual master of Orthodox Unity of the Three Heavens whose surname is Zhang and given name Daoling. After bowing to him, relate the circumstances and reasons for your petition and memorial. The Heavenly Master approves them.[48] Then go on to the Phoenix Pavilion and enter through the door. In a moment, a divine lad clad in vermilion robes and black cap emerges to receive the petition from the petition-submitting jade lad. He enters [the Phoenix Pavilion], then after a short while comes out again and leads [you] to see the Most High [Lord Lao] … as well as the Great One. … Submit the petition to the Most High. The Most High reads through it. The Great One, in accordance with the wishes of the Most High, assigns [the petition] to the Jade Platform of Great Purity [office] [whose clerks] will jot "Comply" on it. Then this is finished. … Bid farewell to the Great High, and take your leave. … Bow on your knees twice again to bid farewell to the Heavenly Master. Along with the perfected officials in charging of petitions and memorials, you return elated.
>
> 科曰，… 便於案前伏地，便存赤紅炁從己心中出，上昇天。直到紫雲，見天門。門度一丈八尺，諸侍衛悉住，唯與周將軍及直使功曹，傳章玉童擎章表至闕門之下西，謁見正一三天法師姓張名道陵。載拜訖，具陳章表事由。天師九拜[sic., should be 允諾]，即往鳳凰閣門之下入。須臾，有一仙童朱衣玄冠出，就傳章玉童手中接章表，入，少頃，復出，引入見太上。… 又見太一 … 呈太上章表，太上一覽，太一承太上意，署太清玉陛下，作依字。了 … 辭太上出門。… 又載拜，辭天師。同奏章真官抃躍而迴。

In the traditional protocol described in the *Master Red Pine's Petition Almanac*, the petition is directed all the way to the Most High and the Grand One, even though their approval appears to be only a formality since they are expected to comply. In the "Numinous Writs for Urgent Submission," in contrast, the petition stops at Zhenwu's office; it does not go further up the divine bureaucracy. Zhenwu's compliance alone is sufficient; no higher authority's authorization is necessary. This does not suggest a revolutionary reconstruction of the Daoist pantheon. Zhenwu did not usurp a top position in the hierarchy; the location of his office attests to his

72 *A god in transition*

place in the hierarchy: a side hall off at the left of the court compound. In fact, this makes it all more significant that Zhenwu remained in the middle ranks of the hierarchy. Approval from the ancestral master, albeit secondary in the authority protocol, was all that the ritual master needed. The source of a ritual specialist's authority shifted from the Most High and the Great One to the "holy teacher." The divine ancestral masters were in essence perceived as the ultimate source of the ritual efficacy most essential in facilitating ritual powers; nevertheless, the divine power was domesticated and had to be exercised through a bureaucratic routine.

Bureaucratization of Zhenwu

The assimilation of Zhenwu into the Daoist bureaucratic system has to be examined together with that of the Four Saints of the North Apex, Zhenwu's old team (see Chapter One). The Four Saints as a team were first drafted into the Department of Exorcism (*Quxie yuan* 驅邪院), of the Celestial Heart school and assigned to head a set of four offices. They worked along with a large number of subordinate generals and other stalwart deities to pacify demons at the decree (*chi*) of the North Emperor (ZHDZ 37. 518a–c). Zhenwu's office in this administration was called the Bureau of the Aiding Sage (*Yousheng fu* 佑聖府). The Aiding Sage, or Yousheng, was the title that the state granted him between 1107 and 1113.[49] The appellations of other three members of the quartet also doubled as the titles of their offices, a fact suggesting the bureaucratization was at an early, crude stage.

Then, in the *Tianpeng* ritual system, a popular thirteenth-century or earlier spin-off from the Celestial Heart school,[50] the Four Saints received a new set of offices: the Bureaus of Yuanying taihuang 元應太皇 (headed by Tianpeng), Yuanjing dantian 元景丹天 (headed by Tianyou), Yuanzhao zixu 元照紫虛 (headed by Yousheng), and Yuanhe qianjiao 元和遷校 (headed by Zhenwu) (*Fahai yizhu*, j.46, ZHDZ 41.648c).[51] All four offices begin with the same character, *yuan* 元 ("primordial"), suggesting more formality in the design than that in the Celestial Heart ritual school. The Four Saints were assigned 300,000 soldiers each. The ritual specialists summoned the Four Saints after undergoing the *bianshen* meditations to take on the identity of the North Emperor. These fierce generals, followed by their soldiers, came in response to the summons. They finalized the process of consecrating (*lit.* "enter") the practitioner's talismans (*rufu* 入符) and accordingly empowered the talismans as well as rituals (ZHDZ 41.647a–648c).

Other new ritual schools teamed the quartet and their "primordial offices" with a fifth member. The Tongchu (*Tongchu* 童初) ritual system, begun in early twelfth century relies on a "five bureaus" system headed by the Four Saints with the one who is no less prestigious than Zhang Daoling himself. These offices were collectively referred to as the Five Primordial Plain Bureaus (*wuyuan sufu* 五元素府). The founder of the Youthful Incipience school, Yang Xizhen 楊希真 (1101–1124), "respectively served the images of the Four Saints" since his youth according to his biography in *Records of Mt Mao* (*Maoshan zhi* j.16, ZHDZ 48.442c).[52] He reportedly entered a mystical grotto on Mt Mao in 1120 and was bestowed the ritual programs by the divine bureau of Youthful Incipience (thus the name of his liturgical system). A ritual program codified in writing by the early thirteenth century presented the Five Primordial Plain Bureaus as the core administration of the Youthful Incipience.[53] Jin Yunzhong, himself a Youthful Incipience initiate, wrote a long treatise on this program in which he asserted that the Five Primordial Plain Bureaus oversaw the "life and death, fortune and misfortune, the promotion and demotion of the perfected and transcendent ones" (*Daofa huiyuan* j. 171, ZHDZ 37.532b).

The Four Saints and their "primordial" offices apparently also entered the Divine Empyrean ritual system. The eminent Daoist master Bai Yuchan 白玉蟾 (1194–1229) once explained the significances of the Five *La* days—one of the oldest set of holidays in Daoist history—by saying that they were also the days of the establishment of five bureaus (*kaifu* 開府). The five bureaus in Bai's list were the four "primordial" offices headed by the Four Saints and the Jade Purity Bureau of the Divine Empyrean (Shenxiao yuqing fu 神霄玉清府) which was headed by— instead of Zhang Daoling—the Great Deity of Flame and Code (*Yanhuo lüling dashen* 焱火律令大神) (*Haiqiong Bai Zhenren yulu j.*2, in ZHDZ 19.559c). Bai, the self-styled Vagrant Clerk of the Divine Empyrean (*Shenxiao sanli* 神霄散吏), was likely presenting the Divine Empyrean school's construction of the heavenly court at the time.

Zhenwu's office, Yuanhe qianjiao fu 元和遷校府 or the Primordial Harmony Bureau of Promotions and Record Variation, was highlighted in the rites of the Inferno (Fengdu 酆都) as a personnel registrar department.[54] One of the codes of the Inferno rites instructed that the names of deceased Daoists initiated must be submitted to the Primordial Harmony Bureau (by their disciples) in hope of "verifying merits, pardoning demerits, and then being promoted to the divine."[55] Zhenwu, the battlefield general, thus assumed a desk job as well. The image of him sitting in his office receiving petitions from his disciple-priests, as we see in the "Numinous Writs For Urgent Submission," derived from the bureaucratization of his power. The bureaucratization process not only authenticated Zhenwu's power in the Daoist context but also enriched his godhead.

Daily audience with Zhenwu

Daoist clerics who wished to access to Zhenwu's authority had to meditate with him regularly. As instructed in the "Numinous Writs For Urgent Submission," the initiated ought to diligently meditate with Zhenwu on a daily basis. The text terms the meditational meeting as "audience" and describes it in some detail under the subject-line of "everyday audience" (*meiri chaoli* 每日朝禮):[56]

> Every day at dawn or in the dead of night, sit straight, click your teeth, and swallow the saliva 24 times. Silently recite the full title of the Dark Emperor three times. Visualize a bright spot between the two kidneys, seeing light shoot up along the spine to the back of the head and entering the Niwan Palace.[57]

Visualize the golden radiance blinking and chant "The Heavenly Worthy of the Transformation at the Golden Gate" 21 times. In a few moments, the radiance spreads and shines in all ten directions. See the Dark Emperor [i.e. Zhenwu] sitting upright on the Mountain of Jade Capital, which [internally] is the Niwan Palace.

Sit as still as a mountain. Next, meditate on the four agents on duty: the agent of the heart emerging from the left eye, the agent of the liver emerging the right eye, plus the two agents of the lungs and kidneys emerging from the ears. They stand completely still in the clouds and pay obeisance. Next, see yourself—in the form of a perfected with a writing tablet in hand—come out forward from the Yellow Court. Kneel upright and make your report [*qishi* 啓事]. After finishing, visualize the golden radiance joining together from the four directions and returning to what it was like earlier. You return to the Scarlet Palace. Look down on the spot between the kidneys; it is bright and still; this means the process (*shi* 事) is finished.

If [the audience is for] the capture of malicious spirits, visualize the Dark Emperor with his loosened hair, bare-feet, and ferocious expression surrounded by divine soldiers guarding him carefully on each side. If [the situation is more] ordinary, visualize the god's cheerful face. Should it be to rescue someone from misfortune, visualize his compassionate face.

每日清旦，或靜夜，正坐，叩齒二十四通，咽液二十四過，念玄帝全號三遍。 存兩腎中間一點光明，衝自夾脊上腦後，至泥丸宮，存金光閃爍，口念金闕化身天尊三七聲。 須臾光散，遍映十方。 見玄帝端坐玉京山上，即泥丸也。兆身如山分明。次存四直，自心出左目，自肝出右目，自肺腎出兩耳根，立雲中朝拱，兆自身如真人狀，自黃庭端簡出前朝禮，長跪啟事。 畢，存光四合如故。 兆還絳宮，俯視兩腎中間，光明大定，是為事畢。 若捉祟，存玄帝披髮跣足，聖容念怒，神兵羅列，左右森嚴。 若平常，存聖容喜悅。 若解厄，存聖容慈悲。

This visionary audience started with a pre-operational exercise. The practitioner visualizes a bright point generated between the kidneys. This bright point quickly moves up to the brain (*niwan* or the Mud Pill) through the spinal column (the Spinal Handle Pass). The space between the kidneys, often called that the Ocean of the *Qi*, is the source of both the semen/essence and *qi*. Isabelle Robinet pointedly observed this space to be "the place of the union of the Primordial Couple. It is also the place of the infant who inhabits the cinnabar field and is the result of the union" (Robinet 1993: 82). The Spinal Handle Pass, located on the spinal column between the shoulder blades at the 24th vertebra, is the middle of the Three Passes (*sanguan* 三關) in the *qi*-circulation practices of inner alchemy. It is also the locus where the *qi* is refined into spirit (*shen*). Thus, the starting, middle, and final points where this "bright spot" travels are all places meaningful in inner alchemy meditative practices. The "Diagram of Internal Pathways" (Neijingtu 內經圖), a metaphorical landscape of the human body presented through the perception of the inner alchemy, states it directly: "From the Double Pass of the Spinal Handle all the way through the head, this is the root of the paths of cultivation."[58] Thus, through a *neidan* style of *qi* exercise, the practitioner visualizes himself making an audience with Zhenwu. The "daily audience" in question was also internal cultivation, that demanded rigorous practice. It was only through unremitting cultivation that the practitioners could appeal to Zhenwu's authority at any time they needed. They invested a good deal of time and energy in faithfully meditating on Zhenwu. There is, then, no surprise that we encounter the portrayal of Daoist priests in lay anecdotes as Zhenwu devotees.

Actualizing the heavenly court within his head, the practitioner proceeds to make the virtual audience. Corporal deities are called out from the heart, liver, lungs, and kidneys one by one to assemble an entourage, a common meditative liturgy known as "summon and unifying" (*zhaohe* 召合).[59] The "self" of the practitioner, in the meantime, emerges from the center of his body, the Yellow Court (*hunagting* 黃庭). All five then are called out ("summoned") and meet together ("unifying") to make an audience with Zhenwu. The god's appearance depends on the nature of the audience. Zhenwu. During a routine audience, the practitioner should imagine the god to be compassionate, but when exorcism is needed, the god would be seen barefoot with loosened hair in his old exorcist image (in contrast to the majestic royal appearance that matches the title of Dark Emperor used in the citation).

Thanks to ritual programs like the "Numinous Writs for Urgent Submission," Daoist priests acquired a routine that facilitated daily access to the ultimate source of ritual power. This access greatly enhanced their ritual efficiency. In the pre-Song ritual compendiums *Master Red Pine's Petition Almanac*, the very first subject discussed was the importance of observing the liturgical calendar (*Chisongzi zhangli* j.1, ZHDZ 8.620b; Verellen 2004: 295–296). Petitions sent to the heavenly court on incorrect days would be discarded automatically. Then, there came the "Numinous Writs for Urgent Submission" proposing a ritual program involving a meeting with the divinity every day. It undermined the traditional almanac taboo thanks to the close mentorship that was expected to take precedence over bureaucratic regulations. The Daoist specialists now could carry out ritual remedy on behalf of their clients on the same day that they were consulted. Access to the divine authority on a daily basis is of remarkable value in improving ritual efficiency in Daoism of the Song period and later.

The efficacy improvement was a timely one for Daoist ritual specialists of Song times who found themselves in an increasingly competitive market for ritual services. This revised bureaucratic model—with ritual authority coming from imperial protocol but the access to this source of authority coming through a private channel (the master-disciple bond)—naturally became popular among Daoist ritual practitioners. As the model caught on, Zhenwu's role as a popular ancestral master was added to his godhead.

In modern times in the Daoist Offering ritual, or *jiao*, one finds the image of Zhenwu placed opposite to that of the Zhang Daoling, the first Heavenly Master (see, for example, Schipper 1993 [1985]: 94). The arrangement suggests a matching status between the two in the liturgical setting. Given the reverence of

76 *A god in transition*

Zhang Daoling in Daoism, this was no small success for a god who was fairly obscure until the mid-tenth century. More importantly, his story of success embodied the evolution of Daoism during the transition period of China from middle to late empire.

The growth of Zhenwu's cult in Daoism was closely related to the Thunder Rites that quietly developed in the mid-eighth century and flourished by the early twelfth century. The liturgical manuals of the Thunder Rites often instruct the practitioners to transform themselves into divinities in order to swiftly dispatch the violent macho thunder deities, and Zhenwu was one of the recommended choices. Assuming the identity of a god arguably increased the perceived efficacy of the ritual. However, the conventional interpretation for such identity-change was divine possession, and Daoist adepts could not accept this interpretation. They regarded divine possession as a crude practice, good only for their assistants or village spirit mediums. To create a replacement, Daoists, probably inspired by Tantricism, turned to *cunxiang* or visualization-meditation, the core practice of Daoism, and generated the method of "transformation into the divinity through internal refinement" or *bianshen neilian*. Grounded in the classical Daoist belief of a fluid metamorphosis through meditation, *bianshen neilian* imparted visualization exercises from the old Supreme Clarity school and adapted the classical Heavenly Master incantation of metamorphosis. Yet, more importantly, this meditation technique was constructed around a framework combining correlative cosmology with the idea of growing an inner-infant to ritually replace the adept's physical body. This framework is characteristically inner alchemy. Thus, the liturgical breakthrough of "transformation into the divinity" as is would not have been possible without the progress of self-cultivation techniques in inner alchemy methodology in the tenth century. The praxis and intellectual development within Daoism is foundation of the liturgical evolution.

With the successful re-theorization of subjugating one's identity to that of the divinity, the practice of transformation into Zhenwu (or other deities) during ritual practices was legitimated and quickly became a common practice by the twelfth century. "Transforming" oneself into the divinity via *bianshen* required intensive meditation and created an intimate relationship between the impersonating practitioner and the impersonated god, a relationship not unlike that between the divine lineage patriarchs and the initiated practitioners in Tantrism. Indeed, in many ritual programs Zhenwu was perceived as a patriarch, or "ancestral master" (*zushi*), which eventually became a standard way to address Zhenwu among his devotees in Ming times and later. The seventeenth-century vernacular novel *Journey to the North* (*Beiyou ji* 北遊記), for example, uses the appellation of *zushi* to refer to Zhenwu throughout the book. The ancestral master was the patron saint and the source of ritual efficacy to those who were initiated into rituals administered by him.

While it was through a master–disciple metaphor that Daoist priests explained their access to the power of Zhenwu, it was the bureaucratic chain-of-command model in which Zhenwu's power and authority were projected. In both the *Scripture of Zhenwu* and the early Celestial Heart ritual manuals, Zhenwu descended from the celestial realm only after receiving an edict from the supreme emperor. He exercised his power in the position of a military commander authorized by the celestial court. In liturgical manuals codified in the late thirteenth and fourteenth centuries, he no longer took orders from others; he gave orders. Ritual specialists appealed to him in accord with courtly formality in order to seek for favors. His role had changed but the model was intact; the request was still presented through bureaucratic procedures. His power was always exercised through formal channels.

In the Daoist ideal, gods are bureaucratized. Zhenwu's rise from a general to Supreme Emperor corresponded with the administrative systems of the new ritual lineage schools. As a member of the Four Saints, he was depicted as the head of an office of ritual lineages of the Celestial Heart, Divine Empyrean, and, most elaborately, of the Youthful Incipience. Finally, he was integrated into the core liturgy of classical Daoism, "submitting the petition" (*baibiao* 拜表). Within the Daoist realm, he grew into a symbol of its bureaucratized ritual metaphor.

Scholars have argued that the Song dynasty witnessed the beginning of modern Daoism. The development proceeded not only because of socio-economic growth but also because of a liturgical and theological needs within Daoism. The popular response to the clerical innovation was an important albeit little understood factor of lay devotion to Zhenwu. The growth of Zhenwu worship and that of many other Chinese deities must be situated not only in the socio-economical context but also within the internal logic of Daoism.

4 A god and his mountain

"In China, sacred sites are places where the power of a deity is manifest, places that are *ling* (numinous, efficacious)," as Susan Naquin and Chün-fang Yü note (1992: 11). While sacred sites need deities, deities also benefit in more than one way from having a "home base". In the case of Zhenwu worship, the god's home base is Mt Wudang in central China, where he was believed to have spent some 42 years in self-cultivation and where he ascended to heaven in broad daylight. The mountain has been one of the most prominent sites on the Chinese spiritual atlas since the fourteenth century, in particular for Zhenwu worship.

A space by itself is neither sacred nor profane; its sanctity derives from human experience and exists only in human perception. Sacred space is constructed by human agents who compete and negotiate with each other in shaping and reshaping the hegemonic system of their society. Thus, as Bernard Faure elegantly puts it, "the sacred site was never entirely a given but was in constant flux, incessantly modified by the actions and perceptions of residents and visitors" (1992: 150). In the case of Mt Wudang, the site had made its way onto the religious map long before the birth of anthropomorphized Zhenwu. The mountain had an earlier religious existence before Zhenwu became part of the picture. Daoist clerics wrote their own version of the mountain's history that inserted Zhenwu into the sacred space; they "superscribed" Zhenwu, using Prasenjit Duara's terminology, on top of an older reading of the mountain. This was done by projecting the mountain as a stage of Zhenwu's life story, complete with pilgrimage routes—designated by clerics who themselves labored to lay down the paths and erect the temples—by which the story was reenacted. Through tactful reinterpretation and reconstruction, Daoist clerics transformed Mt Wudang into the seat of Zhenwu worship. Mt Wudang was so successful that it served as a model that other Zhenwu sites could employ in designing their sacred space (Wang 2010).

While the Daoists were successful in altering the previous image of the mountain they did not manage to establish absolute hegemony over the reading of sacred space. Like pilgrimage sites in other religions, Mt Wudang is "an arena for the interplay of a variety of imported perceptions and understandings, in some cases finely differentiated from one another, in others radically polarized" (Eade and Sallnow 1991: 10). In re-enacting the life of the deity, pilgrims, mostly lay believers, added their own imprint to interpretations of Mt Wudang. And finally, the state, represented by the monarchy, functioned as another competitive power in molding the image of the mountain to its own ends. While all three factors contributed to the creation of Mt Wudang as we know it today, the Daoist clerics on the mountain were the primary force.

Mt Wudang before the Southern Song

The name Wudang first appears in written records in the Western Han period as a district under the jurisdiction of the Nanyang *fu* 南陽府 prefecture, which covered an area boarding present-day northwest Hubei and southwest Henan provinces (*Hanshu* 28.1564). Mt Wudang is located in the southern part of Wudang county. The Dan River (Danjiang 丹江) flows to its northeast and then enters the Han River (Hanshui 漢水), a tributary of the Yangzi River. The mountain thus is included in the reaches of the Yangzi River, and is a beneficiary of one of China's greatest water-route networks, affording manageable communications to pilgrims in eastern, southwestern, and northwestern China (see figure 4.1). On the other hand, this meant that the mountain was comfortably distant from the political center throughout most of its history.

Almost 5300 feet at its summit, Mt Wudang is not particularly high. Yet "[a] mountain, tall or not, is famous as long as it has transcendent beings," asserted the ninth-century poet Liu Yuxi 劉禹錫 (772–842) in verses that were memorized by generations of men and women of letters. Mt Wudang made its fame initially as a refuge for hermits and recluses. The first plausible account in this regard concerns

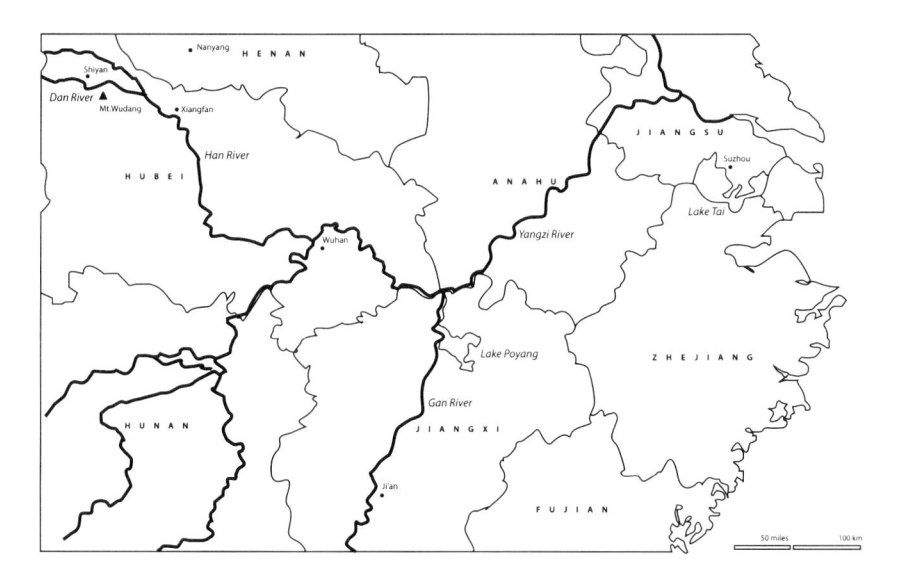

Figure 4.1 Map of the middle and lower reaches of the Yangzi River. Mt Wudang is at the top left-hand corner.
Source: Drawn by Edyth Kuciapa.

Dai Meng of the first century CE, a legendary transcendent (*xian*) and miracle-worker based there (*Zhengao* 14, ZHDZ 2.203a). In CE 150, the Eastern Han dissident Zhao Kang 趙康 "withdrew to Mt Wudang," and "taught the classics and their exegesis" (*Hou Hanshu* 43.1463). His circle of disciples included Zhu Mu 朱穆 (CE 100–163), a well-known prodigy since his youth and a future Regional Inspector, the highest ranking local administrator.[1] Thus by the mid-second century, Mt Wudang has become a locus of intellectual circles and a special attraction for scholar-recruits.

By the fifth century, Mt Wudang played host to numerous "persons learning the way." It was said to be so sacred that those who were not sincere in their spirituality would "be banished by various animals [on the mountain]" (*Taiping yulan* 43.5b).[2] The records do not tell us exactly what "way" the learners were practicing. During this period, a "person of the way," or *daoren* 道人, could be either a Daoist or a Buddhist practitioner (*Nanshi* 76.1705). The "learners of the Way" on Mt Wudang could include both. An account in the long lost fifth-century *Record of South Yongzhou* stated that according to local tradition, Yin Xi, the legendary sixth-century BCE gatekeeper who had reportedly requested Laozi to write down the *Daode jing* had withdrawn to Mt Wudang (*Taiping yulan* 43.5b). The legend of Yin Xi retiring to Mt Wudang, fictional or true, suggests that during the fifth century (when the *Record of South Yongzhou* was written) the locals of the Wudang area perceived a strong connection between the mountain and followers of Daoism. Meanwhile, Buddhists also recognized the spirituality of Mt Wudang. In the mind of the great monk Huisi 慧思 (515–577) of the Tiantai 天台 Buddhist school, the mountain was one of the two ideal locations for practicing *samadhi*, or meditation (*Xu Gaoseng zhuan* T.50.563a.22–T.50.563a.23).

With so many hermits practicing their religion on Mt Wudang, it was only natural that more permanent religious structures would be built. Contrary to its present image as a Daoist mountain, Buddhist monasteries were the dominant presence on the mountain from the mid-Tang to mid-Northern Song periods. The eminent Buddhist monk Huizhong 慧忠 (d. 775), venerated by both Emperors Suzong (r. 756–762) and Daizong (r. 762–779), chose Mt Wudang to establish his famous monastery, the Great One Prolonging the Prosperity Buddhist Temple (*Taiyi yanchang si* 太一延昌寺),[3] with generous support from Emperor Daizong. The monastery survived the Tang and the ensuing Five Dynasties. During the Song dynasty, Emperors Taizong, Zhenzong, and Shenzong all bestowed favors on it one way or another (*Ji'nanji* 5:14a–15a, esp. 14b).[4] The temple was still in excellent condition at the end of the eleventh century.

Daoists monasteries on the mountain, however, developed slowly. The Five Dragons Palace (*Wulong guan* 五龍宮) claims an origin as the Five Dragons Shrine (*ci*) in the early seventh century, but there is no contemporaneous record to verify this claim.[5] Even if it were true, the shrine remained obscure for four centuries or so. It was not until sometime between 997 and 1022 that the shrine was elevated to the status of monastery (*guan*) in the government temple registration accounts. During the state's temple recognition campaign in 1074–1075, however, the Five Dragons Monastery received no imperial acknowledgement. The campaign was a massive project driven by New Policy reformists at the court of Emperor Song Shenzong. The local magistrates, as Robert Hymes' research shows, were actually under pressure to report temples of any significance within their jurisdictions.[6] Thus the fact that the Five Dragons Monastery failed to attract attention from either the administrators or local elite indicates that it held little significance in the second half of the eleventh century.

A quarter of a century later, in 1099 when Li Zhi 李廌 (1059–1109), a well known scholar of his times, visited Mt Wudang, he did not mention any Daoist institutions in his "Verses of Mt Wudang" composed after his visit (*Ji'nan ji* 5: 8a–17b). Li was not oblivious to temples on the mountain; he took note of the Great One Extending the Prosperity Buddhist Temple. Nor was Li prejudiced against Daoism. He devoted substantial space in the "Verses of Mt Wudang" to eulogizing Zhenwu. This tribute also demonstrated his familiarity with and fondness toward Daoist scriptures. The only reasonable explanation for Li's silence about Daoist temples is that none of them was worth mentioning at the time.

During 1119–1125 (the reign of Xuanhe), a new monastery called Purple Empyrean (Zixiao 紫霄) was founded on Mt Wudang (*Zongzhen ji*, middle; ZHDZ 48.567b). In time, this would develop into a great monastery, but the date of its foundation was rather unfortunate since soon the area was invaded by the Jin dynasty of the Jurchen people in their attempt to take over northern China. Clerics fled from the warfare and left the temple in ruins. In sum, at the end of Northern Song times, Daoist monasteries were still in the developing stages.

The Southern Song: Daoist monasticism on Mt Wudang

It was the Southern Song that witnessed the growth of Daoist monasticism on Mt Wudang as Daoist clerics migrated to the mountain and colonized it. As soon as the Song–Jin warfare ceased in 1140, Daoists returned to Mt Wudang and built monasteries dedicated to the worship of Zhenwu. Among the best-known Daoists was Sun Jiran 孫寂然 from Mt Mao, the headquarters of the Supreme Clarity school and the birthplace of the Youth Incipience school (see Chapter Three). Sun Jiran "mastered the various methods of the Five Thunders [ritual] of the Supreme Clarity tradition and many other techniques" (*Zongzhen ji*, xia, ZHDZ 48.577c). He settled down in the Five Dragons Monastery and began to "carry out exorcism by talisman-water to heal people's tormenting diseases. The crowd flocked to him." Within several years, Sun revitalized the Five Dragons Monastery, and his fame reached the court of Emperor Song Gaozong (r. 1127–1162). Sun went to the court, satisfied the emperor's ritual needs, and returned to Mt Wudang with ten licenses to ordain Daoists priests (state-issued licenses were required for clerical ordination and they were expensive to acquire). After his death, his disciples were confirmed as successors by the local magistrate and continued to expand the monastery. In 1182, the Five Dragons Monastery received imperial recognition (*chidie* 敕牒), thanks to a petition by the magistrate of Junzhou (*Zongzhen ji*, middle; ZHDZ 48.566c). This recognition was an evidence of the monastery's growth in size and popularity.

In the second half of the twelfth century, we find records indicating Daoist priests on Mt Wudang receiving Zhenwu worshippers in the temples. The first known to us was Wang Yan 王炎 (1112–1178, courtesy name Gongming 公明).[7] In 1170, upon leaving Hangzhou for Sichuan to assume his new position (*Yijianzhi*, kui, 2.1231), he learned that Sichuan had suffered from a long drought. Even though Hangzhou boasted the most magnificent Daoist monastery dedicated to Zhenwu, Wang "desired to make a detour (*yulu* 迂路) to visit Mt Wudang to pray at the hall of the Zhenwu shrine (*cidian* 祠殿) in person." He said a prayer in a temple on the mountain and a golden snake suddenly appeared on the altar. A Daoist priest (*daoshi*) told Wang, "Ordinary people desire to see it but cannot." The priest's words suggested that he was accustomed receiving common pilgrims and Zhenwu worshippers on Mt Wudang.

Another example of pilgrimage to Mt Wudang concerns the military commissioner (*zhizhi shi* 制置使) of Jinghu 荆湖 stationed in Xiangyang, Zhao Fang 趙方 (*jinshi* 1181),[8] who wished to "present incense" on Mt Wudang around 1217. Before taking the trip, Zhao made an inquiry about his prospects via spirit writing. The message was far from favorable: "The High Perfected One descended via a brush pen, saying: 'Zhao Fang from Xiangyang desires to ascend Mt Wudang; [however, as a] lesser soldier of Fengdu [of the underworld, he] is not invited to burn incense" (*Qiantang yishi* 3.8b). Although Zhao's request was denied, the point of the story should not be lost on us: despite the availability of direct communication with Zhenwu in the city of Xiangyang, Zhao Fang still felt the desire to go to Mt Wudang to make his prayer.

Thus, during the Southern Song period, lay people also perceived Mt Wudang as the primary *axis mundi* of the universe of Zhenwu. In the thirteenth century, we began to see new temples dedicated to Zhenwu were named after the mountain. For instance, a Daoist monastery built between 1228 and 1233 in the southeastern coast province of Fujian, thousands miles away from Wudang, was named *Wudang daochang* 道場 ("daoist field"; *Linding zhi* j. 70, no page number). And, in Leping county in north Jiangxi, a Wudang Daoist Monastery (*guan*) was established between 1265 and 1274 (*Jiangxi tongzhi* 113.5).

Nevertheless, Mt Wudang did not develop smoothly as a pilgrimage center for Zhenwu in the thirteenth century as this was an era of violent warfare. A critical disadvantage was its location in a border area during the rise of the Mongol empire. In 1231, the Mongol prince-general Tolui (Tuolei 托雷 in Chinese history; d. 1232) led his troops in an attack on Kaifeng, Henan, the capital of the Jin. For strategic reasons, he moved through Song territory and Mt Wudang was directly on the route. The Jin army, in the meantime, also crossed the Song border in an attempt to ambush Tolui. The two forces met on Mt Wudang and a brutal battle ensued (*Yuanshi* 115.2886). Further devastation came between 1234 and 1235, when the Mongols raided the area twice within a four-month period. A contemporary, Zhang Duanyi 張端義 (1179–after 1248),[9] recalled that even elderly Daoist priests could not escape the slaughter (*Guier ji*, xia, 25). More military raids in the area in the following year. Residents on the mountain had to flee, and those who insisted on remaining jeopardized their lives. The abbot of the Five Dragons Monastery, Cao Guanmiao 曹觀妙, stayed behind and was slaughtered by soldiers in 1236 (*Zongzhen ji*, xia, ZHDZ 578a).

Mt Wudang lay abandoned for the next three decades until Mongol forces broke the siege of Xiangyang (see Introduction) and moved south of the Yangzi River in January 1275 to conquer southern China. With the departure of the army, monasticism on the mountain revived almost immediately.[10] In 1275, the Purple Empyrean Monastery, or at least the main hall, the only surviving part of the complex, reopened its doors. In the same year, the veteran Wudang Daoist Lu Dayou 魯大宥 (style name Dongyun 洞雲, d. 1285) who had left for the north to study the teachings of the Complete Perfection school, returned with his fellow Complete Perfection Daoist Wang Zhenchang 汪真常 (style name Sizhen 思真). Wang brought six disciples with him and settled down in the Five Dragons Monastery, of which he eventually took charge. Under Wang's abbotship, in 1279 (Zhiyuan 16), the monastery was promoted to "palace" (*gong*) in the state's registration records. Lu Dayou, in the meantime, started a new hermitage on the mountain's South Cliff (Nanyan 南岩), also known as Purple Empyrean Cliff.[11] In the following years, more Daoist monastics, male and female, Han and non-Han, came to Mt Wudang. Some looked for seclusion while others led restoration projects. The priestess Xiao Shoutong 蕭守通, a Khitan by ethnicity, extended the Purple Empyrean Palace, and Zhao Shoujie 趙守節, along with his disciples, rebuilt the Aiding Sage Daoist Monastery. Still others came to study; Lu Dayou had more than 100 disciples and some of whom came from greater distances, such as his future successor Zhang Shouqing 張守清 (1254–?) from Shaanxi province.

After Lu Daoyou passed away in spring 1285, Zhang Shouqing succeeded to the leadership and started to construct a new monastery at the South Cliff. In 1295, a bronze statue of Zhenwu was enshrined at the main hall of the South Cliff Monastery, thanks to a fundraising campaign led by two Daoist clerics, Wang Daoyi 王道一 and Mi Daoxing 米道興, otherwise unknown (*Zongzhen ji*, middle, ZHDZ 48.563a). The statue was cast in Luling (present-day Ji'an) in Jiangxi, the province east of Hubei (Mt Wudang is on the western side of Hubei). The project, from the initial fundraising to casting and transporting, suggested a trans-provincial network formulated by Daoists and Zhenwu worshippers. The monastery was completed in 1311 and named "The Palace of the Perfected and Celebrated Heavenly One" (*Tianyi zhenqing gong* 天一真慶宮),[12] but Daoists and pilgrims often referred to it simply as the South Cliff Palace.

Thus, in the early fourteenth century, the three major monasteries on Mt Wudang—Five Dragons, Purple Empyrean, and South Cliff—were completed and in full operation. Located on the nexus of the pilgrimage routes, they were dedicated to Zhenwu and doubled as houses of worship for ordinary visitors. They offered public places where visitors could make prayers and remain for both spiritual and social purposes. The monasteries were also focal points and highlights of the Zhenwu pilgrimage tour. In a sense, they functioned as fortresses of the Daoist "colonizing" forces, reshaping Mt Wudang and proclaiming it as a sacred site of Zhenwu.

84 *A god and his mountain*

Transforming Wudang into "Zhenwu's mountain"

The first half of the Yuan dynasty in the late thirteenth and early fourteenth centuries engendered the process by which Mt Wudang was turned into an *imago mundi* of Zhenwu. The Daoist clerics on the mountain replaced local beliefs and practices rooted in nature with new teachings that centered on the importance Zhenwu. This long and delicate process is showcased in the re-packaging of the Five Dragons Peak, where the Five Dragons Palace and other temples were located, into a space exclusively devoted to Zhenwu.

The Five Dragons Palace

According to the prominent priest Liu Daoming 劉道明 (fl. 1285–1301), one of the three officially appointed superintendents of Mt Wudang and a resident of the Five Dragons Palace, the origin of his monastery was as follows:

> When the Dark Emperor [i.e. Zhenwu] ascended to the realm of the perfected, five dragons upheld him in ascending. His old hermitage was made into a shrine to venerate the perfected. The *Fangyu shenglan* says: "the Five Dragons Monastery was where he [Zhenwu] taking hermitage." In 1182 (the ninth year of the Chunxi reign of Emperor Song Xiaozong), magistrate of Junzhou county petitioned to the court to grant the temple the title of Numinous Response Daoist Monastery. A stele [commemorating the event] is preserved.
>
> 玄帝昇真之時，五龍披駕上昇，以其舊隱為奉真之祠。方輿勝覽曰：五龍觀即其隱處。宋孝宗淳熙九年，均州知州王德顯奏，降敕牒，賜靈應觀為額，有碑存焉。

The above quotation came from Liu's *Comprehensive Collection of Facts Concerning the Blissful Land of Wudang* (*Wudang fudi zongzhen ji* 武當福地總真集), written and compiled in 1291. Liu cited the *Excellent Views of the Realm* (*Fangyu shenglan* 方輿勝覽) by Zhu Mu 祝穆 (ca. 1200) to support his claim of the connection between the Five Dragons Palace and Zhenwu. The *Excellent Views of the Realm* was not the only topographic work of the early thirteenth century that connected Zhenwu to this monastery. The *Scenery of the Empire Recorded* (*Yudi jisheng* 輿地紀勝), a work which made the author Wang Xianzhi 王先之 (*jinshi* 1196) famous, also made the same assertion. Nevertheless, both sources limit their references to a simple connection, stating the "the Five Dragons Monastery was where he [Zhenwu] taking refuge." It was priest Liu Daoming who provided the new information that the temple was built for the purpose of venerating Zhenwu. In addition, Liu gave the impression that the temple received the name "five dragons" because Zhenwu had been escorted by five dragons upon his ascension to heaven. Liu also listed the leaders responsible for building and rebuilding the temple. It was a selective list; only six in total were mentioned for a period of three centuries, starting from Chen Tuan 陳摶 in the tenth century to Ye Xizhen 葉希真 (fl. 1264–1294). All six men were Daoists. In sum, Liu portrayed the Five

Dragons Monastery as a Daoist establishment dedicated to Zhenwu from the beginning.

There are, of course, different versions of how the Five Dragons Monastery was first established. One endorsed by Jie Xisi 揭傒斯 (1274–1344), a high-ranking official and leading scholar of his time,[13] took the form of a commemorative essay for the temple:

> There are many temples on mountain [Wudang]. Three of them are grand: the Five Dragons, the Purple Empyrean, and the Perfected and Celebrated. The Five Dragons is the grandest. During the era of Tang Zhenguan (627–649), Yao Jian 姚簡, the magistrate of Junzhou, prayed for rain on the mountain. Five dragons appeared. On the spot of the apparition, a Five Dragons Shrine was built. During Song Zhenzong's times, the temple was upgraded from a shrine (*ci*) to monastery (*guan*) and was granted with the temple plaque, "Monastery of the Five Dragons with Numinous Response".[14]
>
> 山多神宮仙舘，其大者有三，曰五龍，紫霄，真慶，而五龍居其首。唐貞觀中，均州守姚簡禱雨是山，五龍見，即其地建五龍祠。宋真宗時，升祠為觀，賜額曰五龍靈應之觀。

In Jie's account the temple was first built to honor the five dragons because, as implicitly suggested, they were responsible for bringing the desperately needed rain. The name of the temple, Five Dragons, thus was a remnant of a local cult of rain-making dragons. Zhenwu was not given any credit at all, not even a mention in this version.

Jie was a contemporary of (though maybe two or three decades later than) the priest Liu Daoming. Nevertheless, his understanding of the origins of the Five Dragons temple was not a later invention than Liu's. On the contrary, it was based on a version that predated Liu's. More than a century before Liu's lifetime, Dong Suhuang 董素皇 (fl. 1183/Chunxi 11), an initiated Daoist, told us that during the reign of Tang Taizong (627–649) Junzhou was suffering from a draught (*Qishenglu*, 1; ZHDZ 30.642b–642c). Yao Jian, as a government official, "received an imperial order to go to the Purple Empyrean Palace on Mt Wudang in person" and carried out an Offering ritual. Five unusual looking Confucian gentlemen (*rushi* 儒士) appeared. They introduced themselves as dragon lords who guarded the mountain under the order of Zhenwu. They were impressed by Yao's righteous, abstemious personality and the meticulousness of his prayer ritual (*zhengzhi guayu, qidao jingyan* 正直寡慾，祈禱精嚴). After the dragon lords left, rainfall ensued, saving crops and people's lives. Yao duly reported the apparition to the court, and Emperor Tang Taizong accordingly ordered the construction of a Five Dragons Daoist Monastery on Mt. Wudang. Meanwhile, Yao withdrew to Mt Wudang with his family to worship Zhenwu. In the end, he was appointed by Zhenwu as the mountain god of Wudang, entitled to receive "animal sacrifice" (*xieshi* 血食) and granted the title of King Awesome Ferocity (Weilie wang 威烈王). Yao Jian was clearly a deified local saint commonly seen in popular religion. This version of the narrative, retold by a Daoist cleric, made Yao Jian the hero who convinced the divinities to grant the needed rains and, more importantly, transformed Yao into a Zhenwu devotee.

Liu Daoming was aware of the legendary encounter between Yao and the five dragon lords. He recorded the encounter in his *Zongzhen ji*. Nevertheless, he did not put it under the entry "History of the Numinous Responsive Five Dragons Palace." Instead, he placed the story in the entry of the "Biography of Yao Jian," and thus obscured the connection between the dragons' rain-making miracle and the establishment of the abbey (*Zongzhen ji*, xia, ZHDZ 48.576c–48.577a). In addition, while the basic story line is the same as that told by the Daoist Dong a century earlier, there are significant variations in the details. In Liu's version, the five lords petitioned the emperor (*di*) in the heavenly court for rain. Permission was granted and the rain would come soon. The five dragon lords were portrayed as agents of the heavenly court; they did not make rain based on arbitrary decisions but followed a prescribed procedure. A bureaucratic model—the standard Daoist perception of ritual efficacy—is clear in the narrative. Liu proceeded to tell readers that the court rewarded Yao for his efforts but failed to mention any rewards for the five dragon lords, certainly not the erection of the Five Dragons Daoist Monastery. This omission concealed the older interpretation of the temple as a commemoration for the five dragon lords' rain-making powers.

The different representations of the origin of the Five Dragons Palace illustrate the progressive attempts of Daoist clerics to replace the old myths of the site by creating alternative readings. Daoist clerics appropriated folk beliefs into Daoist tradition and pushed Zhenwu to the center of the folklore step by step. In the popular religious version cited by Jie Xisi, Zhenwu played no part in the establishment of the temple; the temple was built to honor the five dragon lords who made rain. In the version offered by the Daoist Dong Suhuang of the twelfth-century, Zhenwu entered the picture but was still in the background: he granted permission to the dragon lords to make rain. Then, at the end of the thirteenth century, Liu Daoming asserted that the temple started as a commemorative construction for Zhenwu. Liu acknowledged the legend of the dragon lords as rainmakers but chose not to mention that the temple was named after them in reward for their services. Instead, he implicitly suggested that the temple was so named for the dragons' role in escorting Zhenwu to the heavenly court. Liu's efforts to disassociate the Five Dragons Palace from its legacy in local and popular belief was transparent.

Liu's recasting of the temple's origins was not an immediate success. The scholar-official Jie Xisi shortly after Liu's time, for example, did not accept it. However, Liu and his fellow Daoist clerics on Mt Wudang painstakingly promoted and circulated the *Zongzhen ji*. Ten years after the *Zongzhen ji*'s completion, Liu was still actively soliciting prefaces to the volume from local officials (Wang and Yang 1993). Eventually, the *Zongzhen ji* became the main source of the mountain's history and the Wudang gazetteers in Ming times copied sections of it word for word. It was included in the *Daoist Canon* sponsored by the Ming state. Repeated publications and canonization of the *Zongzhen ji* finally made Liu's reading the "master version" of the origin of the Five Dragons temple (for example, Wang and

Yang 1993: 103). The five dragons faded into the background in the founding mythology of the Five Dragons Monastery.

Daoist clerics' success in making their reading of the mountain the master version did not come easily. To promote their perspective on Mt Wudang, Daoist clerics published not only gazetteers but also albums of paintings. Zhang Shouqing and his disciples, for example, compiled *Album of Auspicious Celebrations* (*Jiaqing tu* with other similar alternative titles). Zhang Shouqing, benefiting from imperial favor, acquired no fewer than seven prefaces for the album by leading figures within and without Daoism, such as Zhao Mengfu and Zhang Yucai (?–1316; the 38th Heavenly Master). The vigorous solicitation of endorsements from leading individuals displayed the editors' determination to promote the collection's prestige, authoritativeness, and thus acceptability. After all, the album was edited in order to "[spiritually] move the readers and initiate their awe and respect" toward Zhenwu.[15]

Mt Wudang as a pilgrimage center

A true test of a god's popularity is the degree to which his places of worship attract pilgrims. The purpose of this section is to provide a basis for discussion on the shaping and reshaping of the sacred landscape of Mt Wudang through the practice of pilgrimage. Pilgrimage to Mt Wudang is an extremely rich topic that a number of scholars have examined. The most influential study in western languages was published by John Lagerwey nearly two decades ago (1992); Pierre-Henri de Bruyn's otherwise extremely informative *Le Wudangshan* (1997) says relatively little about pilgrimage. More recently, Chinese scholars have been adding new insights to our understanding of the topic, such as the work of Yang Lizhi (Yang 2005) and Mei Li (Mei 2007). Thanks to their research, we can discuss pilgrimage to Mt Wudang with confidence and economy.

It is possible that there were Zhenwu worshippers making pilgrimage to Mt Wudang in Northern Song since the *Scripture of Zhenwu* was already in circulation at the end of the eleventh century. However, they, if existed, left no records. Li Zhi, who produced the "Verses of Mt Wudang" discussed earlier, was more a tourist than a pilgrim. In the Southern Song period, however, as new Daoist monasteries were built, Mt Wudang began to attract pilgrims. In addition to the power, or *ling*, of the mountain itself as an *axe mundi*, Daoist masters in residence became famous for their ritual powers and elicited visitors (and donations) to the mountain. Abbots such as Sun Jiran, Zhao Shoujie, and Lu Dayou were highly sought after ritual specialists. Zhang Shouqing trained as many as 4000 disciples at the South Cliff Monastery during his 30-year abbotship (*Xuantian shangdi qisheng lingyi lu* ZHDZ 30.702c). The disciples, like good monastics, sought spirituality through labor. They participated in building the temple complexes and constructed paths, steps, bridges and other parts of the infrastructure. In addition, they also served as guides, hosts, and even security guards.

With expanded facilities and a growing number of Daoist clerics in residence, Mt Wudang developed the capacity to receive large numbers of visitors. They came to "make audience to the mountain to present incense" (*chaoshan jinxiang* 朝山進香)

88 *A god and his mountain*

in the palatial temple complexes managed by Daoists. Cheng Jufu, the prominent Yuan scholar-official, observed in 1314 that tens of thousands of visitors, male and female, flocked to the mountain during annual celebrations of Zhenwu's birth (*Xuelou ji* 5.22b). Some of the visitors brought with them substantial donations and left commemorative steles (charts of the donors and donations below).[16] The information collected was limited but shows that while the overwhelming majority of donors hailed from the vicinity, long-distance pilgrims from Jiangxi and the costal province of Jiangsu also made up part of the contingent.

The imperial court itself, starting from Emperor Yuan Renzong (b. 1285; r. 1311–1320), frequently sent delegates to Mt Wudang to carry out the ritual of Offering. The monasteries obtained both political and material capital from hosting imperial rituals (see the next section). The increasing number of visitors brought even more financial resources to the monasteries, which allowed further and a more elaborate development of the buildings. By the end of the Yuan period, the mountain boasted 17 large temples and more than 60 small ones (Wang and Yang

Table 4.1 Private donations recorded at Mt Wudang during the Yuan Dynasty

Year	Location of the donor	Form or sum of donations	References
1295	Jiaokou village (at the foot of Mt Wudang), Junzhou[17]	Estate for building and supporting a new temple (*Xiuzhen guan*)	CDTSZ 12.167: *Xiuzhen guan beiji* 修真觀記碑
1309	City of Junzhou[18]	Cropland of 100 and plus *mu*	CDTSZ 12.167: *Xiuzhen guan beiji*
1331	Nanzhang district in Xiangyang	Cash	*Wudang Shan Jinshi Lu* 武當山金石錄 3.108: "Heihuyan ji" 黑虎岩記
1333	Anlu in De'an (in Hubei province).[19]	Cash to build a set of statues of divinities, identities unspecified	CDTSZ 12.171: "Yuxuyan gongyuan ji bei 玉虛巖功緣記碑
1336	Unspecified[20]	Cash for beautifying and finalizing a cave temple.	CDTSZ 12.164–12.165: "Yanhuo Leijun cangshui shengdong ji bei" 煙火雷君滄水聖洞記碑
1337a	Kuenshan and Shanghai[21]	Three images (Zhenwu and his parents) along with cash	CDTSZ 12.167–12.168: "Chenxiang shengxiang bei" 沉香聖像碑
1337b	Anlu, Hubei	Cash 750 *min* to build statures of Zhenwu and attendants	CDTSZ 12.171: "Yuxu yan gongyuan ji bei 玉虛巖功緣記碑
1339	City of Ancheng, Jiangxi[22]	Labor cost	CDTSZ 12.168–12.170: "Huayang yan Haoran zi ji bei" 華陽巖浩然子記碑 4. 618, 623
1341	Gongyi, S. Hubei	Cash 200 *ding* for building the path connecting two temples	CDTSZ 12.165–12.166: "Zhenqing gong chuangxiu bei ji" 真慶宮創修碑記

Source: *Chijian Dayue Taihe shanzhi*, hereafter CDTSZ.

1993). Unfortunately, they would all be destroyed when civil war broke out at the end of the Yuan dynasty; one battle in particular, in 1353 between the Yuan government army and Ming-led insurgent groups took place on Mt Wudang itself (*Yuanshi* 142.3396).

The monasteries on Mt Wudang were rebuilt in the fifteenth century on a grand scale, thanks to Emperor Yongle, discussed in the next section. Visitors to the mountain during the Ming period grew to such a significant number that in 1488, the state decided to take advantage of the growth by levying an "incense tax" or *xiangshui* 香稅 (Mei 2007: 272–285) (*Dayue Taihe shan zhi*, j. 7.333a). While there is no quantified data of this tax-revenue that would allow us to estimate the number of visitors, we do know that incense taxes collected on Mt Wudang were a substantial source of revenue. After paying the cost of upkeep for the monasteries (maintenance, incense, candles, and so forth), there was still enough left to supplement local administration for famine relief and for emergency salaries for local soldiers. The tax records also show that a majority of visitors came to Mt Wudang during the first four months of the year. In other words, most visitors were pilgrims coming to the mountain for the main purpose of celebrating the anniversary of Zhenwu birth, a typical way to repay the gods' blessing.

The geographical distribution of Mt Wudang pilgrims is another important area of analysis. Lagerwey, using over 80 inscriptions that he copied and read on the mountain, pointed out that the overwhelming majority of the pilgrims were from the Hubei and Hunan provinces. Thus, he suggests, Mt Wudang was essentially a regional pilgrimage center (Lagerwey 1992: 312). While Lagerwey emphasizes an established custom of pilgrimage-making (in contrast to random individual choices), Yang Lizhi highlights the wide spread of the pool of pilgrims. Agreeing that adjacent prefectures provided the lion's share of pilgrims, Yang nevertheless stresses that pilgrims could be found in most provinces in late imperial China, and thus argues that Wudang was an empire-wide pilgrimage center (Yang 2005). In pursuing Yang's methodology, Mei Li proposes a three-tier model, with Hubei and Henan (not Hunan) as the core reign supplying the majority of the pilgrims, an extended area covering Shaanxi, Shanxi, Anhui, and Hunan provinces, and a periphery that included the rest of the Ming China (2007: 169–213). Her main sources, in addition to local gazetteers, were epigraphs left by "incense associations" or *xianghui* 香會. Beginning in the mid-Ming period, many pilgrims came as members of incense associations, and left records of their visits on steles, cliffs, donated statues and temple utensils. Mei Li collected 95 examples of such epigraphs from Ming times and created a tablet of the geographic distribution of the incense associations (2007: 174). The tablet is reproduced below.

Table 4.2 Geographical distribution of the incense associations that made pilgrimages to Mt Wudang during the Ming dynasty

Province	Hubei	Henna	Shaanxi	Shanxi	Anhui	Hunan	Zhili	Jiangxi	Shandong	Gansu	Fujian	Jiangsu	Yunnan	Not clear	Total
Number	12	30	5	16	6	4	2	1	1	1	0	0	0	17	95

90 *A god and his mountain*

Because not all incense associations left steles and not all pilgrims were connected with incense associations, the table above contains no records about people from Jiangsu, Yunnan, and Fujian. However, evidence confirms the presence of pilgrims from at least Jiangsu and Yunnan.[23] During the mid-Ming period, pilgrimage to Wudang was a major event in Suzhou, the capital of Jiangsu province. (Gu 1989, *Xijin shixiaolu* 1.83). Every year, pilgrims from the Lake Tai area gathered on boats at Beitang 北塘 (North Pone) outside Suzhou early in the second month to set off together up the Yangzi River. There were generally more than 100 pilgrims' boats annually and all were lit with lanterns. The "pilgrim lights on Northern Pond" was a yearly spectacle that local gazetteers proudly recorded.

The presence of Yunnan pilgrims can be seen in the bronze poles that form the fence surrounding the Golden Hall on the summit of Mt Wudang (see figure 4.2). They were donated between 1590 and 1591 by devotees from Kunming, the capital of Yunnan (Yang 2005, Mei 2007, 2010). The poles, 148 in total, each more than 5 feet high and wider than an ordinary person's arm, were cast in Kunming and then transported to Mt Wudang. A project erecting bronze poles in the most symbolic building on the mountain (see discussion below) must have required many details including careful measurements, and negotiation with supervising clerics and government officials. There would have been multiple visits by project leaders and assistant organizers prior to the final trip to deliver the poles, and complex arrangements regarding transportation over hundreds of miles.

It is also worth noting that most of the visiting incense societies came from the province of Henan. The connection between Henan and Zhenwu was longstanding. First of all, the earliest available evidence of Mt Wudang's importance in Zhenwu mythology, the stele containing the *Scripture of Zhenwu*, was located in Henan. Second, Mt Wudang was historically part of Nanyang prefecture, in Henan. Although by the Ming period the area had been transferred to the jurisdiction of

Figure 4.2 The bronze temple on the summit of Mt Wudang.
Source: Picture taken by Mark Nan Tu; © Wikimedia commons.

A god and his mountain 91

Hubei province, its original home location, not unlike that of many Chinese families, remained fixed in people's imagination.

Pilgrimage experience

Records concerning pilgrimage to Mt Wudang during the Song dynasty are scarce. For the Yuan period, however, there is enough information to reconstruct at least one pilgrimage route on the mountain. Two records from the turn of the thirteenth century are useful: the *Zongzhen ji* by Liu Daoming discussed above and the *Record of Scenery of Mt Wudang* (*Wudang jishengji* 武當紀勝集; TC 963). This is a collection of poetry by a Daoist named Luo Tingzhen 羅霆震 from the mid-Yuan period that eulogizes the mountain's sites and associated legends. The poems are arranged according to the order of one of the pilgrimage routes on the mountain. I will use Luo's poetry as a guide to introduce the sites along the route. In Luo's day, there were two ways to approach the mountain, from the east and west, and Luo took the western route. The path begins in Haokou 蒿口, a village at the foot of the mountain, passes the Five Dragons Palace, then the South Cliff Palace at the South Cliff, and reaches the footpath leading to the Great Summit, the desired destination of pilgrims.[24] The return path took a different direction, passing the Purple Empyrean Palace on the way.

At the bottom of the mountain, pilgrims first encountered the Cloister of Reception (Jiedai an 接待庵) where they could rest for tea and refreshment.[25] They then walked past three temples for the earth god, mountain god, and the Marshal Black Tiger (Heihu yuanshuai 黑虎元帥) respectively, who all functioned as the patrol deities of the mountain. The Marshal Black Tiger, states the *Zongzhen ji*, is the "heavenly one of the north" (*Beifang tianyi* 北方天一) who protects the teaching and pacifies the mountain (*Zongzhen ji*, j. xia, ZHDZ 48.575b). The "heavenly one of the north" could take the form of a tiger or a human being, in reality or in the dreams of pilgrims. The Marshal Black Tiger's shrine was located at the Fastening-the-horse Peak (Xima feng 繫馬峰), so named because Zhenwu appeared on the top of the peak riding a white horse.

As the pilgrims exited the Black Tiger Shrine and proceeded to the Five Dragons Peak, they would come across the Grinding the Needle Stone and the betel-nut-plum trees and learn about another episode of Zhenwu's life. During his long sojourn on the mountain, Zhenwu became frustrated by the slow progress of his self-cultivation and decided to quit and take leave. A goddess (whose identity varies in different sources) stepped in to save him from giving up. In the disguise of an ordinary woman, she sat directly on the path near a stream that Zhenwu was to take and began to grind an iron club on a stone by the water. Zhenwu passed by, saw her, and duly asked her the reason for grinding the club. The goddess answered that she was grinding the iron club into a sewing needle. When Zhenwu asserted that this was impossible, the goddess replied that it was only a matter of persistence. Surely enough, Zhenwu got the point and returned to his hermitage to continue his practice. The stream was thus named Grinding the Needle Mountain Stream and the stone Grinding the Needle Stone to commemorate the event. A shrine dedicated to the goddess, the Laolao An 姥姥庵 (Granny's Cloister), was erected at the spot. Liu Daoming told us this deity was a certain Purple Primordial Lord (not to be confused with the Purple Void Primordial Lord, i.e. Wei Huacun), one of the many incarnations of Laozi (*Zongzhen ji* ZHDZ 48.567c). Popular traditions have more versions (Chao 2009). Furthermore, this story is almost identical to one of the episodes that happened to Asanga, the fourth-century Indian co-founder of the Yogacara Buddhist school, during his long-time meditative retreat in search of enlightenment.[26] Nevertheless, what is more important than tracing the sources and verifications of this account is how it once more successfully inserted Zhenwu into the landscape of Mt Wudang.

A short distance ("one hundred steps") south from Grinding the Needle Stone grows the *langmei* 榔梅, a crossbreed of betel nut and plum trees. The betel-nut-plum (in shape resembling kumquats), an indigenous variety,[27] was actually, as the *Zongzhen ji* claims, created by Zhenwu. After encountering the goddess at the riverbank, Zhenwu was ready to retreat to his hut and continue his cultivation of the way. To confirm his decision, he grafted a branch of a plum (*mei*) tree on a dead betel-nut (*lang*) tree and declared this dead tree to be his witness, one that would blossom and bear fruit when he reached perfection. As time went on, the betel-nut tree not only came to live but flourished into a forest. Pilgrims who saw the trees saw the "proof" of Zhenwu's apotheosis. On one side of the beetle-nut forest, one could see a shrine dedicated to a certain *Langmei xianweng* (the transcendent old man of the betel-nut plum) who oversaw the trees. The trees were too tall for anyone to grab the fruit. Yet, if one kowtowed and prayed to the transcendent old man, betel-nut plums would fall by themselves (*Zongzhen ji*, middle; ZHDZ 48.568a). Without the ritual, the fruit was visible but unreachable. The *Complete Collection* informs us that it was Zhenwu who appointed the old man to guard the trees. A local plant—and maybe a local belief—on the mountain was thereby assimilated into Zhenwu mythology.

The pilgrims burned sticks of incense at the Old Granny Shrine and, for obtaining some of the betel-nut-plums, made prayers at the shrine of the old immortals of the betel-plum. It was almost guaranteed that they would hear the story about how the goddess enlightened Zhenwu and how the latter created a fruit tree unique to Mt Wudang. The natural settings of the mountain (i.e. the stone, river, and trees) were reinterpreted as landmarks of Zhenwu legends. The mountain was woven into the Zhenwu story, and Zhenwu was etched into the landscape of the mountain. Little by little, the Daoists "colonized" the mountain and made it into a central stage of the Zhenwu's life.

Finally, the pilgrims came to the Five Dragons Palace, the main stop in the middle of the pilgrimage route. The palace contained several halls, of which that of Zhenwu was the main one. When the pilgrims came to the main hall of the Five Dragons Palace, they would see (*Zongzhen ji*, middle, ZHDZ 48.567a):

> The center of the main hall, in glaring golden and jade color, enshrined the sacred image of the Supreme Emperor of the Dark Heaven. The image is in a dark robe of a pattern of five dragons; it has thick (*lit*. dragon-like) eyebrows and almond-shaped (*lit*. phoenix-like) eyes as glorious as the sun and moon; its

hair loosened and feet bare. The whole image is created from unusual aromatic [wood] and pure lacquer. The Jade Maiden and Golden Lad, holding a sword and seal in their hands are there, along with two ministers in official attire attending at the court. Four great heavenly stalwarts hold flags surrounding and guarding him. The four walls are painted with stories of his birth and his learning of the Way. At the back [of the hall], a green turtle and a huge snake are displayed, showing the ascending and descending aspects of fire and water.

正殿當中，金碧交縈，專以崇奉玄天上帝聖容，帝御五龍玄袍，龍眉鳳目，日彩月華，披髮跣足，皆以異香純漆塑而成之。玉女金童，擎劍捧印，二卿朝服拱侍。庭下四大天丁執纛秉旌扈從環衛。四壁繪降生成道事跡，後列蒼龜巨蛇水火升降之勢。

The Five Dragons temple was no less than a classroom of Zhenwu hagiography. The other halls in the monastery enshrined Zhenwu's parents, the Three Pure Ones, the Jade Emperor, Wenchang (Lord of Literature), and the Three Perfected Lords Mao (San Mao zhenjun 三茅真君). The Three Perfected Lords Mao were the local deities of Mt Mao, the birthplace of Sun Jiran who rebuilt the Five Dragons Palace in the mid-thirteen century . It was most likely Sun who brought the veneration of Three Perfected Lords to Mt Wudang. There were also lesser halls (*tang* 堂) for thunder deities, two of which were devoted to Thunder Marshals Zhao and Meng. The design of this temple compound illustrated not only Zhenwu's life but also his relationship with other Daoist deities. Any visitor to the temple, literate or illiterate, could learn a good deal about Zhenwu mythology: his parents, self-cultivation, image, his attendant generals, and his commander status in the Thunder Ritual.

Although Zhenwu's mother, Queen Shansheng, was mentioned only in passing at the birth of Zhenwu in the *Scripture of Zhenwu*, she was well represented on the mountain. Pilgrims could find a temple called Queen Mother Palace (Wangmu gong 王母宮) on Great Brightness Peak (Daming feng 大明峰) nearby the Five Dragons Palace that was dedicated to her. It was among the "nine palaces" on Mt Wudang during the Yuan period. The *Zongzhen ji* maintains that according to local oral tradition (*qijiu xiangchuan* 耆舊相傳), this was where Zhenwu's mother took residence after coming to search for Zhenwu . A stele erected by pilgrims on the mountain brings the queen into the picture by characterizing Zhenwu's leaving home as "escaping the country and leaving his mother" (*biguo limu* 避國離母) (Mei 2007: 223). This phrase shows a contrast with the *Scripture of Zhenwu*, in which it was the father-king and the throne that being singled out as what Zhenwu had renounced. Priest Liu Daoming, after sketching the serene scenery surround the Queen Mother Palace, asked rhetorically, "Can anyone who did not renounce the world stay (*qixi* 棲息) here?" (*Zongzhen ji*, middle, ZHDZ 567c). Liu's remarks show that he learned about the origin of the Queen Mother Palace through oral tradition and accepted it wholeheartedly despite its lack of scriptural support.

The legend of the origin of the Queen Mother Palace points to another example of the lay people's perspective being incorporate in the Zhenwu lore: the clash between social and religious duties. The *Scripture of Zhenwu* uses only six characters to discuss the parental reaction (actually the father only) to Zhenwu's decision of leaving home in order to pursue a spiritual quest: *fuwang buneng jinzhi* or "the father-king cannot prohibit." The potential conflict in the story, between Zhenwu's spiritual quest and his duty as a son, is minimized. Yet for ordinary people the pursuit of a monastic lifestyle at the cost of one's social responsibilities, especially the duty of filial piety to one's parents, created a serious conflict. To lay people, the scriptural version inadequately justified Zhenwu's failure to fulfill his filial obligations, and omitted any discussion of what happened to his parents. The gravity of the conflict in the popular version is represented in the scenario where the queen climbs the mountain to look for her son, and her loss is compensated with the building of a temple. The laity devised the story not merely to fill in the missing episodes but to implicitly challenge the monastic clergy over their failure of filial piety.

As the pilgrims moved on to the next main temple, the South Cliff Palace, they would walk by the Gold Lock Peak (Jinsuo feng), where Zhenwu imprisoned the demons he captured (*Zongzhen ji*, shang, ZHDZ 48. 563a):

> The Gold Lock Peak: ... The "Biography" said that the Dark Emperor captured demons and killed their leader. The demons were of an odd shape and unusual appearance resembling apes and monkeys. There were locked underneath [the Gold Lock Peak]. The Dark Emperor vowed, "I will release you only after the water in the mountain stream dries out."
>
> 金鎖峰: ...傳云: 玄帝收攝妖魔, 戮其渠魁。奇形異狀如猿如猴, 悉鎖于下。誓曰; 俟此山下澗水枯竭, 方才放爾。

Heading southeast, pilgrims came to the South Cliff located north of the Great Summit. Here, they would see a row of temple buildings extending out along the cliff. The South Cliff, as the *Zongzhen ji* tells us, was where Zhenwu practiced self-cultivation most of the time and where he eventually ascended to heaven in broad daylight. Here we see an inconsistency with Liu Daoming's version of the legend of the Five Dragons Palace as the place of ascension that further supports the theory that Liu imposed a new origin of the Five Dragons Palace to replace the old one. To the west of the South Cliff was the Clothing Changing Platform (*Gengyi tai* 更衣台), where Zhenwu, prior to ascending to heaven, changed his hermit outfit of leaves and ivy made to the attire bestowed on him by the Jade Emperor.

Finally, pilgrims reached the Great Harmony Palace (Taihe gong 太和宮) at *Dading* (Great Summit). For those who planned to pay homage to Zhenwu on the tip of the mountain at dawn, as imperial delegations did, this was the place to stay overnight. Most Pilgrims, on the other hand, would try to continue the last one mile farther, climbing to reach the tip of the Great Summit before heading down the mountain before sunset. In the narrow space of the summit, during Yuan times, there was a stone altar enshrining Zhenwu and a miniature pavilion entirely cast in bronze containing an incense-burner and nine bronze statues with Zhenwu in the

A god and his mountain 95

center.[28] Upon reaching the apex of their journey, literally and figuratively, the pilgrims were told that:

> At the summit, recite scriptures (*xianjing* 仙經) and say prayers for your ancestors; the merits [collected by doing these here] are the biggest. If you keep your heart refined and pious, then the air of the four directions will be clear and the eight sides are [so clear] that are penetrable. Rare birds and auspicious signs will all appear in front.
>
> 至此默誦仙經，祝讚祖禰，善功最大。持心精恪，則四氣清朗，八表洞徹。珍禽異瑞，畢現於前。

The scenery was also magnificent. Pilgrims could have a panoramic view of the hills and see that the mountain was "indeed an enclave for the celestial perfected ones" (*Xu Xiake youji*, xia.23b). However, people were not supposed to linger. The *Zongzhen ji* warns that the summit is not for mortal human beings. The space is limited, the wind is strong, and therefore, a big crowd could cause disaster. In any case, there were more sites to see and more folklore to hear in the Great Summit Peak area for the pilgrims as they headed down. A pond, called the Heavenly Pond (Tianchi 天池), beneath a cliff on the southern side of the Great Summit, was the residence of a dragon. Nearby, they would find traces of the Queen Shansheng once again, in the form of the Queen Cliff (Huanghou yan 皇后巖). It was said that Queen Shansheng, as she was looking for her son, took rest here, and therefore the cliff was named after her (*Zongzhen ji*, shang, ZHDZ 560.a). The mother–son bond, unseen in scriptural tradition, was once again highlighted.

On their return, the pilgrims descended toward the east, and came to the Purple Empyrean Palace to see yet another majestic abbey. The Purple Empyrean Palace was built in the same style as the Five Dragons Palace but with more space and grandeur. In the area nearby, the pilgrims would also see the temple dedicated to Yao Jian, the rain-praying Junzhou magistrate who encountered the five dragon lords discussed earlier. The title granted to him after the apotheosis was King Awesome Fire. However, in the Daoist narratives, he was presented as a "numinous officer," or *lingguan* 靈官, a low-ranking Daoist divinity. Departing the Purple Empyrean Palace and following the mountain path along the Purple Empyrean Torrent (*jian* 澗), pilgrims headed down the foot of the mountain. From there, they crossed the stream at the fort, signaling that the "audience with Zhenwu" was coming to its end.

Daoist priests mapped a scared atlas on the landscape of Mt Wudang comprising locations where episodes of Zhenwu's life were staged, episodes that illuminated the progression of his divination. The power of Zhenwu was "sedimented and preserved" on the mountain after his apotheosis, a process which created the "spatialization" of his "charisma," using Eade and Sallnow's phrasing (1991: 8). The clerics clearly intended to impose on the pilgrims a hegemonic pilgrimage experience by promoting an "official" reading of the landscape on top of altering or conceiving old myths which conflicted with Daoist tradition. However, the pilgrims insisted on their own itinerary and produced a religious experience that reflected the traditions of both Daoism and popular religion.

Imperial recognition of Mt Wudang

Throughout the Song dynasty, Mt Wudang received little attention from the monarchs as a religious site. At this time, the epicenters of Zhenwu worship were the temples dedicated to him by the monarchs in their capitals as discussed in Chapter Two. In Hangzhou, the capital of the Southern Song, the Aiding Sage Daoist Monastery converted from Emperor Xiaozong's old princely residence, hosted annual festivals so magnificent that it was claimed the city's devotion to Zhenwu exceeded that of any other place (*Mengliang lu* 2.1b). Song emperors intentionally established a cultural hegemony that made the monarchy the center of action (Bickford 2006: 486–488). Sublime temples in the capital, where the imperial court was located, served the function of glorifying the monarchy; they were promoted as a religious model for peripheral areas to follow and admire, just as the emperor served as a personalized model for his subjects.

It was under the foreign rule of the Mongols that Mt Wudang finally received its due reverence by imperial authorities. As Lagerwey observes, "the cosmological dimensions of the mountain [i.e. Wudang] … were first clearly defined under the non-Chinese Yuan dynasty" (Lagerwey 1992: 297). Mongolian emperors could not claim an ancestor who was a Chinese cultural symbol as their counterparts of the Tang and Song dynasties had done. Therefore, Chinese scholars in the Mongol court made use of the more traditional strategy of political legitimacy; they appealed to the Five Phases theory so as to enhance Mongol legitimacy in the eyes of the Han subjects.

Yuan emperors, beginning with Emperor Renzong, bestowed special favors on Mt Wudang.[29] Before ascending to the throne in 1307, he had spent two years in exile in western Henan with his mother. Given the close connection between western Henan and Mt Wudang, it was likely that he came to learn about the Daoists on the mountain. Renzong's mother was evidentially acquainted with the clergy on Mt Wudang; she admired Zhang Shouqing so much that she invited him to Beijing to lead ritual services from 1310 to 1314 (*Xuelou ji* 5.21b). In addition, Renzong shared the same birthday with Zhenwu. Every year he sent a delegation of government officials and Daoist priests to Mt Wudang to carry out the Gold Register Offering celebrating both his and Zhenwu's birthday (*Jinshi lüe* 946). His successors continued the practice and added their own birthdays to the ritual calendar as well. Hosting imperially sponsored Offering rituals meant not only recognition of the mountain but also an annual bounty of gifts to the monasteries hosting the rituals.

To comprise the imperial delegations to Mt Wudang, the state recruited Daoist priests not only from the capital but also from provincial temples. One such priest was a certain Tang Dongyun 唐洞雲 from Xuzhou in present-day Jiangsu province. Master Tang was so proud of his participation in the delegation that he asked Zhao Mengfu 趙孟頫 (1254–1322), the leading scholar-official of his time, to compose a commemorative essay on the event. Tang then erected a stele with the inscribed essay at his temple in Xuzhou for visitors to appreciate (*Jinshi lüe* 1150). Thus, when the priests returned to their home temples after the state ritual on Mt Wudang, they brought their experiences with them and incorporated the sacred site of Zhenwu into local memory.

Although Mt Wudang received its first imperial patronage from Mongol rulers, unprecedented support came from the Ming monarchs Yongle 永樂 (r.1403–1424) and Jiajing 嘉靖 (r. 1522–1566). The founder of the Ming dynasty, Emperor Hongwu (r.1368–1398), claimed to have received Zhenwu's support in his march to power.[30] Yet it was the third emperor, Yongle, bearing the title the Prince of Yan (Yan Wang 燕王) before his enthronement, who really demonstrated royal patronage. Yongle was one of Hongwu's younger sons, and was passed over in the succession when the throne was given to the eldest son of the deceased heir apparent, known to history as Emperor Hui (Huidi 惠帝, r.1399–1402). Only 13 months after his nephew had been enthroned, Yongle launched an armed rebellion against the young emperor, an act of sedition that had to be justified post facto. Thus, not unlike the Mongols, Yongle's court addressed its problem of legitimacy by borrowing Zhenwu's credentials. The emperor and court literati advanced the thesis that Zhenwu had sanctioned the rebellion. According to the story, after the decision was made to attack the imperial army, Yongle and his principal advisor Yao Guangxiao 姚廣孝 (1335–1419) could not agree on the date for the operation. Yongle was eager to start but Yao insisted on waiting. When Yao finally determined that the time was ripe for action, the ceremonial rally for initiating military operations, "making offerings to the [spirit of] the [military] banner" (*jidao* 祭纛) took place. As the soldiers lined up to take the pledge, Yongle reportedly saw a divine figure in armor with untied hair surrounded by numerous banners. He asked Yao about the identity of the divinity. Yao answered that the deity was his "teacher" (*wushi* 吾師), Zhenwu, whom he had been waiting all the time. Yongle then "disheveled his hair and held his sword in response" (*pifa zhangjian xiangying* 披髮仗劍相應; *Mingshu* 160. 3156–3157).

Yongle went on to overthrow his nephew and ascended the thrown in 1403. In 1412, he decreed the restoration of the monastic temples on Mt Wudang that had mostly been destroyed during the catastrophic civil war at the end of the Yuan period. The lavish project included 17 large temple complexes, the so-called "nine palaces and eight monasteries" (*jiugong baguan* 九宮八觀) and numerous smaller ones.[31] Among them, one merits a special mention here, the bronze shrine on the top of the mountain that is often referred to as the "golden submit of Wudang." Yougle ordered this one-room pavilion to replace the Yuan miniature bronze pavilion which was intact at the time.[32] Over 400 Daoist clerics with their apprentices were selected to staff the new temples. In 1413, Yougle assigned the 44th Heavenly Master, Zhang Yüqing, to choose an additional 200 Daoist priests to be abbots of the major temples. Even this was not enough; later in the year, Yongle instructed the Daoist registrar (*Daolu si* 道錄司) to find more Daoists who were well trained and pious (*you daoxing, zhencheng* 有道行，真誠的) to inhabit the temples on the mountain.

In addition, Yongle set aside farm land for the monasteries and settled 500 convicts and their families there as the tenants (Ishida 1995). Peasants whose land lay next to the temples were relocated, so the monastery tenants could take over. More uncultivated land in the area was parceled out and assigned to the tenants; in the end, there were 550 households in total listed in the tenant registers. Each was assigned 50 *mu* of land (about 8 acres) and expected to pay a yearly rent of 0.14 *shi* of grain per *mu* to the monasteries. This was on the lower side of the rent scale for state farmland (*guantian* 官田) that was pegged at between 0.1 and 1 *shi* for every *mu*.[33] The state also made itself responsible for the clothing of priests and novices, as well as the daily necessities of the temples, such as incense, candles, and oil (for lanterns and cooking). All imperial support, Yongle repeatedly uttered, was to honor his parents, and to show gratitude for the god's blessing of his campaign to "clear away disorder" (*jingnan* 靖難), a euphemism for his military usurpation. Each decree that he issued to thank the god in reality reinforced the propaganda that his enthronement was divinely sanctioned.

In 1418, the principal buildings were completed, and the emperor issued an edict to be engraved as a monument (*Jinshi lüe* 1251) for every visitor to the mountain to see, to read, or hear others to read. Over the next six years, more auxiliary structures were added and it was not until 1424 that the project was finally regarded as complete. Yongle appointed a court supervisor to visit the temple regularly and report on required repairs or materials. The supervisor oversaw the court's allocation of incense, oil, special offerings to the temple required in the calendar of services, and of food to support the resident monks.

From the beginning of his restoration project, Yongle relied heavily on the professional knowledge of the Daoist masters. He summoned Sun Biyun 孫碧雲 (1345–1417), the right director-in-chief of the Daoist register at the court, to check out the site. Later, he appointed Sun Biyun as abbot of the Southern Cliff Palace. Despite the perception in later Ming times Yongle's project created the sacred space on the mountain, it is clear that what he did was to restore, but not reshape, the sanctity of an older space. The new temples commemorated the old legends represented in gazetteers compiled by Daoists of the Yuan dynasty (see Appendix 2). While Yongle possessed the political capital to restore the mountain, he did not have the symbolic capital to redesign the mountain's landscape. He could only see the sacred geography through the eye of the Daoist clergy.

On the other hand, Yongle managed to turn Mt Wudang into a political platform. His decree claiming divine sanction of his enthronement was displayed on the mountain for every visitor to look at. When he moved the original golden pavilion on the summit to make room for a larger one commissioned by himself, his determination to put his signature on the mountain was clear. As attested in writings from late Ming times, Yongle was given full credit for creating the entire temple complex on Mt Wudang. Thus, in popular eyes, he successfully eclipsed the contributions and influence of the Daoist clerics. In the future, there would even be assertions that the facial design of the Zhenwu stature in the Golden Pavilion at the Great Submit of Mt Wudang derived from Yongle's own face (Chan 1997). In reality, the two do not resemble each other (see figures 4.3–4.5). Thus, just as Daoist clerics used Mt Wudang

Figure 4.3 A statue of Zhenwu inside the shrine on the summit of Mt Wudang.
Source: Picture taken by Yang Lizhi.

to proselytize Zhenwu worship, Yongle used the mountain to expand imperial authority. The mountain began to emanate a political legitimacy of its own. The importance of this new layer of symbolism would be demonstrated by Emperor Jiajing a century later when another controversy arose over succession to the crown.

In 1552, Emperor Jiajing 嘉靖 (r. 1522–1566), the 11th ruler of the Ming, launched a major renovation project of the monasteries on Mt Wudang that cost the court nearly 100,000 ounce (*liang* 兩) of silver, not including supplements from the provincial administration (Wang and Yang 1993: 180). The project included the building of a spectacular arch for the point of entry to the mountain, engraved with the four characters *zhishi xuanyue* 治世玄嶽 ("the Dark Peak that governs the world") that became the new demarcation of the boundary of the sacred territory (Mei 2007: 70). After the renovation was completed in 1553, Jiajing composed "The Stele Record Commemorating the Completion of the Renovations of the Dark [Emperor's] Palaces on Mt Taihe" (Mt Taihe is an alternative name for Mt Wudang) proclaiming his devotion to Zhenwu (*Dayue zhilue* 2.300). In addition to the conventional encomiums for blessing the country, benefiting the people, and protecting sovereignty, Jiajing added another unique reason:

> My late august father was granted the [fiefdom] of Ying. The manor house directly faces the winding numinous vein[34] of the superior Taihe [i.e. Mt Wudang] to which he carefully performed regular rituals. Since I have succeeded [to the throne], I received blessing descending [from Mt Wudang].
> 朕皇考封藩郢邸, 實當太和靈脈蜿蜒之勝, 歲時崇封謹。嗣朕入承大統以來, 仰荷垂佑。

Figure 4.4 Portrait of Emperor Yongle.
Source: © Wikimedia commons.

Here, Jiajing proclaimed a close connection between Mt Wudang and himself, that went beyond the usual imperial blessing from Zhenwu that past monarchs had asserted. Emperor Jiajing was not born to the succession but was a lesser member of the royal family. In the inscription, he implicitly argued that the mandate of heaven had been transmitted to his branch of the imperial house thanks to his father's close bond with Mt Wudang (and thus Zhenwu). In addition, it was his father bequeathed this relationship to him, inherent in the system of fiefdoms. The unspoken premise of his argument was that Zhenwu had the authority to endorse a new imperial line from a lesser branch lineage. This authority, not surprisingly, found no basis in scriptural tradition of Daoism; it emanated from the state symbolism that Yongle had created for Mt Wudang's heritage.

Thus, Jiajing's renovation project on Mt Wudang propagated his father's importance in the transmission of the heavenly mandate. In reality, Jiajing was chosen by the Empress Dowager Zhang (d. 1541) together with the senior grand secretary Yang Tinghe 楊廷和 (1459–1529) to succeed Emperor Zhengde 正德 (1505–1521), who had died without a son. The grand secretary and the empress dowager had insisted that Jiajing be adopted as a son of Zhengde. Jiajing resented the arrangement, and was recorded asking in distaste: "Can parents be so easily changed?" (Fisher 1990: 56). The relationship between the new emperor and his natural father, and the latter's status in the imperial protocol then became the

Figure 4.5 Portrait of Emperor Yongle, detail.

focus of a three-year political dispute known as the Great Rites Controversy. The dispute ended with Jiajing triumphantly turning his birth father into a posthumous emperor in 1524 after Yang Tinghe' retirement the same year. In 1528, Jiajing denounced Yang and stripped him of his elite status. Yang died the very next year (*Mingshi* 190.5039). Over 200 leading officials who protested against the Emperor's decision to grant his birth father emperor status were jailed, exiled, or disciplined over the next three years; at least 17 of them died due to the injuries suffered from physical punishment (Fisher 1990: 93). Jiajing's anger lasted for another 20 years; when Empress Dowager Zhang died in 1541, Jiajing denied her a proper funeral (Geiss 1988: 463) and executed her brother four years later.[35] His retribution was proof of how deep the anger against the empress dowager ran in his heart. To justify his harsh treatment to the woman who called him in to succeed the throne, he must declare that he was not chosen but born to be the emperor; the empress dowager could claim no credits in his enthronement. Thus, there is no surprise that in 1553 he still intended to glorify his natural father as the source as his legitimacy. The renovation project on Mt Wudang served this purpose.

This is not to say that there was absolutely no personal devotion involved in Jiajing's patronage of Mt Wudang. In the second month of the forty-fifth, and last, year of his reign, Jiajing told grand councilor, Xu Jie 徐階 (1503–1583), that (*Shizong shilu* j. 555, n.p.):

> I have been sick for 14 months. … [I plan to] go down the south to Chengtian Prefecture [i.e. Anlu, where Jiajing was born], to pay respects at my parents' burial mound, and take medicine as well as swallow the *qi* there. It was where I was originally conceived. [Going there] will definitely succeed [in curing my illness].
>
> 朕病十四月矣.…南視承天, 拜親陵, 取藥服氣, 此原受生之地, 必奏功。

102 *A god and his mountain*

Jiajing put aside his plan at Xu Jie's discouragement, and died the end of the year. Thus on his deathbed, at a time when there was no political agenda involved, Jiajing looked to the *qi* of his birthplace which could rejuvenate him and would work miracles. Jiajing's remark on the spiritual connection between him and his birthplace matches his proclamation on the relationship between Mt Wudang and his father. Jiajing betrayed a persistent belief in the geomantic influence a man could receive from his native place, and put it all altogether in a package that brought glory to his family as well.

This chapter investigates the trajectory of Mt Wudang from its incarnation as a general site of spirituality to its crystallization as a sacred mountain dedicated to Zhenwu. The belief in Zhenwu's connection with Mt Wudang began to spread at the end of the eleventh century. By the late twelfth century, the mountain had become a particular attraction to those who wished to pray to the deity. Over the next two centuries it developed into an empire-wide pilgrimage site thanks to the Daoist monasticism that took root and flourished on the mountain, despite periods of warfare and destruction. The clerics themselves attracted followers by their expertise in ritual and their reputation in asceticism; they were also the designers and executors of the construction and infrastructure. They built not only a sizable network of temples but, more importantly, a new map of the sacred geography of the mountain. They shaped the mountain into a pilgrimage center for Zhenwu worship in both a theological and a physical way. They actively communicated their projection of the mountain through writing, drawing, compiling, and publishing gazetteers and albums. Where remnants of local worship lingered, such as mythical creatures and dragon kings, they were subsumed beneath the layers of Zhenwu mythology.

The pilgrims and visitors to Mt Wudang were the lifeblood of the mountain. As they set foot on the mountain paths, the rocks, caves, trees, and cliffs were signposts that allowed them to experience the salient points of Zhenwu's life; the god's dilemma in having to leave his social duties behind, his frustration during the quest for the way, his success in reaching perfection, and his power in exorcism. The route was punctuated by prayer and rest at the temples, where pilgrims were impressed by the majesty of the buildings, the decor, and the statues. They could learn or refresh their memory about Zhenwu's life, which was visualized on the wall murals. They had heard about the greatness of the god; on the mountain, they confirmed it with their own eyes. They read (or listened to other people reading) the steles left by previous pilgrims telling of the profound gratitude for Zhenwu's miraculous deeds. On popular occasions, such celebrations of Zhenwu's birth, they would meet so many fellow pilgrims that the god's glory would be further verified.

While Daoist clerics on the mountain shaped the master version of the sacred geography, secular power, represented by the monarchy, also competed for influence. The Yuan emperors did little for the mountain other than confirming the prestige that it had already acquired. It was the Ming monarchs, especially Yongle and Jiajing, who showered the mountain with lavish patronage. While Yongle essentially followed the contours that the Daoists created, he successfully fashioned a new reading of Mt Wudang that emphasized its role as a state symbol. The greatness of the mountain showcased the greatness of the emperor. This new layer of symbolism was taken advantage of by Jiajing a century later during the Great Rites controversy. The latter attributed his mandate of heaven to the "numinous vein" of Mt Wudang, which his natural father's fiefdom faced and to which his father prayed.

The creation of Mt Wudang into the primary residence of Zhenwu helped to create a human dimension of the god's existence. He was no longer an abstract figure but a real person who lived in a real place in real time. As Zhenwu's center of the cosmos, Mt Wudang offered a theological focus point for worshippers and a physical arena where various social groups could compete with one another. The competition between clerics, devotees, and monarchs enriched the symbolism of the mountain and accordingly that of the god himself.

5 The whole and the parts

A study of divinity cannot end without a look at divine miracles. After discussing what people can do for the god, it is time to ask what the god can do for people. This chapter analyzes some of the miracles attributed to Zhenwu from Song to Ming times in order to capture the perception of the god during the Song–Yuan–Ming transition. Zhenwu's various images projected themselves through numerous anecdotes related by gazetteers and literati-officials. New miracles were ascribed to him by ardent believers, and his persona expanded as he took on the form of a god for all time and for all people.

Double-edged symbol of military

The origin of Zhenwu's military persona is shrouded in obscurity but it is probable that it too derived from his exorcist capabilities.[1] The Jurchen Jin dynasty in the twelfth century first recognized Zhenwu as a military god and required their soldiers to worship him. The Jin leaders order that every military base had to erect a Zhenwu temple for the purpose of strengthening military morale (*Shaanxi tongzhi* 28.27b). The prominence of Zhenwu in the state religious system of the Jurchen Jin is further supported by the theory, attributed to Zhu Xi 朱熹 by Liu Chenweng 劉辰翁 (1232–1297), that Zhenwu was originally a Jurchen god or *nüzhen shen* 女真神 (*Xuxi ji* 4.14a).

The Song dynasty, unlike the Jin did not try to promote Zhenwu's military godhead. After all, the Song state had established its military ritual system before Zhenwu rose to prominence. From an early stage, Song military rituals centered on *maya* 禡牙 (military banners) and the deified mythical figure Chiyou 蚩尤 (*Songshi* 121.2829), the primary rival of the Yellow Emperor in mythical times and, according to some classical traditions, the creator of weaponry (Puett 1998).

It is true that Song soldiers worshipped Zhenwu. When the members of the Gongsheng regiment in Kaifeng saw a snake and a turtle appearing together, for example, they interpreted this as Zhenwu's manifestation (see Chapter Two). The legendary General Di Qing 狄青 (1008–1057), another example, wore the Zhenwu image on the battlefield (*Qingbo zazhi* 2.65). They were also eager participants in celebrations for the god's birth. However, the fact that Zhenwu was worshipped by military men does not necessarily make him a military god. Song soldiers and officers worshipped multiple gods and engaged keenly in religion in general. They were so active in religious affairs that the court felt the needs to curb their involvement in erecting new temples and participating religious activities with lay people (*Song huiyao* li 20.2b, 12b–13a).

The military symbolism of Zhenwu developed outside the government military system. It was in Daoist military rituals where we find Zhenwu being invoked as exemplified in the *Master Guigu's Heavenly Marrow Numinous Writings* (*Guigu zi tiansui lingwen* 鬼谷子天髓靈文). This text, composed during Southern Song times or later, contains rituals that promise to transform beans into soldiers and grass into horses, elements often found in popular fiction and stage opera. The guardian deity of the rituals was again Zhenwu. The text instructs the practitioner to make offerings at the altar to Zhenwu on days of the double-third, the double-fifth, and the double-seventh. In presenting the offering, the practitioner should (*ZHDZ* 32.568b):

> loosen his hair, hold a sword, face the Dipper (*Beidou* 北斗, "north bush"), and recite an incantation as follows: "[I] respectfully invite General Zhenwu of the Emperor of the North Apex to descend to aid my power. Quickly come to the altar where all aromatic delicacies are displayed. I, with the edict of the [Supermen] Emperor, practice the rituals in the realm. Promptly, promptly, in accordance with the laws and commands.

> 對北斗，披頭仗劍持呪，呪曰："奉請北極大帝真武將軍，速令下降，助吾神力。急付壇場，馨香珍味。吾奉帝勁，行法于世。急急如律令。"

With the blessing of Zhenwu, the practitioners started to produce elixir (*jindan* 金丹, *lit.* golden cinnabar) that would transform their bodies. When the transformation was complete, they could perform all kinds of supernatural power, including turning regular soldiers into supermen (*ZHDZ* 32.569c):

> If you are in the army on the battlefield, first prepare an incense burner. A bowl of clean water is also needed. Face north, set up seven black banners and one drum. In a black garment, [you] the master should loosen your hair, recite the incantation, hold a brush-pen to write the talismans, and visualize yourself in the image of Zhenwu. When the talismans are completed, prick your tongue, spit blood along with the water and the talisman ash, bite the drum and wave the banners toward the north. Command the soldiers to call the sacred name together. A black wind will come from the north covering the army; all the soldiers will turn into ten feet tall, blue faced spirit generals of "black killer." Even armies of a million soldiers cannot resist them.

> 若臨軍過之，先用香鑪一枚，須要淨水一椀，向北用皂旗七柄，鼓一面，師人皂背子披頭念呪，執筆書符，想自己真武形像，符成就燒灰，嚼舌噴血并水符灰，向北方振鼓搖旗，教衆軍叫聖字，黑風當北方罩，軍兵皆成一丈鬼神，青面黑殺將軍，百萬軍不可當也。

The text made it clear that the practitioners had to transform themselves into Zhenwu to enforce the power of this ritual. In other words, the ritual was not carried out merely by invoking the god but by substituting one's identity with Zhenwu's martial character during the ritual performance, a context similar to the *bianshen neilian* ritual discussed in Chapter Three of this study. This type of ritual cannot be found in traditional military treatises such as the *Seven Books of the Military Scriptures* (*Wujing qishu* 武經七書) nor in officially compiled military encyclopedia like the *Compendium of Essentials of Military Scriptures* (*Wujing zongyao* 武經總要). Yet it would be readily recognizable to those who were familiar with the vernacular fiction involving the supernatural.

The occultist quality of military ritual carried out in Zhenwu's name suggests that the military symbolism of the god was beyond the state's control. Further evidence comes from the rebellions in the wake of the fall of the Northern Song and the rise of the Southern Song. In 1130 (Jianyan 4), the brigand leader Qi Fang 戚方 (1110 ca.–1170) besieged the city of Xuanzhou 宣州 in modern Anhui province, bordering Jiangsu province. He and his commanders decided to use the *Zhenwu fa* ("ritual") in taking over the city on the grounds that layout of the city was shaped in the form of a turtle and a snake (*Sanchao beimeng huibian* 138.13). The rebel army, in imitation of Zhenwu, unbound their hair. Although the rebels failed to take Xuanzhou, a large portion of the city walls was destroyed after the operation. The implicit power of the "Zhenwu ritual" in the account is unmistakable. More than half a century later, Liu Zai 劉宰 (1166–1239, *jinshi* 1190), a military official (*wei* 尉) serving in Jiangning (江寧, present-day Nanjing, Jiangsu), went so far as to categorize *Zhenwu fa* as one of the forbidden "demonic techniques" (*yaoshu* 妖術; *Songshi* 401.12167–12168).

There were individual cases in which high-ranking officers in the Southern Song army worshipped Zhenwu. These cases show that Zhenwu began to obtain a new symbolism as the state's authority. However, the process was not initiated by the state but by the ordinary local people as seen in the case of the Zhenwu Hall in Yanguan zhen 鹽官鎮 (Salt Office Town) in Xihe 西河 prefecture, modern Gansu. The temple burned down in 1165 during prolonged warfare between the Song and the Jurchen Jin.[2] After the departure of the Jin troops, a Song general, Wang Guangzu 王光祖 (courtesy name Jingxian 景先),[3] arrived and discovered a Zhenwu statue sitting in the ashes without the slightest damage. In 1172, General Wang was appointed by the Song court as head of Xihe Prefecture, with jurisdiction over the Salt Office Town.[4] He began to refurbish the Zhenwu Hall as soon as he took the position. After the restoration was completed, he requested a certain Mi Juchun 米居純 of an adjoining county to write a record in commemoration. The inscription says:

> [The General] recounted to me, Mi Juchun, a humble guest, the following: "In 1165, I was fighting the enemy and came here, but the settlement (*jingyi* 井邑) had already burned down to nothing. Nevertheless, I saw in the ashes the image of the Perfected Lord [i.e. Zhenwu] sitting majestically. The painting that decorated it was unchanged, fresh and clean. His unbound hair was not damaged at all. Even the turtle and the snake remained in good shape. I admired the god's numinosity and already had the intention of restoring the temple but it was beyond my capacity [at the time]. Incidentally, I returned here in charge

of the military. Thus, I organized [the construction project] and gathered together workers. The locals learned about the project and came without being summoned. Timber merchants contributed lumber, potters contributed roof tiles, and masons contributed their skills. The rich donated money and the poor donated their labor. In no time, the temple was built. You may write a record of it."

謂下客米居純曰："予于乾道己酉歲捍禦敵人至此，而井邑已皆焚蕩，惟於灰燼中瞻見真君容像，巍然而坐。所飾丹青不變而鮮潔，所披之髮不壞而俱存，雖龜蛇之形狀亦無損。予欽仰其靈，已有重修之意，恨力無及。適剖符來此，即計度糾工，邦人聞之，不日而集，虞者木，陶者瓦，工自獻技，匠自獻巧。富者以財，貧者以力，不日而成，子可作記。"

General Wang's monologue ended here. It is plainly clear that what impelled him to rebuild the Zhenwu Hall was the need to fulfill his vow. He made the commitment because he was astonished by the sight of the god's statue that survived catastrophe. For him, this was demonstrable proof of the god's power. It was the iconic miracle became the focus of Wang's devotion, and planted the seeds of his rebuilding plan.

I quote the general's speech in full to show not only what was said but also what was not said. The general made no mention of military miracles by Zhenwu or any indication that the god blessed the Song official army. As a general-turned-magistrate who was sent to the newly recovered border region by the central government, Wang would have been the ideal candidate for elaborating on Zhenwu's beneficence to the state and emperor, but he did not. His neglect in doing so indicates that Zhenwu was not yet held as a symbol of state authority. Zhenwu temples may have been recognized by the state but the state did not treat the god as a special military symbol of the state. Rather, Zhenwu was a personal devotional object of military men.

Nevertheless, while General Wang's renovation of the Zhenwu Hall was inspired by personal devotion, he acted in the capacity of a magistrate. He thus unwittingly intermixed the characteristics of individual and official religiosity. As an emissary of the central court, Wang had rescued the area from foreign occupation and embodied state power to the locality. Even though he launched the temple project out of personal devotion, his actions were perceived in a different light by the locals. They surmised a connection between the god and the victory, entertaining the possibility that credit should go to the former. This is well attested to by the author of the inscription writing in his own voice:

Earlier, the enemy abandoned the peace treaty and intended to push [their army] all the way down to take over Sichuan. They were defeated by our government army (*guanjun* 官軍) when they advanced here. Who knows whether or not it was because of the hidden protection of the god? Do I dare fail to write this down in respect?

中前敵人叛盟，意欲長驅而下蜀，至此而為官軍所敗，寧知非陰護之所致耶？敢不敬書。

108 *The whole and the parts*

The connection between Zhenwu and the triumph of the government army was thus established. Yet it was not a result of deliberate state promotion. Instead, it emanated from the projection of the ordinary people of the frontier. Like Mi Juchun, the locals had their own religious protocol. They appropriated Zhenwu as their state symbol, without waiting for sanction by their civilian superiors. The military symbolism of Zhenwu was beyond the imagination and control of the Song state.

When the Mongols conquered China, they brought with them their own military rituals and beliefs. Scholars have argued the Zhenwu was adapted to, or assimilated into, Mahakala, a Tibetan Buddhist god well received in Khubilai's court (De Bruyn 1997). How influential the Mongolian-Tibetan faith was in reshaping Zhenwu's military godhead deserves more investigation. Nevertheless, it is true that the early Ming rulers, who grew up under the Mongolian regime, showed much greater interest than their Song counterparts in manipulating Zhenwu's military symbolism. Emperor Hongwu, the founder of the Ming dynasty, ordered his princesons to pay their respects to Zhenwu and the divinity of military banners when leaving the capital for their fiefdoms. His forth son, Emperor Yongle, further utilized Zhenwu's military symbolism at his rebellious war against the legitimate emperor (see Chapter Four). When Yongle and his chief advisor, Yao Guangxiao, chose Zhenwu to legitimize their seizure of state power; it represented a critical point in the development of the Zhenwu cult. And this was not a random choice. It was Zhenwu position in occult military ritual that impelled them to do this. Through military ritual, Zhenwu had fostered and expanded his martial character, and those who invoked Zhenwu for their own aspirations were merely ratifying this fact.

As discussed in Chapter Four, Yongle was on the whole successful in making Mt. Wudang a symbol of state authority. However, he was unable to take control of the military symbolism of Zhenwu. By default, the state was forced to share Zhenwu's military symbolism. In the *Table-pounding Amazements* (*Paian jingqi* 拍案驚奇, a collection of short stories completed in 1627, Ling Mengchu 淩濛初 (1580–1644) recounted his version of the tireless story of the early Ming female rebel, Tang Saier 唐賽兒 (fl. 1420). While Ling conventionally portrayed Tang as a sexual slut and a sorcerer who mastered the Daoist military occult rituals, he insinuated that she exploited Zhenwu's authority in military occult rituals (*Erke paian jingqi* 453–479). Whether or not Tang Saier solicited Zhenwu as a legitimizing force like Yongle did is not the point here; the point is that Ling Mengchu expressed the belief that Zhenwu's military authority was not monopolized by the state. Metaphysical military power can be harnessed by either side in battle; Zhenwu's status, especially in occult military rituals, was a weapon for the rebellious to challenge the state as well.

Pacification and social norm

Military symbolism lead Zhenwu to be perceived as a protector against the armed force, as we see in the legend of the Daoist monastery Jixian gong 集仙宮 in Jiading 嘉定 (Shanghai) during the Yuan army's victory over the Southern Song in 1275. Upon taking over the city, the Mongol cavalry reportedly saw black clouds covering the top of the temple and soon found themselves surrounded by heavy fog, unable to see. The commander prayed to the heavens: "Which god are you? Please remove the fog and I swear not to kill a single person after entering the city."[5] The sky suddenly cleared and the commander kept his promise. While the Mongol commander did not know who had played the supernatural trick, the Daoist clerics at the temple were certain: It was Zhenwu who enshrined at the right side of the Hall of the Three Pure Ones in their temple, the Gathering of the Immortals Palace. A half-century later, in 1317, the Refined Master (an honorific title for Daoist clerics) Lu and his disciple, also the abbot of the Gathering of the Immortals Palace built a new chapel for Zhenwu. A commemorative stele was duly erected to recount the 1275 siege when "the power of the emperor [i.e. Zhenwu]" saved the entire city.

Foshan zumiao

Zhenwu's role as tutelary deity was further enriched by the symbolism of the orderly social norms in Ming times. One of the best documented cases is the Lingying miao, or the Numinously Responsive Temple, in Foshan township, 60 miles from Guangzhou. Better known as Zumiao ("original temple"),[6] it was the main Zhenwu temple in Foshan, built some time during the Song–Yuan period (*Foshan zhongyi xiang zhi* 8.3a) although it had only several enclaves at the end of Yuan times. The significance of Zhenwu, referred to as the North Emperor locally, and the Zumiao in Foshan is well illustrated in the insurgency of Huang Xiaoyang 黃蕭養 (d. 1450).

Huang Xiaoyang, a native of Guangdong, launched an armed rebellion after breaking out from prison. With a naval force of 300 boats, he besieged the city of Guangzhou in 1449. The provincial navy was utterly defeated at first (*Mingshi* 146. 4111) while Huang raided adjacent towns and villages for supplies. In fright, the local elders (*fulao* 父老) of Foshan prayed to Zhenwu at the Zumiao and inquired whether or not their town might be the next target of attack (*Foshan zhongyi xiang zhi* 8.2b). The answer was yes. A militia was quickly organized and rallied in front of the Zumiao to make a vow in blood. "Whoever cowers down upon facing the enemy or betrays [the town]," those taking the oath said, "the god will strike him dead" (*Foshan zhongyi xiang zhi* 8.12b).

The rebels came exactly as the divination had predicted. The militia constructed a strong fortification and successfully defended their town. They asked Zhenwu's oracles for all their strategic battlefield decisions and attributed their success to the god. In the fourth month of 1450, Huang was killed during a battle with official troops reinforcing the area and the rebellion was essentially over (*Ming Shi* 175.4657). Once the Huang Xiaoyang rebellion was suppressed, a provincial official, Chen Zhi 陳贄, made the rounds of the areas which had been attacked. When he came to Foshan, amazed by the fortification, he summoned the elders for praise. The latter took the chance to ask Chen to write a commemorative inscription for the temple and detailed for him various miracles that Zhenwu had performed during the siege. Chen duly composed the inscription (*Foshan zhongyi xiang zhi* 8.12b-13b) and the stele was erected in 1452. However, the underlying tone in Chen's narrative was cautious; he tactfully treated the miracles as local people's interpretation rather than as matters of fact. Again, it was the local people who emphasized Zhenwu's role as a protector and pacifying power; the magistrate—the representative of the state—accepted the correlation only conditionally and with some suspicion.

As the principal temple of the town's tutelary deity, the Zumiao received constant donations from the locals. A certain He Kang 何康 asked for a son and, after receiving one, donated a piece of cultivated land. Another Foshan native, Liang Tao 梁韜, prayed successfully for a son on his friend's behalf. The two men together donated close to an acre of cultivated land (*Foshan zhongyi xiang zhi* 8.8b). Nevertheless, as the records show, lands donated to the Zumiao were mostly in small pieces, suggesting that the god's appeal embraced a large base of small landholders rather than a small section of the elite. By the mid-fifteenth century, the Zumiao, as a registration unit on the government's household records, was rich enough for its abbot to be selected as the *jiashou* 甲首, or head of the district, responsible for tax collection and organizing labor service among the district dwellers. Furthermore, with its sizable estate and income, the Zumiao was an important resource for various public projects. It sponsored two shelters for male and female homeless people (thus upholding sexual morality among the poor), granaries for charity seed loans (for spring sowing), and hosted a community school. The temple and its god provided important service to the community and even reinforced its social norms.

The temple festival of Zumiao on the third day of the third month, the "double-three fair" (*chongsan hui* 重三會), brought together much of the town's population. Organized by the temple's association heads (*huishou*), there were the ritual of Offering (*jiao*), feasts, and music performances. The Zhenwu statue procession was carried through the town, a parade taking two days to complete. The procession route was carefully designed to pass through the outlaying areas of Foshan—another indicator of Zhenwu's function as the town's tutelary god. While the Zumiao itself was the epicenter of the gala, every district (*fang* 坊) in the town put up decorative displays and staged plays in their neighborhoods. One of the excitements of the celebration was the fireworks show, with firecrackers that had to be lit from the incense burner in the temple. Poor households were not excluded from participating, although the price they paid could be dear; some families sold their children in order to pay for the firecrackers.[7] A gazetteer criticized such sacrifice to be "shocking." As shocking as it was, the celebrations for Zhenwu's birth were all-inclusive, as befitting a local patron saint.

The New Year also witnessed a Zhenwu celebration in Foshan. On the sixth day of the first lunar month, the townsmen brought Zhenwu's statue from the Zumiao and carried it through the city in a palanquin with musical bands and a large entourage. It was believed that whoever placed their hands on the divine palanquin handles would receive good luck. Thus, the crowds swarmed to get closer to the images in the procession to such an extent that the procession was frequently stuck in traffic.

Nearly a hundred years after the Huang Xiaoyang rebellion—the event that authenticated Zhenwu as Foshan's tutelary god—a new temple record for the Zumiao was composed in 1642. The inscription, by Li Daiwen 李待問—a native son and a *jinshi* degree holder (1604)—credited the god not only as a protector but also the single benefactor of the prosperity that Foshan had enjoyed over the last century (*Foshan zhongyi xiang zhi* 8.14a):

> My county, Foshan, has traditionally been the crown of the Southern Seas region. All who took shelter here could gather their community together. The reason that the population grew day by day and carriages [of traders] from every direction converged on Foshan was due precisely to the efficacy of the Emperor [i.e. Zhenwu].
>
> 吾鄉佛山舊為南海之冠。凡庇茲宇者，咸獲鳩其妻保聚，生齒日繁。四方之舟車日以輻輳者，實惟帝之靈爽有以致之也。

A stone inscription at the Zumiao from 1685, at the beginning of the Qing dynasty, shows a further evolution in the popular perception of Zhenwu; it alludes to the god as a loving mother (*Foshan zhongyi xiang zhi* 8.14b):

> [The god's attitude] toward the people of Foshan is no less than that of a loving mother nurturing a newborn infant. … Why is it like this? Could it be that the south is the land of fire while the Emperor [i.e. Zhenwu] associates with the virtue of water; [the contrast of fire and water] stimulating each other here in our place? Or is it because Foshan follows the metal-casting trade, and the blazing of the fire is so extreme, that the water virtue also becomes extreme? … How could it be accidental that the Emperor is enshrined and receives offerings in this land?
>
> 其於佛山之民不啻如慈母之哺赤子，… 若是者何也？豈以南方火地，以帝為水德，於此固有相濟之功耶？… 抑佛山以鼓鑄為業，火之炎烈特勝，而水德之發揚亦特甚耶？…帝之廟食乎茲土者，豈偶然哉？

Here, the inscription noted the interesting circumstances in which a god of the north bestowed loving protection on a location at the southern tip of the empire. The inscription sought to justify this claim of the special favoritism in the light of the obvious theological contradictions. The Five Phrases cosmology provided the needed legitimacy, and the classical association of Zhenwu/Xuanwu and water was once again brought back to the picture. Prosperity grew in an orderly cosmos, one in which the opposites attract and complement each other. The old cosmological symbolism of Zhenwu (see Chapter One) was therefore reinterpreted to make the theology relevant to the current place and time.

Savior and child-grander

The *Record of the Listener* tells of a certain Mao Xuan 毛璿, a native of Quzhou (Zhejiang) and a student during the last decades of the Northern Song period. He returned home to sell the family house, due to his "incompetence in making a living" (*buneng zhisheng* 不能治生). One morning, he saw the apparitions of his grandparents and parents sitting in the main hall (*ting* 廳) of the house. "Xuan, in shock, bowed and asked: 'You have been dead for a long time; how could you be here?' The only one who answered was the father, who said, 'We see your situation is not good.' [The father] looked around the house and sighed, saying, 'you have a good future in your career; be patient'" 璿驚拜問曰:"去世已久，安得至此?" 皆不答。惟父曰:"見汝無好情況。" 因仰視屋太息曰:"汝前程尚遠，可寬心。" (*Yijian zhi*, jia 15.134–5, esp. 135). The father and son continued their conversation but switched to a different topic, that of postmortem life. The father pointed to the Zhenwu's image enshrined, admonishing the son to "carefully serve him; you will not go to hell after death but directly to the North Dipper (*beidou* 北斗) to be a disciple."

Mao's vision apparently reflected his need for self-assurance in face of losing the family legacy. During the conversation, the ancestors were concerned about him, not shamed by him. The father's ghost (or the young man's subconscious) predicted a prosperous career for the young scholar (undoubtedly in officialdom, thus canceling out his incompetence in momentary management). The financial crisis, by implication, was only temporary and eventually he would restore the family's fortunes. In light of this, the father's advice to worship Zhenwu was a surfacing of the debate in Mao's subconscious between his beliefs and doubts: What was the point of continuing to worship Zhenwu when the god did not even lift a finger to prevent him from bankruptcy? Worshipping trickster gods like Wutong or fox spirits seemed to be much more profitable (von Glahn 1991; Kang 2006). The answer was that the real benefit would come posthumously, when he would escape the purgatorial process through his newfound devotion.

Anxiety about postmortem fate was stronger and more pervasive in Song China than earlier periods for a variety reasons and resulted in the rapid growth of cults that rescued suffering souls from infernal punishments (Von Glahn 2004: 135–144). This psycho-religious trend also likely helped the growth of the worship of Zhenwu who was believed to have the power to protect his devotees from adverse judgment and lift them directly to heaven.

While Zhenwu might not be willing to rescue a man from financial torment, he was certainly sympathetic to couples facing the heirless crisis. Zhenwu's reputation or function of granting offspring became well developed in later imperial times. This was particular clear when we look into records of pilgrims. John Lagerwey, after studying a vast number of the steles on Mt Wudang, concludes that the main reasons motivating pilgrims going there during later imperial and early republic times were to pray for a son, to give thanks, and to fulfill a vow (Lagerwey 1992: 312). Among these three, praying for a son is the only clearly spelt out purpose. Wang Daokun 汪道昆 (1525–1593; *jinshi* 1547), a native of the neighboring Anhui province and a scholar-official, specified that he went to Mt Wudang with his childless friend to pray to Zhenwu for an offspring. Xu Xuemo 徐學謨 (1522–1593, *jinshi* 1550), another high-ranking scholar-official, took his junior colleague, a *jinshi* degree-holder and a native from Zhangpu, Fujian province, all the way to the summit of Wudang in order to pray for a son ([Wanli] *Xiangyang fuzhi* 48.17, 28). Another Zhenwu pilgrimage site that was believed to be specifically responsive to prayers for sons was Mt Qiyun in Anhui province. Emperor

Jiajing of the Ming dynasty ordered the Heavenly Master to carry out a *Jiao* ritual there in 1532 to pray for a son (*Qiyun shan zhi*). The very next year, his first son was born. Li Rihua 李日華 (1565–1635), another example, was a native of Jiaxing, Zhejiang, and a scholar-official, whose sons died in infancy. He learned from his father that their neighbors who had new born children would conducted pilgrimages to Mt Qiyuan to pray to Zhenwu on the behalf of the infants and these babies all survived well. Li accordingly made a pilgrimage and soon his wife became pregnant and gave birth to a healthy son. Li's story tells us not only his personal belief but also the local belief in Zhenwu's power to grant and protect children.

Weather, illness, and water

Weather and disease were another two concerns for which people prayed to Zhenwu. During the period from 1195 to 1200 in Chengdu (Sichuan province), a local elite, Liu Dingxing 劉鼎新, and a Daoist cleric (*daoshi*), Zhang Yuanjian, made a collaborative petition to the magistrate: they would like to establish a temple dedicated to Zhenwu in order to pray to him at "flood, drought, and epidemics" (*shuihan jiyi* 水旱疫疾). The petition was granted and the temple was soon completed. People went to the new temple to pray for rain, fair weather, and the cure of diseases. The god was so responsive in answering prayers that the locals—this time, including ordinary people and government clerks (*limin* 吏民)—went to see the magistrate again to petition for an official honorific title for their Zhenwu temple, and they got it. They then erected a stele to commemorate the official recognition.

Zhenwu's power over weather grew out of his prominence in the Thunder Rites, whose main functions were to exorcise demons and regulate the weather. His ability to secure favorable weather then came to be recognized on its own. Beginning in the mid-Northern Song period at the latest, his proficiency in this regard was demonstrated by the attention paid to him in state rituals. During periodic droughts in Kaifeng, Emperors Song Renzong and Song Yingzong came to pray for rain at the Auspicious Fountain—Sweet Spring Monastery which was dedicated to Zhenwu (*Songshi* 11.220, 13.225).[8] Local administrators also requested Zhenwu's support in weather-related matters when their jurisdictions suffered from weather conditions. In the summer of 1049, Zhang Fangping 張方平 (1007–1091), prefect (*zhifu* 知府) of Jiangning (present-day Nanjing, Jiangsu province) at the time, included Zhenwu in his prayers to stop excessive rain (*Lequan ji* 35.10b). Chen Zao 陳造 (1133–1203, *jinshi* 1175), a scholar-official, composed ritual memorials to be submitted to Zhenwu for snowfall and rain (*Jinaghu changweng ji* 39.4–5, and 39.32).

Furthermore, the god's power in weather control was perceived as going beyond the limitation of locality. When courtier Wang Yan 王炎 in Hangzhou in the east Zhejiang province received a new appointment in Sichuan in the west which was undergoing a devastating drought, he decided to seek help from Zhenwu (discussed in Chapter Four). Wang took a detour to Mt Wudang to make a pilgrimage to

Zhenwu to bring rain to Sichuan. According to a staff member in Wang's administration, the appeal resulted in rainstorms across Sichuan even before Wang reached there, thereby saving the harvest and preventing famine (*Yijian zhi*, kui 2.1231).

One of Zhenwu's most beneficial qualities was his ability to bring relief from sickness. As an exorcist deity, Zhenwu's job descriptions included chasing away harmful spirits who possessed human beings and caused them to be sick (both physically and mentally). The Auspicious Fountain—Sweet Spring Monastery in Northern Song Kaifeng (see Chapter Two), for example, boasted a water fountain with therapeutic powers that cured people suffering from epidemics. The *Yijian zhi* recounts a woman hanging up a Zhenwu portrait after her husband became so ill that he fell unconscious (*Yijian zhi* bu 24.1770), and another woman recited Zhenwu incantations day and night when her son developed a high fever and was incapacitated for several days (*Yijian san zhi* jen.8.1538–9). Their direct appeal to Zhenwu indicated that the belief in Zhenwu's therapeutic power among the laity grew firm and clear during the Song dynasty.

While acquiring new symbolism and power during the course of the growth of his worship, Zhenwu retained his old cosmological force as the symbol of water. In the Jiangnan area of Southern Song, people worshipped Zhenwu at home to ward off (*yan* 厭) fire disasters (*Xishang futan*, shang 16b). A similar practice was observed in the Forbidden City in Beijing where Zhenwu statures were enshrined many government bureaus for protection against fire (Hsü 1947).

The multivocality of Zhenwu's symbolism was reflected in the various miracles attributed to him. His adherents also expected him to bring a variety of blessings. Indeed, these powers extended from Zhenwu's original role in exorcism, and were the contributions of his devotees. While soldiers and common people worshipped Zhenwu as an individual choice, their personal devotion could be transformed into a public gesture. The Zhenwu temple that the soldiers of the Gongsheng regiment built went beyond a monument of religiosity; it became a landmark of state power to the provincial population without deliberated enforcement of the central court. The Song emperors, whatever their belief in Zhenwu, did not comprehend the significance of using him to enhance state authority. The only instance in which we found Zhenwu being turned into such a symbol was the Zhenwu temple that General Wang Guangzu rebuilt because of his private belief in the god's power.

The religious aspects of the art of war were best preserved in Daoist liturgical manuals. Occult rituals for military purposes, in texts such as the *Heavenly Marrow* that heavily invoked Zhenwu, added a new dimension to the power of the god. The military symbolism made him the prime candidate for use as a tutelary god in the Ming dynasty for ambitious men like the Prince of Yen, the future Emperor Yongle, and his consult, Yao Guaoxiao. The ramifications of this choice can be observed in the massive reconstruction of Mt Wudang, the headquarters of the Zhenwu cult, by Yongle after his successful usurpation. In the meantime, local people also credited him with protecting their communities and came to worship him as a tutelary god. They appealed to him for all sorts of benefits. By the end of the Ming dynasty Zhenwu had become a god for all people with a legacy that would last to the present day.

The religious landscape of China is as complex as the gods who inhabit it. Many actors and groups have been involved in giving it shape and focus. This study argues that the Daoist priests played the major role in promoting Zhenwu at the early stages of the god's career. Zhenwu veneration was popular among Daoist clerics because he was the "ancestral master" with whom they practiced meditation at a daily basis. Meditative innovation allowed priests to appropriate shamanic practices, such as falling in trances, and transform them into legitimate Daoist techniques. Through the proper methods, priests could thus turn themselves into Zhenwu. These practices not only introduced an innovative ritual to Daoism but also created a close bond between Zhenwu and those participating in the religious services dedicated to him.

Daoist clerics who carried out rituals in Zhenwu's name brought the worship of the god to the people. In the meantime, Daoist monastics on Mt Wudang reinvented the mountain into an axis mundi of Zhenwu. While the religious experts controlled most of the resources that allowed them to mold the mountain's symbolism, ordinary pilgrims managed to add their own perceptions and build on the clerics' foundation. At the top of the hierarchy, the sovereigns, with even more resources to draw on, played their part in the game of negotiating the symbolism of Zhenwu and Mt Wudang.

In the mix, different legends and miracles were created. On the one hand, Zhenwu represented the established order; he was a god who exorcised demons, and removed harmful elements from society. He embodied a military power that could bring security to a locale but was not fully controlled by the state and civil officials. This made Zhenwu accessible to members of the lower orders and virtually anyone who paid him homage. While trickster deities could serve as a tool of negotiation for marginal social groups (Shahar and Weller 1996; Kang 2006), a state-endorsed deity could also side with the rebellious. Watson (1985) famously argued that the Chinese state was more concerned about orthopraxy than orthodoxy and thus left space for negotiation. As people took advantage of the opportunity, the symbolism of Zhenwu was interpreted and reinterpreted. New theological characteristics developed from old ones and added new material. Like the roof of a temple composed of imbricated tiles, the Zhenwu godhead grew to encompass a variety of traits but maintained its distinct character.

For centuries the worship of Zhenwu was an empire-wide phenomenon whose depth and breadth are beyond the scope of this work. Among the many aspects that have been omitted are the manner in which Zhenwu was projected in popular literature, such as in *The Journey to the North*, in spirit writings, and in pilgrimage sites other than Mt Wudang. It is hoped that this study will inspire further investigation and bring all aspects of the Zhenwu story to fruition.

Appendix 1

The *Qisheng lu*

The *Daoist Cannon* completed in 1453 includes 18 titles devoted to honoring Zhenwu (see the list below). There are additional ritual anthologies in the *Canon* containing chapters of the liturgy paying veneration to him, such as the "Ritual of Grand Offering to the Perfected Warrior, Numinous and Responsive" (Zhenwu lingying da jiaoyi 真武靈應大醮儀) in the *Grand Complete Collection of Models for Rites of the Portal of Dao* (*Daomen kefan daquan ji* j.63–68, ZHDZ 42.415–42.429). Among them, the most informative one for Zhenwu miracles is arguably *Xuantian shangdi qisheng lu* 玄天上帝啟聖錄 (hereafter, *Qisheng lu*). This study admittedly made minimum use of the *Qisheng lu* in recounting the history of Zhenwu worship. Here, through a critical reading of this text, I first discuss the problems of the text and then the methodology of utilizing it.

There are three issues that undermine the *Qisheng lu* as a historical record: the uncertainty of its alleged origin, its repeated redaction, and, most importantly, the editorial style that distorted factual reality in order to reveal the "higher truth." Daoist texts often went through extended enlargement after they first took shape; a good example is the *Scripture of Salvation* (Strickmann 1978; Schipper and Verellen, eds. 214–215, 1083–1084). On the other hand, a latter-day corpus may incorporate some much older texts extensively, the *Master Red Pine's Petition Almanac* quickly comes to mind. Thus, a text in the *Daoist Canon* could be of ancient origin but contain materials of a later time, and vice versa. It is true that the past two decades or so have witnessed the publication of a number of monumental reference works that are partially or entirely devoted to bibliographical discussions on the Ming *Daoist Canon*, and this study benefits from them enormously (Boltz 1987; Ren *et al.* 1991; Kohn 2000; Schipper and Verellen 2004; Pregadio 2006). Nevertheless, the dating of the *Qisheng lu* is still under question.

The current version of the *Qisheng lu* is made up of nine chapters: The first chapter is primarily an episodic narrative of Zhenwu's life from his birth as the prince of the Pure and Joy kingdom to his apotheosis. Chapters 2–9 consist exemplary, edifying, or miracle stories related to Zhenwu or his worshippers. The text self-claims to be the result or product of an imperial project decreed by Emperor Song Renzong to collect accounts about Zhenwu in order to honor the god. Yet some obvious historical errors contained in the volume raise questions over this alleged origin. A story in chapter 2 told that Zhenwu provided special protective services during the birth of Princess Jingguo 荊國, the 11th daughter of Renzong (*Qisheng lu*, j.2, ZHDZ 30.647b). However, it gave the wrong year of the princess's birth and claimed that she died at the age of 13 while in reality she lived to be 24 (*Songshi* 248.8778). These may be trivial details, but they are not the kind of errors that would appear in a court project.

In addition, the *Qisheng lu* was re-edited more than once after its completion and thus the materials contained are not necessarily from the Song. As Hung-I Chuang (1994) points out, chapter 1 of the current version is a later addition since, in one of the most obvious examples, it quotes the *Zongzhen ji* compiled by Liu Daoming in the late thirteenth century. Zhang Shouqing, the prominent abbot and contemporary of Liu Daoming but slightly later (see Chapter Four of this study), re-carved the printing blocks of the *Qisheng lu*, under the title of *Xuanwu qisheng ji* 玄武啓聖記.[1] It is probably in this version that the current chapter 1 made its way into the *Qisheng lu*.[2] Scholars used to accept chapters 2–9 of the *Qisheng lu* as legitimate Song sources, although not without accompanying footnotes to indicate some reservations about the date of their compilation (Davis 2001). The controversy, nevertheless, reached a new dimension when Pierre-Henry de Bruyn challenged the authenticity of the entire text in his meticulously researched dissertation on Mt Wudang (1997). In a more recent article, de Bruyn contends that the current version of the *Qisheng lu* was the product of redaction by Ming Daoists to "convince its readers that 'the true Loard Zhenwu was the god of the imperial family of the Song dynasty'" (2004: 555). The Ming Daoists altered the text to such an extent that, according to de Bruyn, it can no longer be treated as a Song source. De Bruyn has a good point. Nevertheless, the *Qisheng lu* was already cited by gazetteers in Southern Song. The citations show that the basic form of the text had already taken shape by then.

What really hindered the *Qisheng lu* being deployed as an historical account, I would suggest, is its hagiographic nature. The original compilers and later editors deliberately altered facts in order to tell a "higher truth." A good example is the story about a séance in which Zhenwu predicted the birth of Emperor Song Renzong (*Qisheng lu*, j.3, ZHDZ 30.653ab). In the story, Zhang Shouzhen, the founding abbot of the Supreme Clarity Great Peace Palace, took in his monastery a certain Fu Hong 傅鴻. Later, Zhenwu possessed Fu Hong to deliver a message (*tuoshen jiangyan* 托身降言) for Zhang Shouqing to "pass on to the emperor of the Song dynasty on my behalf" (*wei wu chuanbao Songchao tianzi* 為吾傳報宋朝天子). The divination announced that the Barefoot God (Chijiao daxian 赤腳大仙) was to descend from heaven to earth. The implication is clear, a new emperor was to be born. Zhang Shouzhen duly reported the prophecy to local administer who then reported it to the court. "At the time, the emperor read [the report] personally; he was both surprised and pleased. Later, as predicted,… the crown prince was born. This was Emperor Renzong" (時，皇帝御覽，驚喜交集。 後，果… 降慶太子，即仁廟是也。ZHDZ 30.653b).

The belief that Emperor Renzong (1010–1063, r. 1023–1063) was an incarnation of the Barefoot God was in wide circulation in Song times. The editor of the *Qisheng lu* deliberately assimilated it into the Zhenwu lore, as attested by the chronological flaw contained. Zhang Shouzhen, the key figure in the story, died before Emperor Taizong (939–997, r. 976–997) in 996.[3] If Zhang ever passed on the divine message to the court, it would be that of Taizong, grandfather of Renzong. Taizong, had multiple adult sons. A prophecy announcing a future imperial grandson to be a divine incarnation would be interpreted as an implicit endorsement for the father-to-be as the next emperor. This would make Zhang dangerously suspicious of Taizong.[4] The oracle could be great news only to Zhenzong (968–1022, r. 998–1022), father of Renzong, who was desperate for a male heir for since his sons born earlier had all died when the emperor reached age 40. A prophecy of another son soon to be born to him (with a bonus of being divine incarnation) would definitely make the emperor "surprised and pleased." However, Zhang Shouzhen, dead by then, could not possibly have delivered the prophecy to Zhenzong's court.

The editor of the *Qisheng lu* was aware of the dilemma and thus skipped the identity of the emperor in the story. While the editor probably thought he was telling a higher truth that Zhenwu was "the family god of the Song emperors," he nevertheless took the liberty to scramble together elements from different sources that were originally unrelated to Zhenwu. This liberal attitude in editing undermined the credibility of the *Qisheng lu* as a source of historical facts.

The central question here is whether the *Qisheng lu*, in its current version, possesses any value for the study of the Zhenwu cult in Song times. It does, but not for the reconstruction of the cult's chronology. As Glen Dudbridge expressed in his study of the *Guangyi ji* by Dai Fu 戴孚 of the Tang dynasty, "flaws in chronology disqualify any claim to record actual events as they happened, but we can adopt a style of reading which sees the story expressing public perceptions; and these respond to echoes of the same perceptions in other—and other kinds of—sources" (Dudbridge 1995: 102–103). The perceptions in the *Qisheng lu* indeed echo other sources from Song times.

De Bruyn is correct in asserting that the redaction of the *Qisheng lu* in the *Daoist Canon* was not finalized until Ming times. Yet it would be misleading to ignore the fact that the basic form of the text took shape by the early Southern Song period. The text's origin as an imperial project is questionable and the royal worship described in it are not necessarily historical facts. However, it preserves materials consonant with other sources, and provides rich detail of veneration practices otherwise unavailable. As it stands, the *Qisheng lu* cannot and should not be used as a prime source to reconstruct the actual events (especially the imperial patronage) of the Zhenwu cult but it is valuable for studying the general practices of Zhenwu worship during Song times when employed with caution and with the same discretion as employed in using secular records.

List of texts in the *Daozang* dedicated to the worship of Zhenwu

1. TC 27   *Yuanshi tianzun shuo Beifang Zhenwu miaojing* 元始天尊說北方真武妙經
2. TC 203   *Xuandi dengyi* 玄帝燈儀

Appendix 1   119

3. TC 655   *Taishang shuo Ziwei shenbing huguo xiaomo jing* 太上說紫微神兵護國消魔經
4. TC 663   *Xuantian shangdi shuo bao fumu enzhong jing* 玄天上帝說報父母恩重經
5. TC 754   *Taishang shuo Xuantian dasheng Zhenwu benzhuan shenzhou miaojing* 太上說玄天大聖真武本傳神咒妙經 (With commentary)
6. TC 775   *Taishang shuo Xuantian dasheng Zhenwu benzhuan shenzhou miaojing* 太上說玄天大聖真武本傳神咒妙經 (Scripture alone)
7. TC 776   *Zhenwu lingying zhenjun zengshang yousheng zunhao cewen* 真武靈應真君增上佑聖尊號冊文
8. TC 814   *Zhenwu lingying hushi xiaozai miezui baochan* 真武靈應護世消災滅罪寶懺
9. TC 815   *Beiji Zhenwu puci dushi fachan* 北極真武普慈度世法懺
10. TC 816 *Beiji Zhenwu yousheng zhenjun liwen* 北極真武佑聖真君禮文
11. TC 958 *Xuantian shangdi qisheng lu* 玄天上帝啟聖錄
12. TC 959 *Daming Xuantian shangdi ruiying tulu* 大明玄天上帝瑞應圖錄
13. TC 960 *Yuzhi Zhenwu miao bei* 御製真武廟碑
14. TC 961 *Xuantian shangdi qisheng lingyi lu* 玄天上帝啟聖靈異錄
15. TC 962 *Wudang fudi zongzhen ji* 武當福地總真集
16. TC 963 *Wudang jisheng ji* 武當紀勝集
17. TC 1213 Taishang Xuantian Zhenwu wushang jiangjun lu 太上玄天真武無上將軍錄
18. TC 1482 *Xuantian shangdi baizi shenghao* 玄天上帝百字聖號

Appendix 2

Monasteries in Emperor Yongle's Mt Wudang project

Name of the monasteries in Emperor Yongle's project	Description in Chijian Dayue Taihe shan zhi 敕建大岳太和山志 (Column A)	Description in Chijian Dayue Taihe shan zhi 敕建大岳太和山志 (Column B)
Taixuan zixiao gong 太玄紫霄宮	"It is the old Purple Empyrean Primordial Saint Palace." P. 138	
Taihe gong 太和宮		New; beneath the Golden Pavilion
Golden Pavilion 金頂	"There was a small bronze hall before." P. 137	
Xingsheng Wulong gong 興聖五龍宮	"It is the old Numinous Response Palace of the Five Dragons." P. 137	
Nanyang gong 南岩宮	"It is the old Palace of the Perfected and Celebrated Heavenly One ." P. 138	
Yuzhen gong 遇真宮	"Zhang Sanfeng built a cloister here." P. 139	
Jingle gong 淨樂宮		New; located in city of Junzhou, not on Mt Wudang
Qingwei gong 清微宮	"…where Zhang Shouqing practices self-cultivation in the past." P. 139.	
Chaotian gong 朝天宮	"… there had been good-sized functional shrines before, but was in ruin [by 1412]" P. 140.	
Wulong xinggong 五龍行宮	"There were temple-complex which were ruined due to wars." P. 140	

Appendix 2 121

(continued)

Name of the monasteries in Emperor Yongle's project	Description in Chijian Dayue Taihe shan zhi 敕建大岳太和山志 *(Column A)*	Description in Chijian Dayue Taihe shan zhi 敕建大岳太和山志 *(Column B)*
Taixuan guan 太玄觀	"The entrance cloister of the Laozi Cliff [temple] of old times." P. 140	
Yuanhe guan 元和觀	"There was an old shrine here but not majesty enough." P. 140	
Fuzhen guan 復真觀	"There had been a shrine here, but did not survive [by 1412]." P. 140	
Huilong guan 回龍觀	"There had been a shrine here but did not survive [by 1412]." P. 141	
Renwei guan 仁威觀	"It was in a [different] old location [before 1412]." P. 141	
Weilie guan 威烈觀	"There were shrine-complex for worshipping King Awesome Ferocity (Weilei) [i.e. Yao Jian]." P. 141	
Baxian guan 八仙觀	The shrine here had been empty [by 1412]." P. 141.	
Longquan guan 龍泉觀	"It was in a [different] old location [before 1412]." P. 141	
Taichang guan 太常觀	"There was an old temple here." Pp. 141–142.	
Ziran an 自然庵		New. Alleged hermitage of Chen Tuan. No temples there before 1412.
Langmei xianweng ci 榔梅仙翁祠	"The old temple complex did not exist due to wars; only the ruining remained [by 1412]." P. 142	
Wuya miao 烏鴉廟	There had been a shrine but did not exist [by 1412]." P. 142.	
Heihu miao 黑虎廟	"It was in a different old location." P. 142	
Guanwang miao 關王廟	"There was an old Shrine of the Perfected Lord who Exalt Peace (Chongning zhenjun) here [before 1412]." P. 143	
Sanqing guan 三清觀		Post-Yuan but not related to the 1412 project.
Taishang guan 太上觀		
Yuxu gong 玉虛宮		New. Not on the mountain.

(continued on next page)

(continued)

Name of the monasteries in Emperor Yongle's project	Description in Chijian Dayue Taihe shan zhi 敕建大岳太和山志 (Column A)	Description in Chijian Dayue Taihe shan zhi 敕建大岳太和山志 (Column B)
Chongfu yan 崇福岩		New temple built in 1412
Qingshui yan 清水岩	"There were shrines here but all in ruin [by 1412]" P. 93.	
Xianlü yan 仙侶岩	"There were statures here but no worshipping activities [by 1412]." P. 93.	
Lingxu yan 靈虛岩		Alleged residence of Sun Simiao and Chen Tuan. No temples until the 1412 project.
Yinxian yan 隱仙岩		A site where ascetics live historically. No temples until 1412 project.
Taishang yan 太上岩	A cave temple began in 1038 (Song Tiansheng 9)	Not included in the 1412 project.
Laolao dian 老姥殿		New in 1412
Heilong tan miao 黑龍潭廟	"There was a temple here, the ruin is still there."	
Heilong tan 黑龍潭廟	"There is a temple within the cliff; prayers said there are answered all the time."	Not included in the 1412 project.

Column A shows monasteries and temples that were built on the locations where old temples had been; Column B shows the monasteries and temples built on new sites.

Notes

Introduction

1 The day corresponded to the 19th day of the 12th month of the 10th year of Khubilai's regime (known to Chinese history as the sixth year of the Zhiyuan 至元 era) in the Chinese calendar. The calendar conversion in this study uses the "Western–Chinese Calendar Converter—2000 years" (http://www.sinica.edu.tw/~tdbproj/sinocal/luso.html) provided by the Institute of History and Philology, Academia Sinica.
2 The following account is based on "Yuan chuangjian Zhenwu miao lingyi ji" 元創建真武廟靈異記 and "Yuan chuangjian Zhaoying gong bei" 元創建昭應宮碑, both written by Xu Shilong 徐世隆 (CE 1206–1285), and a second "Yuan chuangjian Zhaoying gong bei" by Wang Pan 王磐 (CE 1202–1293). They are collected in *Xuantian shangdi qisheng lingyi lu* 玄天上帝啓聖靈應錄 (TC 961; hereafter *Lingying lu*) j.1 (see ZHDZ 30.699a–700c). Also see *Jinshi lüe* 1100–1102.
3 The Golden Water River is often confused with the nearby and much better known Sorghum River (*Gaoliang he* 高梁河) in later records of this event. They are two different rivers; see *Qinding rixiao jiuwen kao* 欽定日下舊聞考 43.8a (SKQS edn).
4 The personal beliefs of Chabi and Khubilai tended toward Tibetan Buddhism (Rossabi 1988: 14, 39; Jing 1994: 41).
5 It is in accordance with the theory of the Cycle of the Five Virtues (*wude zhongshi* 五德終始) related to the all-inclusive Five Phases cosmology. This cyclic model was one of the most influential political legitimacy theories in China since classical times.
6 For example, the *Scripture of Quelling Demons by the Divine Soldiers for the Protection of the State, Spoken by the Most High* (Taishang shuo Ziwei shenbing huguo xiaomo jing 太上說紫微神兵護國消魔經; TC 655).
7 See "Edict of changing the characters [that are same as those in] the name of the holy ancestor" (Shengzu ming yi qi zi zhao 聖祖名易其字詔) in *The Collection of the Grand Edicts of the Song* (*Song da zhaoling ji* 宋大詔令集), 135.475. For a more detailed account of the entire event, see "Stele of the Celestial Celebration Monastery (Tianqing guan bei 天慶觀碑)," erected in 1014 (*Jinshi lüe* 249–250). For an analysis of the political background and theological implication behind this event see Cahill 1980 and Jing 2002: 73–84.
8 The same decree also ordered that gods' names containing the other character of the divine ancestor's name, *lang*, had their names changed to *ming* 明. Both characters mean "bright."
9 Of course, some sources returned to the use of Xuanwu. However, the word *xuan* became taboo again during the Qing dynasty (1644–1911), thanks to its second emperor, Kangxi (r. 1662–1722), whose personal name was Xuanye 玄燁. Written records that used Xuanwu were changed to Yuanwu 元武. In sum, the god was rarely addressed by his original appellation, Xuanwu.
10 A rubbing of this stone inscription is in *Beijing tushu guan cang lidai shike shiliao* 北京圖書館藏歷代石刻史料 (Collection of Chinese stone rubbings throughout the dynasties in the Peking Library), vol. 41.7. For a modern print version, see *Jinshi lüe*, 306–308.

124 *Notes*

This scripture is included in the Ming *Daoist Canon* under an identical title except for one additional character, "wondrous" (*miao* 妙), in front of the word "scripture" (see ZHDZ 30.522). The stele and the canonical versions are virtually the same; the canonical version includes two extra invocations near the end of the main text while the stele contains an additional appendix.

11 Kaihuang, or "Inaugural Luminary," was originally a Daoist *kalpa*-cycle of antique times. It was adopted as a reign name by Emperor Sui Wen (r. 581–604) between CE 581 and 600.
12 *Daofa huiyuan*, j. 253, ZHDZ 38.426.a.
13 A good example is Chen Pu (fl. 1078); see Eskildsen 2001.
14 For example, Zhenyan 證嚴 *fashi* of the Tz'u-chi 慈濟 Association.
15 During the Song period and later, by law, ordination required obtaining licenses from the state first (*Song huiyao*, Daoshi, 1.22b). The ordination licenses were so monetarily valuable that they became a commodity (Lin 1962). Many religious specialists were not ready to pay this license fee.

1 A god in formation

1 The Year Star was an imaginary star (a "shadow Jupiter" as David Hawkes termed it) created by ancient Chinese astronomers for the convenience of describing and calculating the motions of the Sun and Moon; for a detailed explanation, see Hawkes 1985: 80.
2 The transformation from a turtle alone to a turtle encircled by a snake was not a simple linear development. The turtle by itself was still used during the Eastern Han period, for example, Zhang Heng 張衡 (CE 78–139), in his "Lingxian 靈憲," used *linggui* ("spiritual turtle") where normally the term Xuanwu would be used; see *Quan Houhan wen* 55.4a–6b, esp. 5a.
3 *Shuowen jiezi zhu* 13, xia, 9a–b. Modern scholars have different opinions regarding the possible symbolic meanings of the image of the entwined turtle and snake; see Major 1986: 65–86.
4 *Shiji* 27.1289–1308. At present, there are no pre-Han archeological discoveries presenting the Four Animals in full. The design of a dragon and a tiger opposite each other was discovered at a tomb from the Yangshao period (Li 1999) and on a side of the coffin of Duke Yi of Zeng (Zenghou yi 曾侯乙), dated to 433 BCE (Sun & Kistemaker 1997: 19). Minao Hayashi maintains that the combination of a dragon and a tiger represent the Four Animals, and the other two were dropped because of limited space on the coffin (Hayashi 1989: 17). Yet there were other combinations of zoomorphic quartet in classical times that included a dragon and a tiger but not a turtle (Major 1986: 67). Thus, we cannot presume that Xuanwu was implied in representations of a dragon and a tiger on the coffin of the Duke Yi of Zeng.
5 *Xiu* or "lodges" referred to the 28 asterisms that ancient Chinese astronomers selected as measurements for observing and describing the motion in the nocturnal sky. The earliest known record of the complete "28 lodges" was discovered on the coffin of Duke Yi of Zeng.
6 *Liji zhushu* 3.12a. Kong Yingda of early Tang times noted in his commentary that the Four Animals were also used in military banners during his lifetime.
7 The term, Four Animals or *sishou*, was used by Zheng Xuan 鄭玄 (CE 127–200) in his commentary, see *Liji zhushu* 3.12a. The Four Animals were also known as "four divinities" (*sishen* 四神). To avoid confusion, it is worth mentioning another set of four symbols that are very similar, the "four numinous" (*siling* 四靈), consisting of a dragon, phoenix, turtle and, instead of a tiger, a *lin* 麟, commonly rendered into English as a unicorn.
8 Alternative labels for the categories included *wucai* 五才, or Five Materials, and *wude* 五德, or Five Virtues (reads: powers). For a survey of the scholarly debate over the rendering of *wuxing*, see Wang 2000: 3, 76.
9 See "Heavenly Pattern," translated by Major 1993: 72, with my own emphasis and minor modifications.

10 The Green Dragon Gate and Xuanwu Gate were cited in *Shiji* 8.386, note 2; the White Tiger Gate was mentioned in *Hanshu* 99.4191, and the Vermillion Bird Gate (called Zhuniao instead of Zhuque) in *Hanshu* 99.4145.

11 There are no systemic records of the construction of the capital of the Six Dynasties. We know of the Vermillion Bird Gate from accounts of the punishment of Yang Quanqi 楊佺期 (CE ?–399). After losing a battle with Huan Xuan 桓玄 (CE 369–404), Yang Quanqi was decapitated. His head then was sent back to the capital, Jiankang, to be held up for display, and the site chosen for the spectacle was the Vermillion Bird Gate (*Zhuque men* 朱雀門); see *Jinshu* 84.2201.

12 Emperor Xiaoming (r. 512–528) of the Northern Wei named his era as Shengui or Divine Turtle (CE 518–519). However, the Chinese characters used was *gui* 龜, not Xuanwu.

13 "Xuanwu is an alternative name of the black turtle" (*Xuanwu ji wugui zhi yiming* 玄武即烏龜之異名), see *Xishang futan*, shang, 6a.

14 The text was first written down by Yang Xi 楊羲 (330–386?) in séances between CE 364–370 and reedited by Tao Hongjing 陶弘景 (CE 452–536); see Strickmann 1977; Robinet 1984: 137–138; Bokenkamp 1997: 193 and 200 n. 20.

15 This geographic arrangement matches classical numerology in that six is the number of the north. In addition, in correlative cosmology north is associated with the great *yin* force and death.

16 The Celestial Masters school appeared to go through a profound change after the Supreme Clarity revelations; see Bokenkamp 1997: 189. I am aware of the debate over the dating of this text; for a detailed discussion, see Kleeman 2004.

17 According to the *Inner Explanation*, Lord Lao issued three different kinds of practices designed for the three regions of humankind according to the specific geographic pneumas: the Great Way of Inaction for the Central Kingdom, the Way of the Buddha for barbaric kingdoms outside the Central Kingdom, and the Way of the Pure Contract for Chu and Yue; see Bokenkamp 1997: 209.

18 For a discussion of the text, see Schipper and Verellen eds. 2004: 543–544. The text also can be found as a chapter in the *Wondrous scripture of North Emperor's Divine Incantations for Subduing Demons Set Forth by Heavenly Worthy of Primordial Beginning* (*Taishang Yuanshi Tianzun shuo Beidi fumo shenzhou miaojing* 太上元始天尊說北帝伏魔神咒妙經, TC 1412).

19 There are two editions of the *Evidential Miracles* extent: one is an individual book and the other comprises chapters 117–121 of the *Yunji qiqian* (TC 1032). The story of Fan Lingyan is available only in the *Yunji qiqian* version.

20 *Taishang zhuguo jiumin zongzhen miyao* j.3, ZHDZ 30.332a. For a biographical account of Deng, see "*Tang Dongjing Futang guan Deng tianshi jie* 唐東京福唐觀鄧天師碣" by Li Yong 李邕 (*Jinshi lüe* 125–126).

21 The citation is from the *Daode jing*, j.39.

22 See, for example, "Section of the Palaces of the Thearchs and Masters of Clarity and Tenuity" (*Qingwei dishi gong fenpin* 清微帝師宮分品) in *Daofa huiyuan* j.3, in ZHDZ 36.18. For more discussion on the offices of the Four Saints, see Chapter Four.

23 The name of Su Zhongchang is found in the eulogy of Su Song's fourth son, Su Xi, see "Gu Huiyouge Daizhi zhishi Sugong muzhi ming" 故徽猷閣待制致仕蘇公墓誌銘, in *Fuxi ji* 浮溪集 25.1a–6a, esp. 1b. Su Zhongchang's age is found in *Chengxiang Weigong* 2.3a. For Ms Zhang's family background and the content of her dowry, see *Chengxiang Weigong* 2.5a.

24 The abbey was built under the auspices of the Empress Dowager Wei 韋, the mother of the first emperor of the Southern Song, Gaozong (r. 1127–1162). She was a devotee of the Four Saints from her days as an imperial concubine of Huizong. She was convinced that the Four Saints protected her son, the future Emperor Gaozong, when he served as an emissary to and hostage of the army of the Jurchen Jin during the siege of Kaifeng in 1126. She herself was held as a hostage of the Jin from 1127 to 1142 and she kept the portraits [*huixiang* 繪像] of the Four Saints with her. After returning to the Song court in Hangzhou, she financed

126 *Notes*

   the building of the Four Saints Daoist Monastery with her own "rouge stipend" in order to repay their blessing (*Mengliang lu* 8.12b–13a; *Xianchun Lin'an zhi* 13.11).
25 The quotation is as follows: "At the Four Saints Daoist Monastery in Lin'an [present Hangzhou] in the 6th month [of the lunar calendar], men and women of the entire city gathered to pray and worship. Someone wondered how it could appeal to people to such an extent; [Lu Jiuyuan] replied: 'Simply because of divine favoritism [*lit.* injustice] in rewarding and punishing [i.e., playing favoritism to whoever prayed there]"; see *Xiangshan quanji* 34.25b.

2 A god in full: the Song dynasty

1 According to a stele inscription of CE 1294, the Huxiu si 虎岫寺 in Jinjiang 晉江 county, Fujian, originally called Zhenwu Palace (*gong*) was established during the reign of Zhenguan 貞觀 (627–649) of Emperor Tang Taizong (Li, Guohong 1998: 210). There is a gap of 650 years between the composition of the inscription and the claimed origin, and there was no earlier source cited in the inscription to support the claim. The Five Dragons Palace on Mt Wudang, coincidentally or not, also claimed a history back to the reign of Zhenguan, but if true, it is unlikely that palace was built to honor Zhenwu; see the discussion in Chapter Four.
2 Emperor Song Taizong dedicated the abbey to the Black Killer in order to express his gratitude for the god's reported oracles endorsing his assumption of the throne (*Yunji qiqian* 103.2223; Davis 2001: 72).
3 Three different sources are used here to piece together the time and location of the incident: For the year of Kong's *jinshi* degree, see *Kongshi zuting guangji* 7b. Kong's tomb inscription by Wang Anshi indicates the time he took the *tuiguan* position in Ningzhou as well as the fact that the snake appeared when the Daoists were producing a Zhenwu image (*Linchuan xiansheng wenji* 91.6b–9a). The *Songshi* informs us that the venue was the Zhenwu Hall of the abbey (*Songshi* 297.2883).
4 The Celestial Celebration Monastery was a network of temples throughout the empire established by Song Zhenzong's decree in 1009; see "Ling Fu, Zhou, Jun, Jian, Guan, Xian, wu gongguan chu jian Tianqing guan zhao 令府州軍監關縣無宮觀處建天慶觀詔" *Song da zhaoling ji* 179.647.
5 For example, the Celestial Celebration Monastery in Jizhou (present-day Jining 濟寧), Shandong, hosted no Zhenwu Hall until the final decades of the Northern Song dynasty (*Lejing ji* 6.1a-3b).
6 The Gongsheng regiment of mounted troops, created in CE 965, was part of the Palace Command (Dianqian si 殿前司) whose base was located in the southeast corner of the inner city (*neicheng* 內城) of Kaifeng; see *Tōkei mukaroku* 139.
7 The shrine was called alternatively the Zhenwu ci or Zhenwu tang (堂). The *Song huiyao* (li 5.14.472) supplies the most detailed description of the event and the development of the temple. Other standard sources for Song history are misleading if not erroneous on this topic. The *Songshi*, for example, scattered information across different chapters (*Songshi* 8.165, 260.9074 and 283.9562), and the fragmentary narrative causes confusion. Zhou Cheng's *Song Dongjing kao* (13. 239–40), a standard reference work on Kaifeng during the Northern Song period, gives a fairly clear presentation but is mistaken about the imperial investiture granted to Zhenwu, evidently because the source from which Zhou Cheng copied, Li Lian's *Bianjing yiji zhi* (10.166), was wrong to begin with.
8 In addition, Zhenzong conferred on Zhenwu the title of the Numinous Response (Lingying 靈應) Perfected Lord in the 6th month of 1018; see "The Edict of Investing Zhenwu as the Numinous Responsive Perfected Lord" (Feng Zhenwu lingying zhenjun zhao 封真武靈應真君詔) in *Song da zhaoling ji* 136.480. The *Wudang fudi zongzhen ji* (j. xia, ZHDZ 48.573bc) claims additionally that the attendant turtle and snake were also invested. However, no non-Daoist primary source can verify this claim. Given the fact

that the *Zongzhen ji* took the liberty to alter the "Edict of Investing Zhenwu" to make the investiture granted to Zhenwu longer and grander, this text has a tendency to exaggerate the imperial honor received.

9 Emperor Zhenzong fell sick in the 2nd month of 1020 (Tianxi 4) and recovered in the 10th month (*Songshi* 8.168–9). Thereafter, he was taken ill from time to time and finally passed away in the 2nd month of 1022 (*Songshi* 8.171).
10 It burned down again when the Jurchen Jin conquered Kaifeng in 1127; see *Song Dongjing kao* 13.239.
11 *Songshi* 11.220, 13.255, 18.353, 113.2699. Renzong could have prayed for rain at the abbey at least one more time if it had not been for the criticism of a remonstrator (*jianguan* 諫官); see *Songshi* 320.10403.
12 The law was cited by Sima Guang 司馬光 (1019–1086) in a memorandum of 1062; he served as a remonstrator (*jianguan* 諫官) at the time (*Xu Zizhi tongjian changbian* 197.14b). Nevertheless, the law was barely enforced. Even within the four capitals (*sijing* 四京), there were temples consisting of more than 100 bays not registered with the government. Emperor Renzong considered pardoning these temples by granting them name plaques, which meant that they would automatically be registered in government records. It was this decree that provoked Sima Guang to quote the temple-building restriction in the Song legal code cited above.
13 See "Record of Restoring the Divine Cranes Daoist Monastery" (Chongxiu Xianhe guan ji 重修仙鶴觀記) by Wang Yizhong 王夷仲 and "Verified record of restoring the Divine Cranes Abbey" (Chongxiu Xianhe guan shilu 重修仙鶴觀實錄, no author); both are collected in *Jinshi lüe* 270–272. The "restoration" was only in name. The old Divine Cranes Daoist Monastery, built during the Tang period, was located three *li* outside the city wall and was in ruins before the Song dynasty was founded. The new Divine Cranes Daoist Monastery was situated in the center of the city, only 100 steps away from the magistrate's office. The Song state required permission to establish larger scale temples, as discussed in note 12. To get around the restriction, people appropriated the name of an abandoned temple that existed in records of the local government, and claimed to "restore" the old temple while actually building a new one. They did this because permission to establish a new temple required protracted bureaucratic hassle. It was easier to adopt the name of an old temple that had ceased to function but still remained in the register. For this, only the local administrator's consent was needed.
14 The four new halls were dedicated to four groups of deities: the Jade Emperor (accompanied by the Eleven Stars), the North Apex (accompanied by the divinities of the Twelve Earthly Branches), the Three Officials of Heaven, Earth and Water (by themselves alone) and, finally, Zhenwu accompanied by the North Dipper (*beidou*).
15 Fan had been appointed vice military commissioner to Shaanxi in 1041 during the war with the Xi Xia kingdom (982–1227), the Song's neighbor to the northwest. In planning his defense strategy, Fan had his eye on a military outpost called Mapu zhai 馬鋪砦 which bordered on Xi Xia territory. In early 1042, Fan fortified Mapu zhai into a fortress and re-named it Dashun ("All Smooth"); see *Songshi* 314.10270–10271; Li Huarui 1998: 217.
16 The *Song huiyao*, which recorded the grant of the title, does not give a reason for the enfeoffment. There had been no major combat at Dashun for decades since 1070. There was, however, a severe drought in Qingzhou in 1074 (Xining 7), under whose jurisdiction Dashun was, one year prior to the enfeoffment (*Xu Zizhi tongjian changbian* 256.4a; cited from Li Huarui 1998: 423). Another possibility is that this was part of the state's 1074–1075 temple regulation campaign that requested local administrators to report temples in their jurisdiction for state recognition.
17 The temple record, "Xianyou xian Fushi Jinshi shan Fushen daoyuan ji" 仙遊縣傅氏金石山福神道院記 is preserved in Wang Mai's *Quxuan ji* 5.24–27, SKQS edn.
18 Madam Chen here refers to Qianshou's wife. Fu Ji's wife, whose maiden name was also Chen, died and was buried in Yixing along with her husband (*Luofeng Fushi zupu*).

128 *Notes*

19 This is probably a symbolic reminiscence of human sacrifice. Since classical times, ritual blood smearing (*xin* 釁) was part of the ceremony to consecrate a temple bell and drum.
20 Having passed the *jinshi* degree during Shenzong's reign at the relatively young age of 26 *sui*, Fu Ji built his reputation, but damaged his political career, by attacking the leaders of the reformist New Party. After Huizong (1082–1135; r. 1100–1125) ascended the throne in 1100, Fu Ji, as a former tutor of the current emperor, rapidly ascended the bureaucratic ladder when Huizong's grandmother, who tried to balance the Old and New Parties, was in power. However, after the empress dowager passed away, the political wind changed. Huizong's favor tilted toward the New Party. Fu Ji was removed from the central court and assigned a local office in Yixing Jiangsu province. He died there three months later. For more of his career, see *Xianyou xianzhi* 33.10.
21 When the court granted an individual a tomb-tending temple, a temple whose clerics would look after his tomb, it was too great an honor for the family to refuse (Chikusa 35–36). In addition, there was an economic benefit: the family now owned the estate attached to the tomb-tending temple. In Song times high-ranking officials often requested the court to grant them rich temples designated as their tomb-tending temples in order to appropriate the temple riches.
22 *Yijian zhi*, *dingzhi*, 2. 551. The story is also discussed in Hansen 1990: 43–44. For a discussion about the nature of the *Yijian zhi* (*The record of the listener*); see Hansen 1990: 17–23.
23 See "Qingzhen guan Haotian ge ji 清真觀昊天閣記" by Chen Zhen 陳振 in 1219, collected in *Gusu zhi* 30.7b–9a.
24 For the discussion on why they preferred to use the name of an old temple instead of a new one, see note 13 of this chapter.
25 It is difficult to believe that there was not a single Zhenwu temple in Chengdu at the end of the twelfth century. The statement might be better understood as referring to a community-oriented Zhenwu temple.
26 "Record of the Mysterious Primordial Daoist Court (Xuanyuan daoyun ji 玄元道院記)" in *Yechu ji* 1.10b–12a by Shao Hengzhen 邵亨貞 (1309–1401); also see *Jinshi lüe* 954.
27 *Yijian jia zhi* 15.134–135. According to Hong Mai, Mao was a student in the Three Halls school system which was a government education institution initiated in 1071 and abolished in 1121 (*Songshi* 155.3623).
28 *Yijian yi zhi* 8.250–251. For a full translation, see Hansen 1990: 171–172; for Hong Hao's biography, see *Songshi* 373.11557–11562 and Hansen 1990: 17.
29 The painting was discovered during the excavation of the ruins of Khara Khoto in the Kozlov expedition of 1908; see Piotrovsky 1993. Khara Khoto was destroyed by the Mongols in 1226–1227 and was never rebuilt (Dunnell 1966), thus the painting must have been produced before then.
30 Daoist faithful meeting in congregations to recite scriptures can be found in Nanjing (*Jinshi lüe* 1049) and Hangzhou (*Mengliang lu* 19. 9ab). According to Wu Zimu, rich households in Hangzhou during the Southern Song organized and financed monthly meetings called "society of Numinous Treasure" (*lingbao hui* 靈寶會) for fellow believers to recite the Zhengyi scriptures together.
31 However, Zhenwu, disguised as a Daoist priest, came down to admonish the abbot that the "release of living beings" ritual could only create extra demands for captured animals and thus contribute to the avarice of hunting and fishing. In addition, the animals were often injured during capture, and would not have suffered if not for the ritual. The abbot accordingly realized his mistake and abolished the practice.
32 A similar record of the same event can also be found in *Mengliang lu* 2.1a–b.

3 A god in transition

1 The citation is from the section of "The Classics of Regions Within the Seas: The East" in the *Shanhai jing* translated by Anne Birrell. Birrell (1999: xv) dates the section to 6 BCE. It

should be noted that the original Chinese text does not indicate whether there were many thunder deities or only one.
2 *Taiping guangji* 394.1b–3a: "Chen Luanfeng." There are additional stories suggesting thunder gods have pig-heads, see *Taiping guangji* 393.12a: "Xu Yu" 徐誧 and *Miscellaneous Morsels from Youyang* (*Youyangzazu*酉陽雜俎) 8.9b.
3 *Taishang Dadao yuqing jing*, j.9 (ZHDZ 4.635b & 636b). Another often cited story in tracing the sources of Thunder Rites is the story of Ye Qianshao 葉遷韶 of Tang times (*Taiping guangji* 394.8a–9b). As Edward Davis (2001: 25) points out, however, bureaucratization, which is a defining trait of Daoist Thunder Rites, was missing in this story.
4 *Yunji qiqian* 115.2547–2549; Schipper 1993. The story is also collected in *Taiping guangji* 53.4a–5b: "Wang Fajin." Both credit their sources to Du Guangting. *Taiping guangji* gives the year of Wang Fajin's death as "the 12th year, *renchen* 壬辰, of Tianbao"; actually the year of *renchen* during the Tianbao reign corresponded with the 11th year (CE 752). Whether or not Wang was a fully ordained and government-licensed Daoist priestess can not be determined. Yet it is evident that Wang was an initiated Daoist. Both records state that she was a disciple of a Daoist priestess (*nüguan* 女官) and received the Small Life Extending Register of the Orthodox One (Zhenyi yansheng xiaolu正一延生小錄). Another Daoist source described her as "a disciple who upheld the Way, carrying the registers and cultivating the golden elixir" (*fengdao peilu xiujindan dizi* 奉道佩籙修金丹弟子); see *The Scripture of the Protection of the Country and the Destruction of Demons by the Lord of Heaven* (Taishang Dongshen tiangong xiaomo huguo jing 太上洞神天公消魔護國經), TC 654, j. zhong, ZHDZ 6.225c.
5 See *The Scripture of the Protection of the Country and the Destruction of Demons by the Lord of Heaven* j. xia (ZHDZ 6.229a). Kristofer Schipper first points out the connection between Wang's ritual and this particular text (Schipper 1993: 830–831). He renders *Tiangong* in accordance to the conventional way.
6 The story is preserved in *Taiping guangji*, j.395.5b and is credited to *Beimeng suoyan*北夢瑣言.
7 *Protocol for the Practice of the Way of the Three Caverns* (*Sandong xiudao yi* 三洞修道儀, TC 1237, j.1; ZHDZ 42.259c). Although the *Protocol* was written in 1003 (Schipper and Verellen 2004, 973–974), it contains information from the first half of the tenth century. Its source was the Daoist master Liu Ruozhou 劉若拙 who was already eminent during the Kaibao era (968–975); see *Comprehensive Mirror of Successive Generations of Perfected Immortals and Those Who Embody the Dao* (*Lishi zhenxian tidao tongjian* 歷世真仙體道通鑑, TC 296, j. 47, ZHDZ 47.531a).
8 Even the *Songshi*, which denounces Lin Lingsu as a fraud, has to recognize, albeit reluctantly, Lin's capability in performing the Five Thunder rite (*SS* 462.13529).
9 The Tang story of Ye Qianshao saving a thunder god is a good example. Out of gratitude, this thunder god promised that he and his four brothers would respond to Ye's call for help at any time. He also warned Ye, however, that the fifth brother was violent and should not be casually sent for. The story is preserved in *Taiping guangji* (j.394.8a–9b, SKQS edn).
10 For example, "All thunder deities who were summoned by ritual officers but failed to arrive, 100 strokes," see "Taishang hundong chiwen Nüqing zhaoshu tianlü 太上混洞赤文女青詔書天律" in *Daofa huiyuan* j. 251, in ZHDZ 38.413c.
11 The old *bianshen* 變身, with *shen* in the character of "body," is typically rendered into English as "transformation of the body." The ritual underlies the parallel between the human body and the cosmos; see, for example, *Scripture of the Divine Continent on the Dance in Heaven in Seven Revolutions and Seven Transformations* (*Shenzhou qizhuan qibian wutian jing* 神州七轉七變舞天經, TC 1331) and *Chisong zi zhangli*, j. 2, ZHDZ 8.630c. For more details, see Andersen 2006.
12 The date of this liturgical manual is unclear. It is found in *Fahai yizhu* 法海遺珠 (*Retrieved Pearls from the Ocean of Rituals*), *j*.15.1–15.2, in ZHDZ 41.454c–455a. The *Retrieved Pearls* is "a loose collection of various methods of Five Thunder magic"

130 *Notes*

(Schipper and Verellen 2004: 1090). It took shape sometime after the mid-fourteenth century but contains materials from the Song–Yuan period (Boltz 1987: 51).
13 The following account of the early history of the Celestial Heart school is based on Hymes 2002: 26–46 unless otherwise noted.
14 *Shangqing tianxin zhengfa* j. 1 in ZHDZ 30.245.8b. The *Secret Essential* (j.1; ZHDZ 30.313b) also asserts that it was Rao Dongtian on whom heaven bestowed the Celestial Heart ritual program.
15 Yuan Miaozong was a reputed master of the Celestial Heart school specializing in exorcism. According to his preface to the *Secret Essentials*, he joined the imperial court's project, compiling a *Daoist Canon* in 1115 and quickly became aware of the lack of ritual programs in the royal collection that could "save the world and cure [disease]" (*jiushi zhiliao* 救世治療), that is, exorcist-therapeutic rituals. He took it on himself to compile such a collection, based on his three decades of learning and practice experience. The result is the *Secret Essential*. The *Secret Essential* contains information on ritual sequences, talismans, invocations, ritual seals, *mudra*, rosters of the divinities associated with the ritual system, penal codes (for both the spirits and the ritual masters) and meditative techniques. For more details, see Poul Andersen's discussion on this text in Schipper and Verellen 2004: 1057–1060. *Shangqing tianxin zhengfa* (TC 566) in its current form was completed sometime after the mid-twelfth century, but was originally put together by Deng Yougong who was active in the late eleventh century, according to Poul Andersen (in Schipper and Verellen 2004: 1060–67, esp. 1061 and 1064). Judith Boltz (1987: 35) gives different dates. For a critical review of Boltz' and Andersen's different opinions regarding this issue, see Hymes 2002: 171–177. I incline to accept Andersen's argument.
16 The other two core talismans are the Three Radiances (*sanguang* 三光) and the Dipper (*Tiangang* 天罡). In later Celestial Heart texts, the Zhenwu Talisman is sometimes replaced by the Black Killer (*Heisha*) Talisman; see, for example, *Correct Method of the Celestial Heart of the Northern Apex* (*Shangqing tianxin beiji zhengfa*; TC 567, not to be confused with TC 566 which has a similar title), j.1 (ZHDZ 30.286a). The Black Killer Talisman is notably different from the Zhenwu Talisman, but the incantation that the ritual master recites while inscribing the former concludes with the phrase: "as decreed by the Zhenwu incantation" (*ru Zhenwu zhou chi* 如真武咒敕). The connection between Zhenwu and the Black Killer Talisman is clear.
17 *Secret Essential* j.2, ZHDZ 30.321b–322b. When drawing the talisman, the text also instructs, the practitioner should visualize the talisman envoy (*fushi* 符使) with loosen hair and barefoot in black outfit riding black clouds and followed by the spirits of the 28 stellar "lodges" (*xiu*) (*Secret Essential* j.2; ZHDZ 30.322 a–b). The iconographic description confirms that the talisman envoy is no one else than Zhenwu.
18 *Shangqing tianxin zhengfa* j. 3 (ZHDZ 30.253.b). Also see Andersen 1996: 153–293.
19 The incantation accompanied with the Xuanwu-Heisha Talisman in the *Shangqing tianxin zhengfa* appears to merge Zhenwu and Heisha (i.e "Black Killer", referred to as Yisheg 翊聖 in the incantation) into one individual (j. 3, ZHDZ 30.253.b); see figure 3.5. The complicated relationship between Perfected Warrior and Black Killer (Heisha) cries for more studies.
20 *Shanxiao*, also known as *muke* ("wonderers in the woods"), was by itself a category in Daoist demonology. In a Thunder Rites' penal code that deals with the spirits, *shanxiao* were subject to particularly harsh punishment. Upon catching *shanxiao* who trespassed on Daoist altars, even if it was on days of celestial pardons (*tianshe ri* 天赦日), a priest had the permission to capture, convict, and execute them by decapitation or dismemberment ("Taishang hundong chiwen nüqing zhaoshu tianlü" 太上混洞赤文女青詔書天律 in *Daofa huiyuan* j. 251; ZHDZ 38.410b).
21 For a historical analysis of the Northern Emperor and his connection to medieval forms of exorcism, see Mollier 1997.

22 The Celestial Pivotal Court (Tianshu yuan 天樞院) is a standard office in the complex Thunder Rites bureaucratic system located in the South Apex ("Nanji you Tianshu yuan" 南極有天樞院; see *Haiqiong Bai zhenren yulu* 海瓊白真人語錄 (TC 1307) j.1 (esp. ZHDZ 19.546c, 550a).
23 See "Imperial Attendant Wang's Eight Elaborate Treatises on Praying" (Wang Shichen qidao baduan jin 王侍宸祈禱八段錦) in *Daofa huiyuan*, j.69, ZHDZ 36.428c.
24 Sign of *mao* is formed by placing the tip of thumb on the lower middle joint of the index finger (Lagerwey 1987:17).
25 The tip of the thumb touches the bottom of the fourth finger.
26 The English translation of the incantation is Andersen's (1995:195).
27 "The supreme divine methods of the Five Ancient Lords of the Feminine One for unraveling the knots of death in the fetus" (Wulao ciyi jie baotai sijie shangxian fa 五老雌一解胞胎死結上仙法) in *Precious Scripture on the Five Ancient Lords, Jade Seal of the Feminine One* (*Dongzhen gaoshang yudi Dadong ciyi yujian wulao baojing* 洞真高上玉帝大洞雌一玉檢五老寶經 TC 1313, ZHDZ 1.92c–93b). Although the text dates from Tang times, Robinet points out that the methods contained are traditional Supreme Clarity practices, see Schipper and Verellen 2004: 588–589.
28 "Dadong ciyi buyang dijun taiyi baishen shangxian fa" 大洞雌一哺養帝君太一百神上仙法 in *Precious Scripture on the Five Ancient Lords, Jade Seal of the Feminine One* (TC 1313, ZHDZ 1.93c–84c).
29 *Chisong zi zhangli*,j.2, ZHDZ 8.630c. I thank Poul Andersen for pointing this out to me.
30 The method is called "Dadong ciyi dijun bianhua cixiong zhi dao 大洞雌一帝君變化雌雄之道" and collected in *Precious Scripture on the Five Ancient Lords, Jade Seal of the Feminine One* (TC 1313; ZHDZ 1.91b–92c).
31 "Method of the Imperial One for the Fusion by the Whirlwind" (Huifeng hunhe diyi zhi fa 徊風混合帝一之法) in *Shangqing dadong zhenjing* j.6, ZHDZ 1.44c–45b, also in *Yunji qiqian* 30.681–692, esp. 690.
32 The meditation practices as the Worthy Lord proceeds to enter the adept's body from the mouth, ascends to the brain, blows the "*qi* of whirlwind" to bring the radiance of the sun and moon that accompany him into a cloud which goes down to penetrate the body, viscera, and all joints. The body turns radiant. The exercise climaxes at the adept reaches the oblivious state and ends as consciousness returns.
33 The text is long thought lost. In the early twentieth century, part of it was unearthed from a cave in Dunhuang, Gansu, in west China. Rao Zongyi restored the fragments with annotations. The English translation is cited from Bokenkamp 1997: 92.
34 It is alternatively known as *Laozi zhongjing* 老子中經. Schipper dates the text to the Eastern Jin (CE 317–420) but speculates that it contains materials from the second century; see Schipper 1985.
35 Red refers to the color of a newborn infant's naked skin. The eighth-century classical authority, Kong Yingda 孔穎達, wrote in his commentary on "Kang Gao 康誥" in the *Classic of History* (*Shujing* or *Shangshu*): "A child is born of red color (*chizi* 赤色), therefore [the text] says 'red child'" (*Shangshu zhushu*13.10b).
36 The mother, the Jade Woman of Mysterious Radiance, provides the infant with nourishment while the father, the Old Man of the Central Ultimate, offers instructions and guidelines (*Taishang laojun zhongjing*, j. shang, ZHDZ 8.213b).
37 Inner alchemy texts use plenty alternative names for the inner elixir, including "mysterious pearl" (*xuanzhu* 玄珠), "perfected person" (*zhenren* 真人), or "embryonic baby" (*tai'er* 胎兒). Ultimately, the "holy embryo" will be mature enough to allow the adept to discard the material body and become a transcendent or *xian*.
38 Exchanging of the middle lines of *kan* ☵ and *li* ☲ transforms them into the trigrams of *kun* (earth) ☷ and *qian* ☰ (heaven). For a succinct introduction to the complex symbolism of *kan* and *li* in the inner alchemy, see Robinet 1997: 236–237.
39 I thank John Lagerwey for this point.

132 *Notes*

40 Letter home in Daoist liturgy refers to the private requests from the ritual masters to the divine lineage patriarchs; see "Taiyi huofu wulei dafa" 太乙火府五雷大法 in *Daofa huiyuan*, j.190, ZHDZ38.79a.
41 In the manual, Nan Bidao 南畢道 (ca.1196–?) is addressed as *dushi* 度師, or the "initiation master", which typically refers to the teacher who initiated oneself. Therefore, the written version of the text appears to have been written by a disciple of Nan Bidao. Nan had only one student who was Huang Shunshen 黃舜申 (1224–1286). Huang was indeed the first codifier of the Pure Tenuity ritual. Nevertheless, we also find Zhang Shouqing (1254–1336) at the end of a list of honors (ZHDZ 31.40a–b), which suggests a re-editing in the mid-fourteenth century.
42 Their full appellations are: Divine Lord of the *Yang* Thunder of Divine Fire of Supreme Purity, Gou Liuji (苟留吉), and the Divine Lord of the *Yin* Thunder of Divine Fire of Supreme Purity, Bi Zongyuan (畢宗遠). General Gou, of black complexion, has three eyes and red hair. General Bi, less frightening, is red-faced.
43 In the exemplary letter itself, we find a fuller title for the recipient: Heavenly Lord of the Grand One, the Purple Sovereign Jade Void Tutorial Primer (*Yuxu shixiang zihuang taiyi tianjun* 玉虛師相紫皇太一天君). This title as part of Zhenwu's exalted appellation can be found in *Zihuang liandu xuanke* 紫皇鍊度玄科 (TC 1451, ZHDZ 44.421c; also see Lagerwey's discussion on the text collected in Schipper and Verellen 2004: 1105) as well as *Xuantian shangdi baizi shenghao* 玄天上帝百字聖號 (TC 1482) in ZHDZ 30.617a.
44 *Daofa huiyuan*, j.5, ZHDZ 36.40c. In addition, Zhang's name is listed in the ritual lineage at the front of the *Secret Methods of the Divine Fire*.
45 *Retrieved Pearls* j.20, ZHDZ 41.488a–b.
46 *Master Red Pine's Petition Almanac* j. 2 (ZHDZ 8.638b–c). The *Great Perfection Code* is a work long lost but preserved in fragmentary form in the *Master Red Pine's Petition Almanac*; see Verellen 2004.
47 Although the text here seems to suggest that the red *qi* ascends to the sky, the following clearly indicates that the priest makes the journey.
48 The original text reads *tianshi jiubai* 天師九拜 or "the Heavenly Master bows on his knees nine times." This is clearly an error. A similar passage found in the *Shangqing Tianxin zhengfa* j.6 (ZHDZ 30.274c) uses 允諾 (*yunnuo*), or "agree," instead of characters 九拜; I made the change accordingly.
49 The *Daoist Cannon* contains an edict of Emperor Song Huizong granting Zhenwu the honorific title of *Yousheng* ("Aiding Sage") on May 6, 1008 ("Zhenwu lingying zhenjun zengshang Yousheng zunhao cewen 真武靈應真君增上佑聖尊號冊文, ZHDZ 30.586). Although the edict cannot be found in the *Collection of the Grand Edicts of the Song*, it is positive that Huizong granted the title *Yousheng* to Zhenwu. In 1107 (Daguan 1), Zhenwu's title in the state registration records contained only the two characters *lingying* 靈應 (*Song huiyao*, li, 20.56b) but grew into four characters *lingying yousheng* by 1113 (Zhenghe 3) (*Song huiyao*, daoshi, 1.31a). The additional two characters, *yousheng*, could only have been granted by Huizong, the reigning monarch during the period.
50 The Tianpeng ritual was popular enough by the thirteenth century to attract criticism form the Daoist master Jin Yunzhong (*Daofa huiyuan* 178, ZHDZ 38.20a).
51 The particular ritual program cited here is preserved in the *Zichen xuanshu* 紫辰玄書 which is collected in the *Retrieved Pearls* j.45–46. The *Zichen xuanshu* was written in 1334 by the fifth-generation recipient Zhang Shunlie 章舜烈. Zhang traced the lineage's history of a hundred years or so. The beholders of the ritual program referred themselves as "successor of the Tianpeng ritual (*sifa* 嗣法)" (*Fahai yizhu* j.46, ZHDZ 41.636c).
52 Although a spin-off of the Supreme Clarity school, the Youthful Incipience ritual program also drew in ample elements from the Celestial Masters and the Celestial Heart schools; see Boltz 1987: 30–33.

53 "Jade Fascicles from the Immaculate Bureaus of the Five Primordial Ones in the Youthful Incipience of the Highest Clarity [School]" (Shangqing Tongchu wuyuan sufu yüce 上清童初五元素府玉冊) in *Daofa huiyuan* j. 171–178 (ZHDZ 37. 532–38.21).
54 The Primordial Harmony Bureau of Promotions and Records occasionally appeared by itself without the rest of the quintet in the liturgical manuals of Pure Tenuity school, for example, the "Shenjie wulei qidao jianshi" 神捷五雷祈禱檢式 in *Daofa huiyuan* j.48 (ZHDZ 36.282b).
55 The ritual program, *Beiyin Fengdu Taixuan zhimo heilü lingshu* 北陰酆都太玄治魔黑律靈書, is collected in *Daofa huiyuan*, j. 266. The text is probably from the fourteenth century. The citation is on ZHDZ 38.497a.
56 The ritual program, "Numinous writs for urgent submission," is collected in *Retrieved Pearls* 20.8 (ZHDZ 41.489c).
57 In Daoist theory, one's brain is divided into nine palaces; *niwan*, or "mud pill" (which is also the old Chinese translation for Nirvana), is one of them. It is located three inches behind the point where the eyebrows cross. It is also referred to as the "upper elixir field," or *shang dantian*, in the *neidan* tradition.
58 The *Neijing tu* was probably produced no earlier than Qing times. Yet, it bears concepts of ancient origin. In addition, the defining characteristic principles of inner alchemy are not specific to certain stages of the tradition's development.
59 This particular interpretation was pervasive enough during the first half of the thirteenth century to attract the attention of Wang Wenqing. Wang argued against it first before offering his own method of Summon and Union.

4 A god and his mountain

1 Regional Inspectors ranked between 2a and 4a of a 9-rank bureaucratic hierarchy with 1a as the highest. In contrast to the Song period and thereafter, the *zhou* in the Eastern Han dynasty was the highest local administrative unit. There were only 13 *zhou* in total across the empire; see Hucker 1985:14. Zhu Mu was appointed Regional Inspector of Jizhou 冀州 in CE 153 (*Hou Hanshu* 43.1461–43.1470). Jizhou covered, primarily, present-day southern Shanxi and northern Henan provinces.
2 The original source is *Nan Yongzhong ji* 南雍州記 (*Record of the South Yongzhou*) by Guo Zhongchan 郭仲產 who was active during the fifth century (420–479; *Taiping guangji* 141.5b). The *Nan Yongzhong ji* has been lost, but its fragments are preserved in the *Taiping yulan*.
3 "Tang Junzhou Wudangshan Huizhong zhuan 唐均州武當山慧忠傳" in *Song Gaozeng zhuan* 9.204–9.207.
4 Emperors Zhenzong and Shenzong were referred to by the names of their tombs, Dingling 定陵 and Zhaoling 昭陵.
5 See Jie Xisi's 揭傒斯 "Stele of the Great Longevity Palace of the Five Numinous and Responsive Dragons" (Da Wulong lingying wanshou gong bei 大五龍靈應萬壽宮碑) collected in *Jinshi lüe* 946. The extended collection of Jie's works, *Wenan ji* 文安集, however, omits it.
6 The administrator of Fuzhou 撫州 in Jiangxi, for example, ended up nominating a non-existent temple (Hymes 2002: 102).
7 Wang Yan had been appointed to the position a year earlier, see *Songshi* 34.645 and 167.3957. To avoid confusion, it should be noted that there was another Wang Yan (1137–1218; courtesy name Huishu 晦叔) active at a slightly later time.
8 For Zhao Fang's biography, see *Songshi* 403.12203–12207.
9 His birth year was indicated at the end of the first *juan* of his *Guier ji*.
10 Information in the paragraph is derived from *Zongzhen ji*, middle, ZHDZ 48.564. a–48.567b.

134 *Notes*

11 The South Cliff was called the Purple Empyrean Cliff in *Zongzhen ji* but the name is no longer in usage. To avoid confusion with the Purple Empyrean Palace, I use the name South Cliff throughout the study.
12 The remainder of this paragraph is based on the "Junzhou Wudangshan Wanshou gong bei" in *Xuelou ji* (5. 21b–5.24b) by Cheng Jufu 程鉅夫 (1249–1318), a leading scholar of his time and a high-ranking official. The passage is also available in *Jinshi lüe* 743–744, under the title "Da Tianyi zhenqing wanshou gong bei 大天一真慶萬壽宮碑."
13 Jie Xisi was born and raised in Ji'an, Jiangxi. For a brief biographical account of Jie in English, see Gerritsen 2007: 92, n. 66. As discussed earlier, the two Wudang Daoists raised funds to cast a bronze Zhenwu stature in Ji'an in 1295. Zhenwu worship was positively popular enough in Ji'an. Jie probably learned about Zhenwu lore from sources other than the clerics.
14 "The Inscription of the Great Longevity Palace of the Five Numinous and Responsive Dragons" (Da Wulong lingying wanshou gong bei), in *Jinshi lüe* 946.
15 A preface of the *Qisheng tu* by Yu Ji, collected in *Xuantian shangdi qisheng lingyi lu*, ZHDZ 30.704c.
16 The chart is based on Wang and Yang's chart (2003: 153) with my own minor modifications.
17 The donation was made to *Xiuzhen* guan.
18 The donors included a military official, his wife, and his mother.
19 The donors were five men of different surnames who noticed that the new monastery at the Jade Void Cliff did not have an image of Zhenwu in the hall and made a donation to commission a statue of the god.
20 The donors were two married couples (four persons). Judging by their names, the four persons were not related to each other by blood.
21 The donors included one man from Shanghai, a member of the Shen 沈 family, and two men from Kunshan 崑山, in present Jiangsu. The Shen family group contained a Mr. Shen and his wife, along with his father and her parents. The three other men show no trace of kinship with the Shens.
22 The donation was made to complete a hermitage for Haoranzi 浩然子, abbot of the Palace of Jade Void (Yuxu gong 玉虛宮), so the master could enjoy his retirement.
23 Although there were no records of pilgrims from Fujian on Mt Wudang, Fujian folklore recounts local people's pilgrimages to the mountain (Li 1998: 192).
24 Pilgrims who took the eastern route entered the mountain from Jiaokou village, crossed the Jiudu Mountain Stream, leading to the Purple Empyrean Palace, then the South Cliff Palace, and then headed to the Great Summit (Wang and Yang 1993: 147–148; for a detailed map, see de Bruyn 1997: 2/b).
25 Luo's poem on the Temple of Reception reads: "Treat yourself to a full stomach of blue essence rice at the post station, and work hard climbing the mountain to be close to cloud nine" (*Jishengji*, ZHDZ 48.580a).
26 I thank Janice Willis for bringing this to my attention.
27 *Langmei* eventually made the list of articles of tribute to the emperors during Ming times. When Xu Hongzu requested some *langmei* from Daoist priests on Mt Wudang, the latter told him that giving it away without official authorization was a crime subject to harsh penalty. Xu obtained some anyway after entreaty and bribery. He described the fruit as shaped like kumquats (*jinju* 金橘), and preserved by being candied in honey (*Xu Xiake youji* 1xia.24).
28 It was removed to the Lesser Lotus Peak (Xiaolian feng) in the early fifteenth century in order to make space for the life-size bronze shrine created by Emperor Yongle's order.
29 The third emperor of the Yuan, Chengzong, granted new titles to Zhenwu's parents but did not bequeath special patronage to Mt Wudang.
30 Hongwu wrote that while his fleet was sailing to do battle with his rival for the throne, Chen Youliang 陳友諒 (1320–1363), he saw a turtle and a snake swimming alongside his boat

(*Yuzhi xizheng ji* (I first encounter this material in Cai Xianghui 1989). During this crucial campaign, known in Chinese history as the "determining battle (*juezhan* 決戰) of Lake Boyang," Chen Youliang lost his life, signifying Hongwu's future success (Dreyer 1974). Although it was never clearly spelled out, the turtle and snake could be easily interpreted as a sign of Zhenwu's blessing. After the enthronement, Hongwu made sure Zhenwu's temple in Nanjing, the capital at the time, received sacrifices from state officials. Yet, he did not show any particular interest in Mt Wudang.

31 The following paragraphs on Yongle's temple project on Mt Wudang are based on Wang and Yang 1993: 165–168, 174–177; and Lagerwey 1992, unless noted otherwise.
32 This Yuan bronze pavilion survives. It has been relocated within the Taihe Palace near the submit. Pilgrims are told to walk around it in order to obtain good luck.
33 The rent on official farmland (*guantian zu*) was between 0.1 and 1 shi per *mu*. See *Mingshi* 78.1897 (Shihuo zhi).
34 The "vein" here refers to a mountain's "dragon vein" (*longmai* 龍脈), visible only to the trained eye of a geomancer. The dragon vein is the channel along which the *qi* or vital energy of a mountain moves (Smith 1991: 141).
35 While the brother was indeed guilty of manslaughter, he undoubtedly fell victim to Jiajing's revenge (Geiss 1988: 463).

5 The whole and the parts

1 The metaphorical parallel and overlaps between military rituals and Daoist exorcism have just began to attract scholarly attention; see Katz 2008.
2 This war was started by Wanyan Liang (1121–1161; r. 1149–61) in 1161 and lasted for another four years after his death.
3 Not to be confused with the much more prominent General Wang Guangzu (fl. 1068–77) whose courtesey name was Junyu 君俞 (*Songshi* 350.11076–7).
4 "Yanguan zhen chongxiu Zhenwu dian ji 鹽官鎮重修真武殿記," *Jinshi lüe*, 363–4. The quotation in translation below is from the same source.
5 "The Record of the Hall for the Supreme Perfect [One]" ("Shangzhen dian ji 上真殿記") in *Jinshi lüe* 902.
6 It obtained this name because all of the temples in Foshan, except for the Zumiao, were destroyed in the chaos at the end of Yuan dynasty. To the Ming dwellers of Foshan, it thus became the oldest temple. David Faure has undetaken extensive research on Foshan, see, for example his 1990 article.
7 A local gazetteer comments that "There is an old proverb: 'Set off the big firecrackers in Foshan, shoot sons over to Leigang village.' It means that people have to sell sons to payback the money for the firecrackers. Indeed this is shocking." [*Guangxu*] *Nanhai xianzhi*, ch. 26). Leigang is a neighboring town of Foshan.
8 More monarchs of the Song paid visit to Auspicious Fountain—Sweet Spring Monastery, but it is uncertain whether or not they prayed for rain there.

Appendix 1

1 According to the preface by Zhao Mengfu. The preface, titled as "Xuanwu qisheng ji xu," is preserved in Zhao's *Songxue zhao wenji* 松雪齋文集 7.16b–7.17a (SBCK edn.). The ban on the usage of the character *xuan* was no longer in effect after the fall of the Song.
2 The *Qisheng lu* underwent further editing after Zhang Shouqing's edition. Zhao Mengfu's preface that Zhang solicited, for example, is not found in the current *Qisheng lu*.

3 *Yisheng baode zhenjun* gives the exact date of Zhang Shouzhen's death, the 16th of the leap 7th month of Zhidao 2, which corresponds Sep 1, 996 (j.1, ZHDZ 29.793).
4 First, in general, a divine endorsement of an adult prince as the next emperor threatened the current emperor. Second, Taizong was particularly paranoid about the issue of successor (*Songshi* 281. 9528–9529).

Bibliography

Andersen, Poul. 1995. "The Transformation of the Body in Daoist Ritual." In *Religious Reflections on the Human Body*, edited by Jane Marie Law, 186–208. Bloomington and Indianapolis: Indiana University Press.

Andersen, Poul. 1996. "Taoist Talismans and the History of the Tianxin Tradition." *Acta Orientalia* 57, 141–152.

Andersen, Poul. 2004. "Taishang zhuguo jiumin zongzhen miyao" and "Shangqing tianxin zhengfa." In *Taoist Canon: A Historical Companin to the Daozong*, edited by Kristofer Schipper and Franciscus Verellen, 1057–1060, 1064–1067. Chicago: Chicago University Press.

Andersen, Poul. 2006. "Bianshen" in *The Encyclopedia of Taoism*, edited by Fabrizio Pregadio, 230–231. London: Routledge.

Anhai zhi 安海誌. Kangxi 康熙 reign (1662–1722). In *Zhongguo difangzhi zhuanji* 中國地方志專輯 [pt. 1] *Xiang zhen zhi zhuanji* 鄉鎮志專輯, v. 26. Nanjing: Jiangsu guji, Shanghai: Shanghai shudian, and Chengdu: Bashu shushe, 1991.

Baldrian-Hussein, Farzeen. 1986. "Lü Tung-pin in Northern Sung Literature." *Cahiers d'Extrême-Asie* 2: 133–169.

Baldrian-Hussein, Farzeen. 1989–1990. "Inner Alchemy: Notes on the Origin and Use of the Term Neidan." *Cahiers d'Extrême-Asie* 5: 163–190.

Bamin tongzhi 八閩通志. 1490. Huang Zhongzhao 黃仲昭 (1435–1508) ed. Re-edited by the Editorial Committee of Gazetteers of Fujian. Fuzhou: Fujian renmin chubanshe, 1991.

Baopu zi 抱朴子 (*Master who Embraces Simplicity*). Ge Hong (284–364). SKQS edn.

Baptandier-Berthier, Brigitte. 1996. "The Lady Linshui: How a Woman Become a Goddess." In *Unruly Gods: Divinity and Society in China*, edited by Meir Shahar and Robertt P. Weller, 105–149. Honolulu: University of Hawai'i Press.

Baptandier, Brigitte. 2008. *The Lady of Linshui: A Chinese Female Cult*. Translated by Kristin Ingrid Fryklund. Stanford: Stanford University Press.

Beijing tushuguan cang Zhongguo lidai shike taben huibian 北京圖書館藏中國歷代石刻拓本匯編. 1989–1990. Beijing tushuguan jinshizu 北京圖書館金石組 comp. Zhengzhou: Zhongzhou guji chubanshe.

Bell, Catherine. 1988. "Ritualization of Texts and Textualization of Ritual in the Codification of Taoist Liturgy." *History of Religions* 27.4: 366–392.

Bianjing yiji zhi 汴京遺蹟志. Li Lian 李濂 (1488–1566). Beijing: Zhonghua shuju, 1999.

Bickford, Maggie. 2006. "Huizong's Paintings: Art and the Art of Emperorship." In *Emperor Huizong and Late Northern Song China: The Political of Culture and the Culture of*

Politics, edited by Patricia B. Ebrey and Maggie Bickfor, 453–513. Cambridge, Mass.: Harvard University Asian Center.

Birrell, Anne. 1999. "Introduction". In *The Classic of Mountains and Seas, translated with introduction and notes by Anne Birrell*. London: Penguin Books.

Bokenkamp, Stephen R. 1997. *Early Daoist Scriptures*. Berkley: University of California Press.

Boltz, Judith M. 1993. "Not by the Seal of Office Alone: New Weapons in Battles with the Supernatural." In *Religion and Society in T'ang and Sung China*, edited by Patricia B. Ebrey and Peter N. Gregory, 241–305. Honolulu: University of Hawai'i Press.

Boltz, Judith M. 1983. "Opening the Gates of Purgatory: A Twelfth-century Taoist Meditation Technique for the Salvation of Lost Souls." In *Tantric and Taoist Studies in Honour of R. A. Stein*, edited by In Michel Strickmann, vol. 2: 488–510. Bruxelles: Institut belge des hautes études chinoises.

Boltz, Judith M. 1987. *A Survey of Taoist Literature, Tenth to Seventeenth Centuries*. Berkeley: University of California, Institute of East Asian Studies.

Bourdieu, Pierre. 1977. *Outline of a Theory of Practice*. Translated by Richard Nice. Cambridge: Cambridge University Press.

Brokaw, Cynthia J. 1991. *The Ledger of Merit and Demerit: Social Change and Moral Order in Later Imperial China*. Princeton, N.J.: Princeton University Press.

Brook, Timothy. 1993. *Praying for Power: Buddhism and the Formation of Gentry Society in Late-Ming China*. Cambridge, Mass.: Harvard University Press.

Butler, M.A. 2008. "Hidden Time, Hidden Space: Crossing Borders With Occult Ritual in The Song Military," in *Battlefronts Real and Imagined: War, Border, and Identity in the Chinese Middle Period*, edited by Don J. Wyatt, 111–150. New York: Palgrave Macmillan.

Cahill, Suzanne E. 1980. "Taoism at the Sung Court: The Heavenly Text Affair of 1008." *Bulletin of Sung-Yuan Studies* 16: 23–44.

Cahill, Suzanne E. 1993. *Transcendence and Divine Passion: the Queen Mother of the West in Medieval China*. Stanford, Calif.: Stanford University Press.

Cai Xianghui 蔡相煇. 1989. *Taiwan de wangye yu Mazu* 臺灣的王爺與媽祖 (The Lords and the Empress of Heaven in Taiwan). Taipei: Taiyuan.

Cammann, Schuyler. 1948. "The "TLV" Pattern on Cosmic Mirrors of the Han Dynasty." *Journal of the American Oriental Society* 68.4: 159–167.

Cedzich, Ursula-Angelika. 1995. "The Cult of the Wu-t'ong/Wu-hsien in History and Fiction: the Religious Roots of the Journey to the South." In *Ritual and Scripture in Chinese Religion: Five Studies*, edited by David Johnson. Berkeley, Calif.: Publications of the Chinese Popular Culture Project, No. 3.

Chan, Hok-lam 陳學霖. 1997. " 'Zhenwu shen, Yongle xiang' chaungshuo" 真武神, 永樂像傳說. In ibid. *Mingdai renwu yu chuanshuo* 明代人物與傳說, 89–127. Hong Kong: The Chinese University Press.

Chao, Shin-yi. 2002. "A *Danggi* Temple in Taipei: Spirit-Mediums in Modern Urban Taiwan." *Asia Major* 15.2: 129–157.

Chao, Shin-yi. 2003. "Daoist Examinations and Daoist Schools during the Northern Song Dynasty." *Journal of Chinese Religions* 31: 1–37.

Chao, Shin-yi. 2006. "Huizong and the *Divine Empyrean Palace* Temple-network." In *Emperor Huizong and Late Northern Song China: The Politics of Culture and the Culture of Politics*, edited by Patricia Buckley Ebrey and Maggie Bickford, 324–361. Cambridge, Mass.: Harvard University Press.

Chao, Shin-yi. 2009. "The *Precious Volume of Zhenwu Bodhisattva Attaining the Way*: A Case Study of the Worship of Zhenwu (Perfected Warrior) in Ming-Qing Sectarian Groups." In *The People and the Dao: New Studies of Chinese Popular Religion in*

Honour of Prof. Daniel L. Overmyer, edited by Philip Clart and Paul Crowe, 63–82. Sankt Augustin: Institut Monumenta Serica.

Chengxiang Weigong tanxun 丞相魏公譚訓. Su Xiangxian 蘇象先 (Song dynasty, active 1091). SBCK edn.

Cheu Hock Tong. 1988. *The Nine Emperor Gods: A Study of Chinese Spirit-Medium Cults.* Singaporee: Times Books International.

Chijian Dayue taihe shan zhi, 敕建大岳太和山志. 1431. Ren Ziyuan 任自垣 (fl. 1400–1425). In Yang Lizhi 楊立志 ed. *Mingdai Wudangshan zhi erzhong* 明代武當山志二種. Wuhan: Hubei renmin chubanshe, 1999.

Chikusa Masaaki 竹沙雅章. 1979. "Sôdai fuji kô 宋代墳寺考 (Study of tomb monasteries of the Song dynasty)." *Tōyō gakuhō* 61.1–61.2:35–66.

Chuang, Hung-I 莊宏誼. 1994. "Les Croyances Concernant La Divinnite Taoiste Xuanwu (Xéme-XIIIeme Siecles)." Doctorial Dissertation. L.É.H.E.S.S.

Chuci zhangju 楚辭章句. Qu Yuan 屈原 et. al, edited and annotated by Wang Yi 王逸 (ca. 89–158). SKQS edn.

Daofa huiyuan 道法會元 (*A Corpus of Daoist Ritual*). TC 1210.

Daojia jinshi lüe 道家金石略 (*Epigraphy of Daoism*). 1988. Chen Yuan 陳垣, Chen Zhichao 陳智超, and Zeng Qingying 曾慶瑛 eds. Beijing: Wenwu chubanshe.

Daojiao lingyan ji 道教靈驗記 (*Evidential Miracles in Support of Daoism*). Du Guangting (850–933). TC 590.

Daomen dingzhi 道門定制 (*Prescribed Practices from the Portal of the Dao*). TC 1224.

Daomen kefan daquanji 道門科範大全集 (*Complete Collection of the Liturgy of the Portal of the Dao*) TC 1225.

Daomen shigui 道門十規. Zhang Yuchu 張宇初 (1359–1410). TC 1232.

Daomen tongjiao biyongji 道門通教必用集 (*Comprehensive and Requisite Manuals of the Portal of the Dao*).TC 1226.

Daoyuan xuegu lu 道園學古錄. 1341. Yu Ji 虞集 (1272–1348). SKQS edn.

Davis, Edward. 2001. *Society and the Supernatural in Song China*. Honolulu: University of Hawai'i Press.

Dayue Taihe shan zhi 大嶽太和山志. 1556. Wang Zuo 王佐 comp. In Dao Zhendian 陶真典 and Fan Xuefeng 范學鋒 eds, *Wudang shan lidai zhishu jizhu* 武當山歷代志書集注. Wuhan: Hubei kexue jishu chubanshe, 2003.

De Bruyn, Pierre-Henry. 1997. *"Le Wudang shan: Histoire des Récits Fondateurs."* Doctorial thesis, UFR Langues et civilisations d'Asie orientale, Universite Paris VII.

De Bruyn, Pierre-Henry. 2004. "Wudang shan: The Origins of a Major Center of Modern Taoism," in *Religion and Chinese Society, vol. II: Taoism and Local Religion in Modern China*, edited by John Lagerwey, 519–552. Hong Kong: The Chinese University Press.

Dieshan ji 疊山集. Xie Fangde 謝枋得 (1226–1289). SBCK edn.

Dongzhen gaoshang yudi dadong ciyi yujian wulao baojing 洞真高上玉帝大洞雌一玉檢五老寶經. Tang dynasty (618–907). TC 1313.

Dreyer, Edward. 1974. "The Poyang Campaign, 1363: Inland Naval Warfare in the Founding of the Ming Dynasty." In *Chinese Ways in Warfare*, edited by Frank A. Kierman Jr. and John K. Fairbank, 202–242. Cambridge, Mass.: Harvard University Press.

Duara, Prasenjit. 1988. "Superscribing Symbols: The Myth of Guandi, Chinese God of War." *Journal of Asian Studies* 47.4: 778–795.

Duara, Prasenjit. 1988a. *Culture, Power, and the State: Rural North China, 1900–1942*. Stanford, Calif.: Stanford University Press.

Dudbridge, Glen. 1978. *The Legend of Miao-shan*. London: Ithaca Press for the Board of the Faculty of Oriental Studies, Oxford University.

Dudbridge, Glen. 1995. *Religious Experience and Lay Society in T'ang China: A Reading of Tai Fu's Kuang-i chi*. Cambridge: Cambridge University Press.

Dunnell, Ruth W. 1996. *The Great State of White and High: Buddhism and State Formation in Eleventh-century Xia*. Honolulu: University of Hawai'i Press.

Eade, John, and Michael J. Sallnow. 1991. *Contesting the Sacred: The Anthropology of Christian Pilgrimage*. London and New York: Routledge.

Eberhard, Wolfran. 1964. "Temple-Building Activities in Medieval And Modern China—An Experimental Study." *Monumenta Serica* 23: 264–318.

Ebrey, Patricia B., and Maggie Bickford eds. 2006. *Emperor Huizong and Late Northern Song China: The Political of Culture and The Culture of Politics*. Cambridge, Mass.: Harvard University Asian Center.

Ebrey, Patricia B., and Peter Gregory, eds. 1993. *Religion and Society in T'ang and Sung China*. Honolulu: University of Hawai'i Press.

Erke Paian jingqi 二刻拍案驚奇. 1627. Ling Mengchu 凌濛初. Taipei: Guiguan chubanshe, 1984.

Eskildsen, Stephen. 2001. "Neidan Master Chen Pu's Nine Stages of Transformation." *Monumenta Serica* 49: 1–31.

Secret Essentials, see *Taishang zhuguo jiumin zongzhen miyao*.

Evidential Miracles, see *Daojiao lingyan ji*.

Fahai yizhou 法海遺珠 (*The Retrieved Pearls of the Ritual Sea*). Ca. 14th century. TC 1166.

Fangyu shenglan 方輿勝覽. 1256. Zhu Mu 祝穆 (Southern Song dynasty). SKQS edn.

Faure, David. 1990. "What Made Foshan a Town? The Evolution Of Rural–Urban Identities In Ming-Qing China." *Late Imperial China* 11.2: 1–31.

Feuchtwang, Stephan. 2001. *The Imperial Metaphor: Popular Religion in China*. Routledge.

Firth, Raymond. 1996. *Religion: a Humanist Interpretation*. London and New York: Routledge.

Fisher, Carney Thomas. 1990. *The Chosen One: Succession and Adoption in the Court of Ming Shizong*. Sydney: Allen & Unwin.

Foshan zhongyi xiang zhi 佛山忠義鄉志. 1926. 汪宗准 *et al*. In *Zhongguo difangzhi jicheng—xiangzhen zhi zhuanji* 中國地方志集成—鄉鎮志專輯. Nanjing: Jiangsu guji chuban she, Shanghai: Shanghai shudian, and Chengdu: Bashu shushe, 1991.

Faure, Bernard. 1992. "Relics and Flesh Bodies: The Creation of Ch'an Pilgrimage Sites." In *Pilgrims and Sacred Sites in China*, edited by Susan Naquin and Chün-fang Yü, 150–189. Berkeley and Los Angeles: University of California Press.

Fu Weilin 傅維麟. 1936. *Mingshu* 明書. In *Conshu jicheng chubian* 叢書集成初編, vols. 3929–3958. Shanghai: Shangwu yinshuguan.

Fuxi ji 浮溪集. Wang Zao 汪藻 (1079–1154). SKQS edn.

Geertz, Clifford. 1973. "Person, Time, and Conduct in Bali: An Essay in Cultural Analysis." In *ibid., The Interpretation of Cultures*, 360–411. New York: Basic Books. Reprint of *Person, Time, and Conduct in Bali: An Essay in Cultural Analysis*. Yale Southeast Asia Program, Cultural Report Series 14, 1966.

Gerritsen, Anne. 2004. "From Demon to Deity: Kang Wang in Thirteenth-Century Jizhou and Beyond. *T'oung Pao* 90.1:1–31.

Gerritsen, Anne. 2007. *Ji'an Literati and the Local in Song-Yuan-Ming China*. Leiden: Brill.

Giddens, Anthony. 1979. *Central Problems in Social Theory: Action, Structure, And Contradiction In Social Analysis*. Berkeley: University of California Press.

Giss, James. 1988. "The Chia-ching reign, 1522–1566." In *Cambridge History of China: The Ming Dynasty*, Part I, edited by Denis Twitchett and Frederick W. Mote, vol. 7: 440–510. Cambridge: Cambridge University Press.

Goosaert, Vincent. 1997 "La création du Taoisme moderne l'ordre Quanzhen." Ph.D. Diss., Ecole pratique des hautes études, Section des Sciences Religieuses.
Goossaert, Vincent. 2005. "The Beef Taboo and the Sacrificial Structure of Late Imperial Chinese Society." In *Of Tripod and Plate: Food, Politics, and Religion in Traditional China*, edited by Roel Sterckx, 237–248. New York: Palgrave Macmillan.
Goossaert, Vincent. 2007. *The Taoists of Peking, 1800–1949: A Social History of Urban Clerics.* Cambridge, Mass.: Harvard University Asia Center.
Graff, David A. 2002. *Medieval Chinese Warfare, 300–900.* London and New York: Routledge.
Graham, A.C. 1986. *Yin-Yang and the Nature of Correlative Thinks.* Singapore: Institute of East Asian Philosophies.
Graham, A.C. 1989. *Disputers of the Tao: Philosophical Argument in Ancient China.* La Salle, Ill.: Open Court.
Granet, Marcel. 1950. *La Pensée Chinoise*, Paris: Éditions Albin Michel. 1st edn., 1934.
Grant, Beata. 1989. "The Spiritual Saga of Woman Huang: from Pollution to Purification." In *Ritual Opera, Operatic Ritual: Mu-lien Rescues His Mother in Chinese Popular Culture*, edited by David Johnson, 224–311. Berkeley: Publications of the Chinese Popular Culture Project, No. 1.
Groot, J.J.M. de. 1892–1910. *The Religious System of China, Its Ancient Forms, Evolution, History and Present Aspect, Manners, Customs and Social Institutions Connected Therewith.* 6 vols. Leyden: E.J. Brill. Reprint by Southern Materials Center, Inc., Taipei, 1982.
Grootaers, Willem A. 1952. "The Hagiography of the Chinese God Chen-wu: the Transmission of Rural Traditions in Chahar." *Folklore Studies* 11.2: 139–181 and illustrations following (without page numbers).
Grootaers, Willem A., Li Shih-yu and Wang Fu-shih. 1952. "The Hagiography of the Chinese God Chen-wu," *Folklore Studies* 11.2: 139–181 and illustrations following. Reprinted in Willem A. Grootaers, *The Sanctuaries in a North-China City: A Complete Survey of the Cultic Buildings in the City of Hsüan-hua* (Chahar), 123–170. Institut Belge des Hautes Études Chinoises, 1995.
Gu, Wenbi 顧文璧. 1989. "Mingdai Wudang shan de xingsheng he Suzhouren de da guimo Wudan jinxiang lüxing" 明代武當山的興盛和蘇州人的大規模武當進香旅行" (The Prosperity of Wudang shan during the Ming dynasty and the vast scale pilgrimages of Suzhou residents to Wudang). *Jianghan kaogu* 江漢考古 1: 71–75.
Guangdong xinyu 廣東新語. Qu Dajun 屈大均 (1630–1696). Beijing: Zhonghua shuju, 1985.
Guichao gao 蛻巢稿. Xie Yingfang 謝應芳 (1295–1392). SKQS edn.
Guier ji 貴耳集. 1241–1248. Zhang Duanyi 張端義 (1179–ca.1248). SKQS edn.
Guigu zi tiansui lingwen 鬼谷子天髓靈文. Anonymous. TC 867.
Gujin shiwen leiju xinji 古今事文類聚新集. Fu Dayong 富大用 (Yuan dynasty). SKQS edn.
Guoque 國榷. 1652. Tan Qian 談遷 (1594–1658). Beijing: Guji chubanshe, 1958.
Gusu zhi 姑蘇志. Wang Ao 王鏊 (1450–1524). SKQS edn.
Haiqiong Bai zhenren yulu 海瓊白真人語錄. Bai Yuchan 白玉蟾 (1209–1224), TC 1307.
Hansen, Valerie. 1990. *Changing Gods in Medieval China, 1127–1276.* Princeton, N.J: Princeton University Press.
Hao, Yen-p'ing, and Hsiu-mei Wei, eds. 1988. *Tradition and Metamorphosis in Modern Chinese History: Essays in Honor Professor Kwang-Ching Liu's Seventy-fifth Birthday.* Taipei: Institute of Modern History, Academia Sinica.
Hargett, James M. 1996. "Song Dynasty Local Gazetteers and Their Place in the History of Difangzhi Writing." *Harvard Journal of Asiatic Studies* 56.2: 405–44.

Hawkes, David. 1985. *The Songs of the South: An Ancient Chinese Anthology of Poems by Qu Yuan And Other Poets Translated, Annotated, And Introduced by David Hawkes*. New York: Penguin Books.

Hayashi Minao 林巳奈夫. 1989. *Kandai no Kamigami* 漢代の神神. Kyōto: Rinsen Shoten.

Henderson, John B. 1984. *Development and Decline of Chinese Cosmology*. New York: Columbia University Press.

Hisayuki Miyakawa 宮川尚志. 1979. "Local Cults around Mount Lu at the Times of Sun En's Rebellion." In *Facets of Taoism: Essays in Chinese Religion*, edited by Holmes Welch, and Anna Seidel, 83–101. New Haven, Conn.: Princeton University Press.

Hou Hanshu 後漢書. Fan Ye 范曄 (398–445). Beijing: Zhonghua shuju, 1973.

Hsü, Tao-ling 許道齡. 1947. "On the Origin of Hsüan-wu and Its Development" (Lun Xuanwu zhi qiyuan jiqi tuibian 論玄武之起源及其蛻變). *Historical Journal (Shixue jikan)* 史學集刊 5: 223–240.

Huainan zi 淮南子. Attributed to Liu An (ca. 180–122 BCE), with commentaries by Gao You 高誘 (fl. 205–212). SKQS edn.

Huang, Zhaohan [Wang Shiu-hon] 黃兆漢. 1988 [1982]. "Xuandi kao 玄帝考." In *ibid., Daojiao yanjiu lunwenji* 道教研究論文集 (*A Collection of Articles of Daoist Studies*), 121–156. Hong Kong: Chinese University Press.

Hucker, Charles. 1985. *A Dictionary of Official Titles in Imperial China*. Reprint by Southern Materials Center, Inc., Taipei, 1995.

Hymes, Robert. 2002. *Way and Byway: Taoism, Local Religion, and Models of Divinity in Sung and Modern China*. Berkeley and Los Angeles: University of California Press.

Iriya Yoshitak 入矢義高 and Umehara Kaoru 梅原郁 trans. and annotate. 1983. Tokei Mukaroku – Sodai no doshi do seigatsu 東京夢華錄—宋代の都市生活. Tokyo: Yanbo shudian.

Ishida Kenji 石田憲司. 1995. "On the Belief in Zhenwu Shen at Southern Taiwan: Investigated Report about Zhen-wu shen under the rule of Qing Dynasty." *The Tiohô Shûkyû* 85: 24–40.

Jiean laoren manbi 戒庵老人漫筆. 1597. Li Xu 李詡 (1506–1593). Beijing: Zhonghua shuju, 1982.

Jing, Anning. 1994. "The Portraits of Khubilai Khan and Chabi by Anige (1245–1306), a Nepali Artist at the Yuan Court." *Artibus Asiae* 54.1/2: 40–86.

Jing, Anning. 2002. *Yuandai bihua—shenxian fuhui tu* 元代壁畫—神仙赴會圖 (*A Yuan mural—Assembly of the immortals*). Beijing: Beijing daxue chubanshe.

Jingding Jiankang zhi 景定建康志. 1261. Zhou Yinghe 周應合 (1213–1280). SKQS edn.

Jinjiang xianzhi 晉江縣志 1990. Zhou Xuezeng 周學曾 et al. compiled and edited by the Editorial Committee of Gazetteers of Jinjiang prefecture. Fuzhou: Fujian renmin chubanshe, 1990.

Jinshi lüe see *Daojia jinshi lüe*.

Jinshu 晉書. Fang Xuanling 房玄齡 (579–648). Beijing: Zhonghua shuju, 1974.

Jiu Tangshu 舊唐書. Liu Xu 劉昫 (887–946). Beijing: Zhonghua shuju, 1975.

Jiu Wudaishi 舊五代史. Xue Juzheng 薛居正 (912–981). Beijing: Zhonghua shuju, 1976.

Johnson, David, Evenly S. Rawski, and Andrew J. Nathan, eds. 1985. *Popular Culture in Late Imperial China*. Berkeley and Los Angeles: University of California Press.

Johnson, David. 1985. "The City God cults of T'ang and Sung China." *Harvard Journal of Asiatic Studies* 45, 363–457.

Jordan, David. 1972. *Gods, Ghosts, and Ancestors: The Folk Religion of a Taiwanese Village*. Berkeley: University of California Press.

Journey to the West. Wu Cheng'en 吳承恩 (ca. 1500–1582). Translated by Anthony C. Yü. Chicago, Ill.: University of Chicago Press, 1977.

Kang, Xiaofei. 2006. *The Cult Of The Fox: Power, Gender, And Popular Religion In Late Imperial And Modern China*. New York: Columbia University Press.

Katz, Paul R. 1995. *Demon Hordes and Burning Boats: The Cult of Marshal Wen in Late Imperial Chekiang*. Albany, N.Y.: State University of New York Press.

Katz, Paul R. 1999. *Images of the Immortal: The Cult of Lü Dongbin at the Palace of Eternal Joy*. Honolulu: University of Hawai'i Press.

Katz, Paul R. 2008. "Trial by Power: Some Preliminary Observations on the Judicial Roles of Taoist Martial Deities." *Journal of Chinese Religions* 36: 54–83.

Kierman, Frank A. Jr., and John K. Fairbank eds. 1974. *Chinese Ways in Warfare*. Cambridge, Mass.: Harvard University Press.

Kleeman, Terry. 1993. "The Expansion of the Wen-ch'ang Cult." In *Religion and Society in T'ang and Sung China* edited by Patricia B. Ebrey and Peter Gregory, 45–73. Honolulu: University of Hawai'i Press.

Kleeman, Terry. 1994. *A God's Own Tale: The Book of the Transformations of Wenchang, the Divine Lord of Zitong*. Albany, N.Y.: State University of New York Press.

Kleeman, Terry. 2004. "Reconstructing China's Religious Past: Textual Criticism and Intellectual History." *Journal of Chinese Religions* 32: 29–45.

Kohn, Livia, ed. 2000. *Daoist Handbook*. Leiden: Brill.

Kojima, Tsuyoshi 小島毅. 1990. "Seikoyō sedo no seiritsu 城隍廟制度の成立." *Shisō* 思想 792: 197–212.

Kongshi zuting guangji 孔氏祖庭廣記. 1227. Kong Yuancuo 孔元措 (fl. 1191–1227). SKQS edn.

Kroll, Paul W. 1996. "On 'Far Roaming.'" *Journal of the American Oriental Society* 116.4: 653–669.

Kuiche zhi 睽車志. Guo Tuan 郭彖 (fl. 1165). SKQS edn.

Lagerwey, John. 1987. *Taoist Ritual in Chinese Society and History*. New York: Macmillan.

Lagerwey, John. 1992. "The Pilgrimage to Wudang shan." In *Pilgrims and Sacred Sites in China*, edited by Susan Naquin and Chün-fang Yü, 293–332. Berkeley and Los Angeles: University of California Press.

Lagerwey, John. 2004. "Taishang Dadao yüqing jing." In *Taoist Cannon*, edited by Kristofer Schipper and Franciscus Verellen, 525–527. Chicago, Ill.: The University of Chicago Press.

Lejing ji 樂靜集. Li Zhaoqi 李昭玘 (d. 1126). SKQS edn.

Lévi-Strauss, Claude. 1969. *The Raw and the Cooked*. Translated by John and Doreen Weightman. New York: Harper & Row.

Lewis, Mark Edward. 1990. *Sanctioned Violence in Early China*. Albany, N.Y.: State University of New York Press.

Lewis, Mark Edward. 2006. *The Construction of Space in Early China*. Albany, N.Y.: State University of New York Press.

Li, Guohong 李國宏. 1998. "Yongning Huxiu si Xuanwu xinyang wenhua diaocha yu fenxi 永寧虎岫寺玄武信仰文化調察與分析 (Investigation and Analysis of the culture of the Xuanwu cult of the Huxiu temple, Yongning)." In *Daoyun* 道韻, edited by Zhan Shichuang, vol. 3: 210–219. Taipei: Zhonghua dadao chubanbu.

Li, Huarui 李华瑞. 1998. *Song Xia guanxi shi* 宋夏关系史. Shijiazhuang: Hebei renmin chubanshe.

Li, Xueqin 李學勤. 1999. "Xishui po "longhu mu" yu sixiang de qiyuan" 西水坡龍虎墓與四象的起源. In *ibid.*, *Li Xueqin juan* (李學勤卷), 101–109. Hefei Shi: Anhui jiao yu chu ban she : Jing xiao Xin hua shu dian.

Li, Yuanguo 李远国. 2003. *Shenxiao leifa: Daojiao Shenxiao pai yange yu sixiang* 神霄雷法：道教神霄派沿革与思想. Chengdu: Sichuan renmin chubanshe.

Libu zhigao 禮部志稿 (*Draft monograph on the Ministry of Rites*). 1620. Yu Ruji 俞汝楫 et al eds. SKQS edn.

Lin Fu-shi 林富士. 1994. "Shamans and Shamanism in the Chiang-nan Area during the Six Dynasties Period (3rd-6th Century A.D.)" Doctorial thesis, Dept. of East Asian Studies, Princeton University.

Lin Tianwei 林天蔚. 1962. "Songdai chushou dudie zhi yanjiu 宋代出售度牒之研究." (A study on the sale of ordination licenses in Song Dynasty). *Chongji xuebao* 崇基學報 2.1: 76–100.

Linchuan xiansheng wenji 臨川先生文集. Wang Anshi 王安石 (1021–1086). SBCK edn.

Linding zhi 临汀志. Hu Taichu 胡太初 (jinshi 1238); Changding xian difangzhi bianzuan weiyuanhui 长汀县地方志编纂委员会 Comp. Fuzhou: Fujian renmin chubanshe, 1990.

Lishi zhenxian tidao tongjian 歷世真仙體道通鑑, TC 296.

Little, Stephen. 2000. *Taoism and Arts of China*. Chicago, Ill.: The Art Institute of Chicago.

Liu, Kwang-ching, ed. 1990. *Orthodoxy in Late Imperial China*. Berkeley and Los Angeles: University of California Press.

Liu, Zhiwan. 劉枝萬. 1987. "Tenhōshin to tenhōju ni tsuite 天蓬神と天蓬咒について." In Dōkyo to shūkyō bunka 道教宗教文化, edited by Akizuki Kannei 秋月觀暎, 403–424. Tokyo: Hirakawa shupppaan.

Liu, Zhiwei 劉志偉. 1994. "Worship of Popular Deities under the Shadow of the Big Clans: The Northern Emperor Cult in Shawan (Dazu yinying xia de minjin shen chongbai: Shawan de Beidi xinyang 大族陰影下的民間神崇拜：沙灣的北帝信仰)." In *The Proceedings of the Conference of Temples and Popular Culture*, 707–722. Taipei: The Center of Sinology.

Liu, Zhiwei 劉志偉. 1994a. "Shenming de zhengtong xing yu difang hua—guanyu zhujiang sanjiaozhou diqu Beidi chongbai de yige jieshi 神明的正統性與地方化－關於珠江三角州地區北帝崇拜的一個解釋." *Zhongshan daxue shixue jikan* 中山大學史學集刊 2: 107–125.

Loewe, Michael. 1979. *Ways to Paradise: The Chinese Quest for Immortality*. London: George Allen & Unwin.

Lu Xiansheng Daomen kelue 陸先生道門科略 *Survey on Rituals of the Daoist Portal by Master Lu*. Lu Xiujing. TC 1127.

Mair, Victor H. ed. 2001. *The Columbia History of Chinese Literature* (NY: Columbia University Press.

Major, John S. 1986. "New Light on the Dark Warrior." *Journal of Chinese Religions* 13–14, 65–86.

Major, John S. 1993. *Heaven And Earth In Early Han Thought: Chapters Three, Four And Five Of The Huainanzi*. Albany: State University of New York Press.

Mano Senryū 間野潛龍. 1979. *Mindai bunkashi kenkyū* 明代文化史研究 *(A study of the Cultural History in the Ming Period)*. Kyōto: Dōhōsha.

Maspero, Henri. 1981. Translated by Frank A. Kierrman, Jr. 1981. *Taoism and Chinese Religion*. Amherst, Mass.: The University of Massachusetts Press.

Matsumoto Kōichi 松本浩一. 1979. "Sōdai no raihō 宋代の雷法." *Shakai bunka shigaku* 17: 45–65.

Mei Li 梅莉. 2007. *Ming Qing shiqi Wudang shan chaoshan jinxiang yanjiu* 明清时期武当山朝山进香研究. Wuhan Shi : Hua zhong shi fan da xue chu ban she.

Mengliang lu 夢粱錄. Wu Zimu 吳自牧 (fl. 1270). SKQS edn.

Meulenbeld, Mark. 2006. "Civilized Demons: Ming Thunder Gods from Ritual to Literature." Doctoral thesis, Princeton University.

Ming Shizong shilu 明世宗實錄. Zhang Juzheng 張居正 (1525–1582) et al comp. Taipei: Institute of History and Philology, Academia Sinica, 1966.

Ming Taizong shilu. 明太宗實錄. Yang Shiqi 楊士奇 (1365–1444) et al comp. Taipei: Institute of History and Philology, Academia Sinica, 1966.

Ming Taizu wenji 明太祖文集. 1374. Zhu Yuanzhang 朱元璋 (Emperor Hongwu) (1328–98). SKQS edn.

Mingshi 明史. 1739. Zhang Tingyu 張廷玉 (1672–1755). Beijing: Zhonghua shuju, 1974.

Mingshu 明書. Fu Weilin 傅維麟 (d. 1667). In *Conshu jicheng chubian* 叢書集成初編, vols 3929–3958. Shanghai: Shangwu, 1936.

Mollier, Christine. 1997. "La methode de l'Empereur du Nord du mont Fengdu : Une tradition exorciste du taoïsme médiéval." *T'oung Pao* LXXXII: 330–383.

Nanhai xianzhi 南海縣志 1910. Gui Dian 桂坫 (*Jinshi* 1894) and Zheng Rong 鄭榮. Taipei: Chengwen chubanshe, 1974.

Nanshi 南史. 659. 李延壽 (Seventh century). Beijing: Zhonghua shuju, 1983.

Naquin, Susan, and Chün-fang Yü eds. 1992. *Pilgrims and Sacred Sites in China*. Berkeley and Los Angeles: University of California Press.

Nikaidō Yoshihiro 二階堂善弘. 1998. "A Transformation of Xuantian Shangdi: – on the relationship among some Taoist scriptures. 玄天上帝の 變容数種の経典間の相互関係をめぐって." *Tōhō shūkyō* 東方宗教 (*The Journal of Eastern Religions*) 91 (May): 60–77.

Ōfuchi Ninji 大淵忍爾. 1983. *Chūgokujin no shukyo girei* 中國人の 宗教儀禮. Tokyo: Fukutakai zuzobu.

Ortner, Sherry. 1984. "Theory in Anthropology since the Sixties." *Comparative Studies in Society and History* 26.1: 126–65.

Ortner, Sherry. 2006. *Anthropology and Social Theory: Culture, Power, and the Acting Subject*. Duke University Press.

Orzech, Charles D. 1989. "Seeing Chen-Yen Buddhism: Traditional Scholarship and the Vajrayana in China." *History of Religions* 29.2: 87–114.

Overmyer, Daniel L. 1999. *Precious Volumes: An Introduction to Chinese Sectarian Scriptures from the Sixteenth and Seventeenth Centuries*. Cambridge, Mass.: Harvard University Asia Center.

Piotrovsky, Mikhail. 1993. *Lost Empire of the Silk Road: Buddhist Art from Khara Khoto (X-XIIIth century)*. Milan: Thyssen-Bornemisza Foundation.

Pregadio, Fabrizio, ed. 2008. *Encyclopedia of Taoism*. London: Routledge.

Pregadio, Fabrizio. 2006. "Early Daoist Meditation and the Origins of Internal Alchemy." In *Daoism in History: Essays in Honour of Liu Ts'un-yan*, edited by Benjamin Penny, 121–158. London: Routledge.

Puett, Michael. 1998. "Sages, Ministers, and Rebels: Narratives from Early China Concerning the Initial Creation of the State." *Harvard Journal of Asiatic Studies* 58: 425–479.

Puett, Michael. 2002. *To Become a God: Cosmology, Sacrifice, and Self-Divinization in Early China*. Cambridge, Mass.: Harvard University Asia Center for the Harvard-Yenching Institute

Qiantang yishi 錢塘遺事. Thirteenth to fourteenth centuries. Liu Yiqong 劉一清. Shanghai: Shanghai guji chubanshe, 1985.

Qinding rixiao jiuwen kao 欽定日下舊聞考. 1782. Yu Minzhong 于敏中 (1714–1779) et al eds. SKQS edn.

Qingbo zazhi jiaozhu 清波雜志校注. 1192 (prefaced). Zhou Hui 周煇 (b. 1127). Edited and annotated by Liu Yongxiang 劉永翔. Beijing: Zhonghua shuju, 1994.

Qingshi gao 清史稿. 1927. Zhao Erxun 趙爾巽. Zhonghua shuju, 1978.

Qingwei xianpu 清微仙譜. TC 171.

Qisheng lu, see *Taishang shuo Xuantian shangdi qisheng lu*.

Qiyun shan zhi 齊雲山志. 1599; printing blocks re-carved in 1830. Lu Dian 魯點 (*jinshi* 1583).Taipei: Chengwen chubanshe, 1985.

Quan Houhan wen 全後漢文. 1893. In *Quan Shanggu Sandai Qin Han Sanguo Liuchao wen*, edited by Yan Kejun 嚴可均 (1762–1843); reprint, Taipei: Shijie shuju, 1963.

Quxuan ji 臞軒集. Wang Mai 王邁 (1184–1248). SKQS edn.

Ren Jiyu 任繼愈 *et al.* eds. 1991. *Daozang tiyao* 道藏提要 (revised edition). Beijing: Zhongguo shehui kexue chubanshe.

Reiter, Florian C. 2007. *Basic Conditions of Taoist Thunder Magic*. Wiesbaden: Harrassowitz.

Robinet, Isabelle. 1989. "Original Contributions of Neidan to Taoism and Chinese Thought." In *Taoist Meditation and Longevity Techniques*, edited by Livia Kohn, 297–330. Ann Arbor: Center for Chinese Studies, the University of Michigan (Michigan Monographs in Chinese Studies).

Robinet, Isabelle. 1984. *La revelation du Shangqing dans l'histoire du taoisme* (Publications de l'Ecole francaise d'Extreme-Orient), no. 137. 2 volumes. Paris: l'Ecole francaise d'Extreme-Orient.

Robinet, Isabelle. 1993. *Taoist Meditation: the Mao-shan Tradition of Great Purity*. Translated by Julian F. Pas and Norman J. Albany, N.Y.: State University of New York Press.

Robinet, Isabelle. 1997. *Taoism: Growth of A Religion*. Translated by Phyllis Brooks. Stanford: Stanford University Press.

Rossabi, Morris. 1988. *Khubilai Khan: His Life and Times*. Berkeley and Los Angeles: University of California Press.

Sahlins, Marshall. 1981. *Historical Metaphors and Mythical Realities: Structure in the Early History of the Sandwich Islands Kingdom*. Ann Arbor: University of Michigan Press.

Sahlins, Marshall. 1985. *Islands of History*. Chicago, Ill.: University of Chicago Press.

Sandong xiudao yi 三洞修道儀. TC 1237.

Sanfu huangtu 三輔黃圖. 1784. Bi Yuan. 畢沅 (1730–1797) ed. SKQS edn.

Schipper, Kristofer M. 1985. "Taoist Ritual and Local Cults of the T'ang Dynasty." In *Tantric and Taoist Studies in Honour of R. A. Stein*, edited by Michael Strickmann, vol. 3:812–834. Bruxelles: Institut belge des hautes études chinoises.

Schipper, Kristofer M. 1985a. "Vernacular and Classical Ritual in Taoism." *Journal of Asian Studies* 45.1: 21–51.

Schipper, Kristofer M. 1993. *The Taoist Body*. Translated by Karen C. Duval. Berkeley: University of California Press.

Schipper, Kristofer and Verellen Franciscus eds. 2004. *The Taoist Canon: a historical companion to the Daozang*. Chicago, Ill.: University of Chicago Press.

Scott, James C. 1992. *Domination and the Arts of Resistance: Hidden Transcripts*. New Haven, Conn.: Yale University Press.

Seaman, Gary. 1987. *Journey to the North: An Ethnohistorical Analysis and Annotated Translation of the Chinese Folk Novel Pei-yu-chi*. Berkeley and Los Angeles: University of California Press.

Secret Essential, see *Taishang zhuguo jiumin zongzhen miyao*.

Shaanxi tongzhi 陝西通志. 1735. Liu Yuyi 劉於義（1675–1748） *et al.* eds. SKQS edn.

Shahar, Meir, and Robert P. Weller, eds. 1996. *Unruly Gods: Divinity and Society in China*. Honolulu: University of Hawai'i Press.

Shandong Yinan Han mu hua xiang shi 山東沂南漢墓畫像石. 2001. Shandong Yinan Han mu bowu guan 山東省沂南漢墓博物館 eds. Jinan: Qilu shushe.

Shangqing tianxin zhengfa 上清天心正法. Deng Yougong 鄧有功 (11th–12th centuries). TC 566.

Shangshu zhushu 尚書註疏. Kong Yingda 孔穎達 (574–648) *et al*. SKQS edn.

Shanhai jing 山海經. Guo Pu 郭璞 (276–324) ed. SKQS edn.
Shanxi tongzhi 山西通志. 1892. Wang Xuan 王軒 (1823–1887). SKQS edn.
Shenzhou qizhuan qibian wutian jing 神州七轉七變舞天經. TC 1331.
Shiji 史記 (*Grand History*). Sima Qian 司馬遷 (ca. 145BC?–ca. 86 BC). Beijing: Zhonghua shuju, 1972.
Shuijing zhu 水經注 (*Commentaries on the Scripture of the Water [Routes]*). Li Daoyuan 酈道元 (466–527). SKQS edn.
Shuowen jiezi zhu 說文解字注 (*Explaining Single-component Graphs and Analyzing Compound Characters, with Commentaries*). Xu Shen 許慎 (ca. 58–147), with commentary by Duan Yucai 段玉裁 (1735–1815). SKQS edn.
Sichuan Xuzhou fuzhi. Kangxi reign (1472–1522). [康熙]四川敘州府志. In *Xijian Zhongguo difangzhi huikan* 稀見中國地方志彙刊, vol. 50. Beijing: Zhongguo shudian, 1992.
Skar, Lowell. 1996–97. "Administering Thunder: A Thirteenth-Century Memorial Deliberating the Thunder Rites." *Cahiers d'Extrême-Asie* 9: 159–202.
Skar, Lowell. 2000. "Ritual Movements, Deity Cults, and the Transformation of Daoism in Song and Yuan Times." In *Daoism Handbook*, edited by Livia Kohn, 413–63. Leiden: Brill.
Smith, Joanna F. Hadlin. 1999. "Liberating Animals in Ming-Qing China: Buddhist Inspiration and Elite Imagination". *The Journal of Asian Studies* 58.1: 51–84.
Smith, Paul J. 2003. "Problematizing the Song-Yuan-Ming Transition." In *The Song-Yuan-Ming Transition in Chinese History*, edited by Paul J. Smith and Richard von Glahn, 1–34. Cambridge, Mass.: Harvard University Asia Center.
Smith, Richard J. 1991. *Fortune-tellers and Philosophers: Divination In Traditional Chinese Society*. Boulder, Col.: Westview Press.
Song da zhaoling ji 宋大詔令集 (*Collected the grand edicts of the Song*). Song Shou 宋綬 (991–1040) and Song Minqiu 宋敏求 (1019–1079) eds. Beijing: Zhonghua shuju, 1962.
Song Dongjing kao 宋東京考. Zhou Cheng 周城 (18th century). Taibei: Wenshizhe chubanshe, 1990.
Song Gaoseng zhuan. 988. Zanning 贊寧 (919–1001). Beijing: Zhonghu shuju, 1987.
Songshi 宋史. 1345. Tuotuo 脫脫 (d. 1362). Beijing: Zhonghua shuju. 1977.
Soushen ji 搜神記. Gan Bao 干寶 (d. 336)
Stein, Rolf A. 1979. "Religious Taoism and Popular Religion from the Second to Seventh Centuries." In *Facets of Taoism: Essays in Chinese Religion*, edited by Holmes Welch and Anna Seidel, 53–81. New Haven, Conn.: Yale University Press.
Steinhardt, Nancy Shatzman. 1990. *Chinese Imperial City Planning*. Honolulu: University of Hawaii Press.
Strickmann, Michel. 1977. "The Longest Taoist Scripture." *History of Religions* 17: 331–354.
Strickmann, Michel, ed. 1985. *Tantric and Taoist Studies in Honour of R.A.Stein*. 3 vols. Bruxelles: Institut belge des hautes études chinoises.
Strickmann, Michel. 1975. "Sōdao no raigi 宋代の雷儀" *Tōhō Shūkyō* 46: 15–28.
Strickmann, Michel. 1979. "The Taoist Renaissance of the Twelfth Century." Paper presented at the 3rd International Conference of Taoist Studies, Unterageri, Switzerland.
Strickmann, Michel and Bernard Faure eds. 2002. *Chinese Magical Medicine*. Stanford, Calif.: Stanford University Press.
Suishu 隋書. 636. Wei Zheng 魏徵 (580–643). Beijing: Zhonghua shuju, 1973.
Sun, Xiaochun, and Jacob Kistemaker. 1997. *The Chinese Sky during the Han: Constellating Stars and Society*. Leiden: Brill.
Szonyi, Michael. 1997. "The Illusion of Standardizing the Gods: The Cult of the Five Emperors in Late Imperial China." *The Journal of Asian Studies* 56.1:113–135.

Taiping guangji 太平廣記. Li Fang 李昉 (925–996) ed. SKQS edn.
Taiping yulan 太平御覽. Li Fang 李昉 (925–996) ed. SKQS edn.
Taishang Dadao yuqing jing 太上大道玉清經. TC 1312
Taishang Dongshen tiangong xiaomo huguo jing 太上洞神天公消魔護國經. TC 654
Taishang jiuzhen miaojie jinlu duming bazui jing 太上九真妙戒金錄度命拔罪經 (*Scripture of the Golden Register for the Redemption of Sins and for Salvation, [including] the Nine True and Marvelous Precepts*), CT 181.
Taishang laojun zhongjing 太上老君中經. TC 1168.
Taishang shuo Xuantian dasheng Zhenwu benzhuan shenzhou miaojing 太上說玄天大聖真武本傳神咒妙經 (*The wonderful scripture of the original hagiography of Zhenwu, the great sage of the dark heaven, the most high*), CT 754.
Taishang shuo Xuantian dasheng Zhenwu benzhuan shenzhou miaojing [zhu] 太上說玄天大聖真武本傳神咒妙經[註] ([*Commentary on*] *the Wonderful Scripture of the Original Hagiography of Zhenwu, the Great Sage of the Dark Heaven, the Most High*), CT 753.
Taishang yuanshi tianzun shou Beidi fumo shenzhou miaojing 太上元始天尊說北帝伏魔神咒妙經.TC 1412.
Taishang zhuguo jiumin zongzhen miyao 太上助國救民總真祕要. 1116. 元妙宗 (fl. 1086–1116). TC 1227.
Tang Daijian 唐代劍. 2003. *Songdai Daojiao guanli zhidu yanjiu* 宋代道教管理制度研究. Beijing: Xianzhuang shuju.
Taylor, Romeyn. 1990. "Official and Popular Religion and the Political Organization of Chinese Society in the Ming." In *Orthodoxy in Late Imperial China*, edited by Kwang-ching Liu, 126–157. Berkeley and Los Angeles: University of California Press.
ter Haar, Barend J. 1996. "Review: *Changing Gods*." *T'oung Pao* LXXXII: 184–194.
ter Haar, Barend J. 2006. *Telling Stories: Witchcraft and Scapegoating in Chinese History*. Leiden: Brill.
Tokei Mukaroku—Sodai no doshi do seigatsu 東京夢華錄—宋代の都市生活. Meng Yuanlao 孟元老. Fl. 1103–1147. Translated, and annotated by Iriya Yoshitak 入矢義高 and Umehara Kaoru 梅原郁. Tokyo: Yanbo shudian, 1983.
Tuhua jianwen zhi 圖畫見聞志. 1074. Guo Ruoxu 郭若虛 (fl. 1070–1074). In *Zhongguo shuhua quanshu* 中國書畫全書, vol. 1. Shanghai: Shanghai shudian, 2000.
Twitchett, Denis, and Frederick W. Mote, eds. 1988. *The Cambridge History of China: The Ming Dynasty, 1368–1644*, Part 1, vol. 7. Cambridge: Cambridge University Press.
van der Loon, Piet. 1979. "A Taoist Collection of the Fourteenth Century." *Studia Sinica-Mongolica*. Wiesbaden: Franz Steiner Verlag.
Verellen, Franciscus. 1989. *Du Guangtint (850–933)—Taoïste de cour à la fin de la China, médiévale* [*A Court Taoist in Late Medieval China*]. Paris: Collège de France. Mémoires de l'IEHC, vol. XXX.
Verellen, Franciscus. 2004. "The Heavenly Master Liturgical Agenda According to *Chisong zi's Petition Almanac*." *Cahiers d'Extrême-Asie* 14: 291–343.
von Glahn, Richard. 1991. "The Enchantment of Wealth: The God Wutong in the Social History of Jiangnan." *Harvard Journal of Asiatic Studies* 51. 2: 651–714.
von Glahn, Richard. 2004. *The Sinister Way: The Divine and the Demonic in Chinese Religious Culture*. Berkeley and Los Angeles: University of California Press.
Wang Guangde 王光德, and Yang Lizhi 楊立志. 1993. *Wudang daojiao shilüe* 武當道教史略 (A Brief History of Wudang Daoism). Beijing: Huawen chubanshe.
Wang Jianmin 王健民 et al. 1979. "Zenghou Yi mu chutu de ershiba xiu qinglong baihu tuxiang" 曾侯乙墓出土的二十八宿青龍白虎圖象. *Wenwu* 7: 40–45.

Wang, Aihe. 2000. *Cosmology and Political Culture in Early China*. Cambridge: Cambridge University Press.
Wang, Zhongshu. 1982. *Han Civilization*. Translated by K.C. Chang *et al*. New Haven and London: Yale University Press.
Watson, James L. 1985. "Standardizing the Gods: The Promotion of T'ien Hou ("Empress of Heaven") Along the South China Coast, 960–1960." In *Popular Culture in Late Imperial China*, edited by David Johnson, Andrew J. Nathan, and Evenly S. Rawski, 292–324. Berkeley and Los Angeles: University of California Press.
Wang, Richard. 2010. "Qiyunshan as a Replica of Wudangshan and the Religious Landscape of the Ming Empire." Paper presented at "An International Symposium: Divinity and Society—The Cult of Zhenwu in Imperial and Modern China."
Weinan ji 渭南集. Li Zhi 李廌 (1059–1109). SKQS edn.
Welch, Holmes, and Anna Seidel, eds. 1979. *Facets of Taoism: Essays in Chinese Religion*. New Haven, Conn.: Princeton University Press.
Wheatley, Paul. 1971. *The Pivot of the Four Quarters*. Chicago: Aldine Publishing Co.
White, William Charles. 1945. *The Lord of the Northern Dipper*. Bulletin of the Royal Ontario Museum of Archaeology.
Wudang shan jinshi lu. 武當山金石錄. 1990. Zhang Huaben 張華本 ed. Danjiangkou shi: Wenhua ju.
*Wulin jiushi, [Zengbu] [*增補*]*武林舊事. Ca. 1290. Zhou Mi 周密 (1232–1298). SKQS edn.
Xianchun Lin'an zhi 咸淳臨安志. 1265–1274. Qian Yueyou 潛說友 (13th century). SKQS edn.
Xiangshan quanji 象山全集. Lu Jiuyuan 陸九淵 (1139–1192). SKQS edn.
Xianyou xianzhi 仙遊縣志. 1771; re-carved, 1872/1873. In *Putian Xianyou xianshi heding ben* 莆田仙遊縣志合訂本. Taipei: Puxian tongxiang hui, 1963.
Xin Wudai shi 新五代史. 1053. Ouyang Xiu 歐陽修 (1007–1072). Beijing: Zhonghua shuju, 1974.
Xiong, Victor. 1996. "Ritual Innovations and Taoism under Tang Xuanzong." *T'ong Pao* 82.4/5: 258–316
Xishang futan 席上腐談. Yu Yan 俞琰 (1258–1314). Hebei: Hebei jiaoyu chubanshe, 1994.
Xu Gaoseng zhuan 續高僧傳. 645. Daoxuan 道宣 (596–667). Beijing: Zhonghua shuju, 1992.
Xu Xiake youji 徐霞客遊記. Xu Hongzu 徐宏祖 (1586–1641). SKQS edn.
Xu Zi zhi tong jian changbian 續資治通鑑長編. Li Tao 李燾 (1115–1184). SKQS edn.
Xuantian shangdi qisheng lingyi lu 玄天上帝啟聖靈異錄. TC 961.
Xuantian shangdi qisheng lu 玄天上帝啟聖錄 (*Record of the Epiphany of the Supreme Emperor of the Dark Heaven*). TC 958.
Xuantian dasheng, see *Taishang shuo Xuantian dasheng Zhenwu benzhuan shenzhou miaojing*.
Yang Wengong Tanyuan 楊文公談苑. Yang Yi 楊億 (974–1020), Song Xiang 宋庠 (998–1066) ed. Shanghai: Shanghai guji chubanshe, 1993.
Yang, Lien-sheng. 1947. "A Note on the So-called TLV Mirrors and the Game Liu-po." *Harvard Journal of Asiatic Studies* 9. 3/4 : 202–206.
Yang Lizhi 楊立志. 2005. "Wudang jinxiang xisu diyu fenbu chuyi" 武当香俗地域分布 芻議. In *Hubei daxue xuebao* (2005.1).
Yanzhou fuzhi [Wanli] 嚴州府志 *[*萬曆*]*. 1578. Beijing: Shumu wenxian chubanshe, 1990.
Yizhou minghua lu 益州名畫錄. 1006. Huang Xiufu 黃休復 (fl. 1006). In *Zhongguo shuhua quanshu* 中國書畫全書, vol. 1. Shanghai: Shanghai shudian, 2000.

Yongcheng jixian lu 墉城集仙錄 (*Record of the Assembled Transcendents of the Fortified Walled City*. Du Guangting 杜光庭 (850–933). TC 783.

Youyang zazu 酉陽雜俎. Duan Chengshi 段成式 (9th century). SKQS edn.

Yu Guang-hong (Yü Kuang-hong) 余光弘. 1983. "Taiwan diqu minjian zongjiao de fazhan: simiao diaocha ziliao zhi fenxi 臺灣地區民間宗教的發展：寺廟調查資料之分析." *Zhongyang yanjiu yuan Minzu xue yanjiusuo jikan* 中央研究院民族學研究所集刊 53: 67–103.

Yuanshi 元史. 1369. Song Lian 宋濂 (1310–1381). Beijing: Zhonghua shuju, 1976.

Yuanshi tianzun shuo beifang Zhenwu miaojing 元始天尊說北方真武妙經. TC 27.

Yuanshi wuliang duren shangpin miaojing 元始無量度人上品妙經. TC 1.

Yunji qiqian 雲笈七籤. 1017–1021. Zhang Junfang 張君房 (jinshi 1004–1007) ed. Beijing: Zhonghua shuju. 1992. TC 1026.

Zerubavel, Eviatar. 1981. *Hidden Rhythms: Schedules and Calendars in Social Life*. Chicago, Ill.: Chicago University Press.

Zhengao 真誥. Yang Xi 楊羲 (4th century). Compiled by Tao Hongjing 陶弘景 (456–536). TC 1016.

Zhuzi yulei 朱子語類. Zhu Xi 朱熹 (1130–1200). SKQS edn.

Zhongjiang xianzhi. 中江縣志. 1991. In *Sichuan fu xianzhi ji*. 四川府縣志輯. Nanjing: Jiangsu guji chubanshe, Shanghai: Shanghai shudian, and Chengdu: Bashu shushe, 1991.

Zongzhen miyao, see *Taishang zhuguo jiumin zongzhen miyao*.

Index

afterlife: and deity veneration, 111–112; and imperial burial site construction, 17–20
Aiding Sage (Yousheng), title of Zhenwu, 72, 132n49
ancestor veneration: and pilgrimage, 95; and ritual specialists, 69–71; temple building for, 35–36
animals: release of, 43–44, 128n31; sacrifices of, 40, 85
anthropomorphosis: of the Four Animals, 20; and General Xuanwu, 27–28; of Xuanwu the turtle, 15, 20, 21, 27–28. *See also* deity evolution
apotheosis, and Daoist *bianshen* rituals, 66–67
architecture: and cosmological orientation, 19–20; Jiajing's renovation project on Mt Wudang, 99–100; terms for religious buildings, 10; Yongle's temple building on Mt Wudang, 97–98. *See also* temple building
astral origins of Zhenwu, 13–14

Bai Yuchan, 52, 73
Beidi, see North Emperor
Beidi Leigong fa yi juan, 52
bianshen neilan (internal refinement): and the Celestial Heart school, 55–59, 67; and correlative cosmology, 76; introduced, 11, 47, 53, 66–67; and Supreme Clarity meditation, 67, 76; transformation into Zhenwu, 53–55, 57–58, 67. *See also* rituals
birth, 4–6, of Zhenwu 93; prayers for sons, 109–110, 112–113, 118; of Princess Jingguo (daughter of Emperor Song Renzong), 117
birthday celebration, 43–45, 87, 96, 110

Black Killer (Heisha aka Yisheng): associated with Zhenwu, 30; and exorcist practices, 25, 105; and the Xuanwu-Heisha talisman, 56–57, 130nn16,19. *See also* Four Saints
Book of Consecration (*Guanding jing*), 65
Bourdieu, Pierre, 8
Bokenkamp, Stephen, 22, 125nn16, 18
Buddhism: life story of Asanga, 92; Mahakala veneration, 108; and meditation, 61, 64–65, 80; Mongolian interest in, 108, 123n4; on Mt Wudang, 80–81; and Zhenwu's biography, 6
bureaucratic metaphor: and visualization techniques, 58, 73–75; and Daoist ritual efficacy, 58, 86; and the master-disciple bond, 67–72; and the six heavens system, 21; thunder forces domesticated by, 47–48, 51, 52–53, 129n9, 131n22; and Zhenwu, 69–72, 72–73, 76–77, 132n49

calamity: apocalypse of the six heavens and, 22; aversion of, 35, 38, 113–114
calendar. *See* liturgical calendar
celebrations: New Year, 45, 110; Zhenwu's birthday, 43–45, 87, 96, 110
Celestial Heart school: and *bianshen neilan*, 55–59, 67; meditative techniques, 59–60
Celestial Masters school: and the apocalypse of the six heavens, 22; and the ritual of the Five Thunders, 52; and the Supreme Clarity, 22
Chabi, Empress and the Illustrious Response Palace, 1–3
Cheng Chengbian, 25
Chen Ruoyu, 20
Chijian Dayue taihe shan zhi, 88, 120–122

152   Index

children: filial piety, 90–91; as mediums, 59; mother-son bond, 95; prayers for sons, 109–10, 112–113, 118; selling of, 110, 135n7
Chiyou, 17, 104
Chuang, Hung-I, 20, 117
Chuci zhangju, 14
collaboration, lay-clerical patronage of temples, 33, 35–36
community building: and dietary observance, 40–41; and liturgical calendars, 41, 44–45; and temples, 109–110
Complete Perfection school: established by Wang Zhe, 10; and Lu Dayou, 83
The Complete Works of Chuang-tzu, 61
constellations: classical astrology, 19; North Dipper (*beidou*), 112; worship of, 20; Xuanwu (celestial dark turtle) ordering of, 15, 27; Zhenwu relationship to Xuanwu, 13–14, 111
Correct Method of the Celestial Heart of the Supreme Clarity (Correct Method), 55–56, 57, 59–60, 61–63, 130n15
correlative cosmology: and *bianshen neilan,* 76; and heavenly mandates, 1, 2–3; introduced, 16–17; and the manipulation of cosmic forces, 17–20
cultural hegemony: and lay-clerical power struggles, 42–43, 46; and resistance, 8, 11. *See also* local traditions; state power

Daodejing, 80
Daoist Canon: introduced, 116, 118; and liturgical manuals, 55; and the Secret Essentials, 130n15; and *Tiangong,* 50; and the *Zongzhen ji,* 86
Daomen kefan daquanji, 116
Daomen shigui, 68
Dark Emperor (*Xuandi*), 58, 68, 73–75, 84, 94
Dashun, 33–34, 127nn15,16
Davis, Edward, 26, 47, 51, 52, 59, 65
Dayue Taihe shan zhi, 89
death: imperial burial site construction, 17–20; postmortem fate and deity veneration, 111–112; prediction of, 61; Supreme Clarity texts on, 61–62; underworld of Fengdu, 21–22
de Bruyn, Pierre-Henri: and the authenticity of the *Qisheng lu,* 117; on Xuanwu and Zhenwu, 13; on Zhenwu and Mt Wudang, 6

Declarations of the Perfected (*Zenggao*), 21, 23, 80
deification, *See also* apotheosis
deity evolution: and correlative cosmology, 27; summarized, 27–28; Zhenwu's astral origins, 13–14. *See also* anthropomorphosis; incarnation
demonic creatures: control over, 22; and the Tiangpeng incantation, 23–25; turtle-snake pair as, 3
Deng Siguan (Ziyang), 23–24
Deng Yougong (*Shangqing tianxin zhengfa*), 55–56, 57, 59–60, 61–63, 130n15, 130nn15,16
descending days: and liturgical calendars, 42–43, 44, 45, 46, 77; rituals associated with, 39–40, 58, 76, 105
devotional community building: and congregational gathering, 41–42; and dietary observance, 40–41; and liturgical calendars, 41, 44–45; and temples, 109–110
devotional practices: and home shines, 46; image veneration, 38–39; offering rituals, 39–40
dietary restrictions, 40–41, 45
Di Qing, 104
Dongyun. *See* Lu Dayou
Du Guangting (*Daojiao lingyan ji*), 22–23, 24–25, 125n19

Eight Trigrams of the *Book of Change*: 54; and *bianshen* ritual, 53, 54; and *neidan* 64–65; the turtle of, 4, 56
epidemics, 38
Evidential Miracles In Support of Daoism (*Daojiao lingyan ji*), 23, 24–25, 125n19
evolution of the deity of Zhenwu, Zhenwu's astral origins, 13–14
exorcist capabilities: associated with Beidi (North Emperor), 23, 67; of the Black Killer, 25; and the *Secret Essentials,* 130n15; and Zhenwu's military persona, 27–28, 58–59, 67, 104–108

faguan (ritual officers): and Daoist terminology, 10; new rituals introduced by, 9; training of, 59–60
Fahai yizhu, 53–54, 69–70, 72, 129–131, 132n51
fashi (ritual master), 10–11
Faure, Bernard, 78

Fengdu (Mt Luofeng), introduced, 21
fire: protection against, 114
fire virtue, 114; snakes associated with, 3, 64; and Song dynasty legitimation, 2–3. *See also* Five Phases
Five Dragons Monastery/Palace on Mt Wudang, 81, 84–86, 91–92, 93, 94, 117
Five Phases (*wuxing*): common associations of, 63–64; correlative cosmology of, 1, 16–17; and political legitimacy, 2–3, 96, 111, 123n5. *See also* fire virtue; human-divine interaction
Five Thunders ritual system, introduced, 47–48
folklore and folk beliefs: methodology for studying of, 8–9; of the turtle-snake symbol, 3; of thunder deities, 48; Daoist appropriating of, 85–86; Daoist perception of, 66; balancing Daoist hegemony, 93, 94, 95
Four Animals (*sihou*) and architecture, 19–20; archaeological discovery, 124n4; cosmological symbolism of, 11, 15–20; early expressions of, 124nn4–7; humanization of, 20; and TLV mirrors, 17–19; worship, 20; Yi'nan tomb engraving of, 17; in Zhang Heng's Lingxian, 16–17. *See also* human-divine interaction
Foshan, Guangdong province, 108–111
Four Saints (*sisheng*), 25–27, 29
Fu Qianshou, 35–36
Fushen Courtyard (*Fushen daoyuan*), 35–36

Gansu, Zhenwu veneration activities in, 30, 33, 46, 106
Gaozang, Emperor (r. 649–83), 20
Gaozong, Emperor (r. 1127–1162), 81
Ge Hong (*Baopu zi*), 17
General Tianpeng, 25–26, 27–28, 30
General Xuanwu, 3, 27–28
Giddens, Anthony, 8
Golden Water River (*Jinshui he*), 1, 123n3
Goossaert, Vincent, 10, 40
Great Rites controversy, 103
Grootaers, Willem, 4–5
Guanding jing, 65

habitus, 8
hagiographic material: and the Five Dragons temple, 93; and pilgrimage routes, 79, 91–96; production of, 6, 7; *Qisheng lu,* 39–40, 43, 116–118
Hanshu, 15, 79, 125n10

Henan, 89, 90–91, 96
Heshan ji, 38
historicity challenges of the *Qisheng lu*, 117–118, 126n7
Hong Mai (*Yijian zhi*), 36, 37, 39, 47, 82, 111–112, 113, 114, 128nn22, 27, 28
Hou Hanshu, 48, 80, 133n1
Hsü, Tao-ling, 6, 20, 114
Huainanzi, 16
Huang Gongjin, 9
Huang Shunshen, 68–69
Huang Xiufu, 20
Huizong, Emperor, 32, 35, 128n20, 132n49
human-divine interaction: and correlative cosmology, 16–17. *See also* Five Phases (*wuxing*); Four Animals (*sihou*)
humanization. *See* incarnation; anthropomorphosis
Hymes, Robert: on local magistrates and temple administration, 81; on perceptions of divinity by clerics and laity, 9

iconography: of the Monkey King, 48; of Zhenwu (the Supreme Emperor of the Dark Heaven), 93–94; of thunder gods, 48–50; turtle-snake pair, 5–6, 39; Xuanwu-Hesha talisman depictions, 56; and Zhenwu's varying appearance, 75
identity transformation: meditation and, 11, 61, 66–67, 76; and ritual efficacy, 105. *See also bianshen neilan*
image worship, 38–39, 114
incarnation: astral origins, 13–14; in the *Scripture of Zhenwu,* 4–6, 93–94. *See also* deity evolution
inner alchemy. *See neidan*
interior infant visualization, 53–55, 60, 62–63, 64, 74, 76
internal refinement. *See bianshen neilan*

Jiajing, Emperor, 99–102, 103
Jie Xisi, 85–86
Jin Yünzhong, and the authentic rituals of the Lingbao school, 9; and the Youthful Incipience school, 73, 132n50
The Journey to the North (Beiyou ji), 76, 115
The Journey to the West (Xiyou ji), 48
Jurchen soldiers, 39, 104

Khubilai Khan: legitimacy of, 1–2; and Tibetan Buddhism, 108, 123n4
Kong Daofu, 30
Kong Yingda, 14, 124n6

Lagerwey, John, 50, 87, 89, 96, 112, 132n43
Laozi: and Four Animals, 17; and North Emperor of the six heavens, 22–23; Zhenwu as reincarnation of, 31
Lejing ji, 34, 42, 46
Lévi-Strauss, Claude, 7
Lewis, Mark Edward, 17–18
Liji (*Record of Rites*), 16
Liji zhusu (*commentary on the Record of Rites*), 15, 124n6, 7
lingbao hui ("society of Numinous Treasure"), 128n30
ling (responsiveness), 45. *See also* miracles and miraculous powers
Lingxian, 16
Lingying: temples named, 38, 109; title of Zhenwu, 126n8, 132n49
Lin Lingsu, 52
Little, Stephen, 20
liturgical calendar: festivals of note, 44–45, 110; and lay-clerical power struggles, 42–43; and religious community building, 41, 42–43, 45; Zhenwu's birthday, 43–45, 87, 96, 110
liturgical innovations, 8, 76, 115
liturgical manuals: *Fahai yizhu,* 53–54, 69–70, 72, 129–131, 132n51; identity transformation within, 11; *Master Red Pine's Petition Almanac,* 62, 71, 75, 116; petition-submission, 69–72, 75
Liu Daoming (*Wudang fudi zongzhen ji*), 84–86, 91–92, 92–93, 94, 117
Li Zhaoqi (*Lejing ji*), 34, 42, 46
local traditions: and the Daoist pantheon, 66; and temple transformations, 36–38; and unauthorized temple building, 32. *See also* cultural hegemony; resistance
Loewe, Michael, 18
Lord Lao. *See* Laozi
Lu Dayou (Dongyun), 83, 87

Madam Zhang (Lady of Dai, great-grand mother of Su Song), 26–27
Mahakala veneration, 108
martial imagery. *See* military symbolism
market metaphor of religion, 9–10, 75
Master Red Pine's Petition Almanac, 62, 71, 75, 116
medicine and cures, and shrine building, 36
meditation: Buddhist practices of, 61, 64–65, 80; and daily audiences with Zhenwu, 73–75, 114; Deng Yougong's innovations, 59–60; and identity transformation, 11, 61, 66–67, 76. *See also* visualization practices
Mei Li, 87, 89–90
metamorphosis. *See* identity transformation
methodology, 78; introduced, 7–9; and liturgical evolution, 76, 115; and pilgrimage at Mt Wudang, 87, 89–90; and the *Qisheng lu,* 116–18
military banners (*maya*), 16, 104
military men: religious devotion of, 104–5; and Zhenwu worship, 44, 104, 106–7; and King Zhang worship, 44
military rituals: Song state concern with, 104; and rebels, 106; for invulnerability, 105; Song, 104, 108
military symbolism: and the Four Animals, 15–16, 27; of the turtle, 14; and thunder deities, 53; of Zhenwu, 104, 108
miracles: (*Daojiao lingyan ji*), 22–23, 24–25, 125n19; and deity persona expansion, 12; and deity responsiveness *(ling)*, 45; holy water (*shengshui*), 31; and image worship, 39–40; miraculous icons, 1, 37; praying for rain, 32, 67, 69, 85–86, 113; in the *Qisheng lu,* 116; salvific intervention, 35, 38, 108–109. *See also* spiritual possession
miraculous power: of soldiers, 105; and tantric unity with the divine, 64–65; Zhenwu's therapeutic power, 114
Mongolian Yuan empire: legitimacy, 1–3, 96; and military symbolism, 108–9; and Mt Wudang, 82–83, 96; and rainmaking rituals, 69
Mt Mao, 72, 81, 93
Mt Wudang: as *axis mundi,* 82; contested symbolism of, 115; demography of pilgrims, 89–90; geographical setting, 79–80; and the human origins of Zhenwu, 6; and political legitimation, 98–101; as symbol of state authority, 11, 96, 108; and Yin Xi, 80; during the Yuan dynasty, 88, 96, 103; during the Ming dynasty, 88–89, 97–102, 103, 108, 114. *See also* Five Dragons Monastery/Palace; temple building

Naquin, Susan, 78
neidan (inner alchemy): and turtle-snake pair symbolism, 3, 64, 67; and daily audience meditation, 75; introduced, 10, 64
Ning Benli, 9

North Emperor (*beidi*): Four Saints associated with, 11; and the six heavens, 21–23; and the Tianpeng incantation, 23–25; Zhenwu as aide-de-camp of, 6, 21, 25, 27–28; Zhenwu as, 11, 109

pantheons: Daoist pantheon of the Six Dynasties, 20; Song period inclusion of Zhenwu, 27, 29, 46, 47–48
patronage: clergy-lay collaborations, 33, 34–38, 46; Song period temple building, 11, 29, 30–31
Pei Zhongfang, 43
piety. *See* devotional practices
pilgrimage: demography of pilgrims to Mt Wudang, 89–90; at Mt Wudang, 10, 11, 87–91, 102–103; routes and hagiographic material, 79, 91–96
popularity of deities, 45; and pilgrimage, 87
popularity of Zhenwu: and biographical elements, 4, 6; during the Song dynasty, 6, 11, 29, 45–46; widespread nature of, 3–4
popular religion, interaction with Daoism, 9, 50–51, 66, 109
Pueet, Michael, 17, 104

Qing dynasty, 111
Qisheng lu: descending days within, 43; dietary restrictions, 40; introduced, 116–118; and Mt Wudang, 87; Zhenwu worship rituals within, 39–40
Quanzhen (Complete Perfection school), 10, 83
Queen Shansheng, 4, 93, 95
Quxuan ji, 35, 127n17
Qu Yuan, 14

Rao Dongtian, 55
rebels, 106, 109
Records of Mt Mao (*Maoshan zhi*), 72
Records of the Listener (*Yijian zhi*), *see* Hong Mai
reincarnations: Zhenwu as Laozi, 31; Zhenwu as Pei Zhongfang, 43
religious markets, 9–10, 75
religious symbols: forces shaping, 7; inner logic of, 8; state appropriation of, 10, 96
Renzong, Emperor of the Song (r.1023–1063), 31–32, 113, 116–118
Renzong, Emperor of Yuan (r.1311–1320), 88, 96

resistance: and cultural hegemony, 8, 11; and lay-clerical power struggles, 42–43, 46, 94; to state power, 106–108, 115. *See also* local traditions
retribution: for killing, 21; against unresponsive thunder deities, 53; violation of food taboos, 40–41
Retrieved Pearls from the Sea of Rituals (*Fahai yizhu*), 53–54, 69–70, 72, 129–30n12–13, 132n51
"Ritual of Grand Offering to the Perfected Warrior, Numinous and Responsive"(*Zhenwu lingying da jiaoyi*), 116
rituals: emergence of new ritual lineages, 47; innovation of, 115; ritual of Offering (*zhibing xingjiao*), 36, 44, 50, 75–76; *Secret Methods of the Divine Fire*, 68–69; Song-Yuan-Ming period growth of, 9–10; to summon rainfall, 50–52; unorthodox "rite of the thunder lord," 51–52. *See also bianshen neilian*; ritual specialists
ritual specialists: efficacy improvement of, 59–60, 73–75; and Mt Wudang pilgrimage, 87; promotion of Zhenwu by, 37–38, 46, 47, 114; rivalry amongst, 9–10; and temple building, 36; terms for, 10–11
"Roaming Far Away" (*Yuanyou*), 14

sacred space: and human agency, 6, 78–79, 98, 102–103; and pilgrimage, 87–90
sacrifice, 40, 127n19
Sahlins, Marshall, 7
salvific intervention, 35, 38, 113–114
Santian neijie jing, 22
Schipper, Kristofer, 8–9, 51, 59, 66
Scott, James, 8
Scripture of Zhenwu: "descending days," 42; dietary restrictions in, 40; and filial piety, 94–95; and Henan, 90–91; introduced, 4–6
Secret Essential: 23–24, 55–57, introduced 130nn15
Secret Methods of the Divine Fire, 69
self-cultivation: and correlative cosmology, 27, 64, 76; Zhenwu's dedication to, 4, 78, 91
Shakyamuni Buddha, 6
Shangqing tianxin beiji zhengfa, 130n16
Shangqing tianxin zhengfa, 55–56, 57, 59–60, 130n15

shengshi (holy master), and divine meditation, 11, 67

Shiji, 15, 19, 48, 124n4, 125n10

Sima Guang, 127n12

Sima Kou, 38

Sima Qian (*Shiji*): five celestial palaces described in, 15, 19; and thunder, 48

Sima Xiangru ("Roaming Far Away"), 14

six heavens, 21–23

snakes: auspicious appearance of, to Wang Yan, 82; as demonic (*yao*), 30; heart and fire associated with, 3, 64; as male turtles, 14. *See also* turtle-snake pair

social integration and diversification, 6, 78–79, 98–99, 103

Songshi, 2, 31, 32, 45, 104, 106, 113, 117, 126n3,7, 127n8, 127n9,11,15, 133n7,8, 135n3, 136n4

spirit medium, 9, 66; Daoist perception of, 59, 76

spiritual communication: petition-submission routines, 68, 69–72, 73, 75; and spirit writing, 82, 105, 115

spiritual possession: and *bianshen neilian* rituals, 11, 66–67, 76; criticism of, 58–59; and diabolic possession cures, 23, 52, 56–57. *See also* miracle working

state power: appropriation of religious symbols in service of, 10, 66, 88–89, 96–97, 98–99, 106–9, 115; bureaucratization of Zhenwu, 69–72, 72–73, 132n49, 76–77; and regulation of sites of public worship, 32, 33, 38, 80–81, 127nn13,16; resistance to, 106–8. *See also* cultural hegemony

Strickman, Michel, 46, 65

Sun Guangxian, 51

Sun Jiran, 81, 87, 93

Supreme Clarity (*Shangqing*) visualization practices: and *bianshen neilan,* 67, 76; introduced, 55–56, 57, 59–60, 61–63

the Supreme Emperor (*shangdi*): and Thunder Rites, 50–52; and the Tianpeng incantation, 24; and Zhenwu's rise in the Daoist pantheon, 69–72, 77

Su Xiangxian, 26–27

Supreme Emperor of the Dark Heaven (Xuantian shangdi), 6, 58, 68, 73–75, 84, 94

taboos: against animal sacrifice, 40; forbidden foods, 40–41, 45, 51; forbidden name words, 3, 123nn7–9; forbidden rituals, 106

Taishang Dadao yuqing jing, 50

Taishang jiuzhen miaojie jinlu duming bazui jing, 6, 22

Taishang zhuguo jiumin zongzhen miyao. See Secret Essentials

Taishang Yuanshi Tianzun shuo Beidi fumo shenzhou miaojing, 6

Taizong, Song Emperor, 30, 80, 118

Taizong, Tang Emperor, 85, 126n1

Taizu, Song Emperor, 2

talismans: and the Celestial Heart School, 55–57, 62, 72, 130n16; the 36 Talismans of Tianpeng, 23–24; and thunder deities, 67–68; transmitted by Zhenwu, 36, 47, 130n17

Tang Dynasty: Daoist Thunder Rites during, 48, 51; local cults during, 66; and the North Emperor ritual, 22–23; Pure Tenuity ritual established during, 68–69; and Xuanwu, 19–20; Zhenwu temples established during, 20, 29, 126n1

Tanguts (Xi Xia), 34, 39

Tantric Buddhism, influence on Daoism, 64–65, 67, 76

Tan Zixiao, 47, 55

Taylor, Romeyn, 13

temple building: during the Northern Song, 33–34; early Song period Zhenwu temples, 30–31; and gratitude for *ling,* 45; joint clergy–lay patronage of, 33; as a measure of deity popularity, 3–4; motivations, 34–38, 46; on Mt Wudang, 80–81, 102; and naming, 127n13; Song statue laws governing, 32, 38; terms associated with, 10; Zhenwu temples during the Tang, 20, 29. *See also* architecture

temples of note: Aiding Sage Daoist Monastery, 37, 44–45, 83, 96; Auspicious Fountain–Sweet Spring Monastery, 31–32, 42–43, 113–114; Celestial Celebration Monastery (*Tianqing guan*), 30, 123n7; Clean Cloud Hall (Jiyun dian), 29; Five Dragons Palace, 83;, 92–93; Fushen Daoist Courtyard (*Fushen daoyuan*), 35–36; Great Harmony Palace, 94–95; Numinously Responsive Temple (Foshan zumiao), 109–111; Purple Empryean Monastery, 81,

83, 85, 95; Zhenwu Daoist Courtyard, 36–37. *See also* Mt Wudang
ter Haar, Berend, 8
terms: associated with *neidan* meditation, 64; for religious buildings and specialists, 10–11
theory. *See* methodology
thunder deities, 48–53; and the imperial court, 48; introduced, 47–50
Thunder Rites: and *bianshen neilian*, 11, 52–53, 76; in the *Fahai yizhu*, 53–55; according to Zhao Zujian (the *Record of the Listener*), 47. *See also* weather
Tiangong Retreat, 50–51
Tianpeng incantation, 23–25. *See also* General Tianpeng
Tianpeng ritual system, 72
Tiantai lineage of the Lingbao school, 9
TLV mirrors, 17–19
tombs: Qianling, 20; "tomb temple" granting, 128n21; Yi'nan, 17
turtle: as forbidden food, 41; Shengui (Divine Turtle) era, 125; symbolism of unitary form of, 14–15, 64, 123n2. *See also* turtle-snake pair
turtle-snake pair: apparitions, 1, 37, 104; and inner alchemy, 3, 64, 67; as same species, 14; and Xuanwu, 1, 20–21; Zhenwu's emblems, 5–6, 37, 39

underworld, 21–22

visualization practices: and *bianshen* rituals, 62, 63, 67, 76; criticism of, 58–59, 66; and daily audience with Zhenwu, 73–75; and efficacy improvement, 59–60, 73–75; in the *Fahaiyizhu*, 69–70; in *Red Pine Master's Petition*, 71; and the Supreme Clarity tradition, 55–56, 57, 60–63, 67, 76; and Tantric Buddhism, 65, 76. *See also* meditation

Wang Bao, 14
Wang Mai (*Quxuan ji*), 35, 127n17
Wang Wenqing, 52, 58
Wang Yi (*Chuci zhangju*), 14
Wang Zhe, 10
Wang Zhenchang (Sizhen), 83
Warring states period: and the Four Animals, 15–19; and Xuanwu, 14

weather: and the *Tiangong* Retreat, 51; Zhenwu's power over, 12, 113. *See also* Thunder Rites
Wei, Empress Dowager, 125–26n24
women: as donors, 33; Lady of Dai, 26–27; Queen Shansheng, 4, 93, 95; Tang Saier, 108; Wang Fajin, 50–51; Xiao Shoutong, 83; Zu Shu's Pure Tenuity school, 69
worship. *See* devotional practices
Wu, Empress (r. 690–705), 20
Wudang fudi zongzhen ji. *See Zongzhen ji*
Wudang shan. *See* Mt Wudang
Wu Zimu (*Mengliang lu*), 44, 96, 125–26n24, 128n30, 32

Xiang'er Commentary to the Laozi, 63
Xi Xia, 33, 34, 39
Xuantian shangdi qisheng lu. *See Qisheng lu*
Xuanwu ("Dark Martiality/Warrior"): dating of the term, 14; Illustrious Response Palace established for, 2–3; turtle-snake pair identified with, 1, 3, 20–21; as Zhenwu's alternate name, 3, 13, 56
Xuanwu Gate of the Taiji Palace, 19–20
Xuanyuan (Yellow Emperor), and the Four Animals, 16–17
Xu Shen (*Shuowen jiezi*), 14

Yang Lizhi, 89, 99
Yellow Emperor (*Huangdi*): and Chiyou, 104; and the Four Animals, 16–17
Yijianzhi, see Hong Mai
Yin Xi, 80
Yizhou minghua lu, 20, 25
Yongle, Emperor, 89, 97–99, 102, 108, 114
Yousheng: divine bureau named after, 70, 72; temple named after, 37; title of Zhenwu, 132n49
Yuan Miaozong (*Secret Essentials*), 55, 130n15
Yuanshi tianzun shuo Beifang Zhenwu jing. *See Scripture of Zhenwu*
Yü, Chün-fang, 78
Yudiechibuhua (imperial delegate), 1
Yunnan pilgrims at Mt Wudang, 89–90

Zhengao, (Declarations of the Perfected), 21, 23, 80
Zhang Daoling, 22, 71, 75–76
Zhang, Empress Dowager, 101
Zhang Heng (*Lingxian*), 16–17, 124n2
Zhang Shouqing, 69, 83, 87, 117
Zhang Shouzhen, 117–118
Zhang Yuchu, 68
Zhao Shoujie, 83, 87
Zhao Xuanlang, 3
Zhao Zujian, 47
Zhenggao, 21, 23, 80
Zhenzong, Emperor, 3, 31–32
Zhou Mi, 44–45
Zhou Mi (*Wulin jiushi*), 44–45
Zhuangzi, 61
Zhuzi yulei, 13
Zhu Xi (*Zhuzi yulei*), 13, 105
Zichen xuanshu, 132n51
Zongzhen ji: Five Dragons Monastery/Palace, 81, 82–83, 84–86, 92–93, 94; introduced, 84; Purple Empyrean Monastery, 81, 95; South Cliff Palace, 83, 94
zushi (ancestral teacher/master), 11, 67–69, 76